100
DANISH
POEMS

100

From the Medieval Period

DANISH

to the Present Day

POEMS

Bilingual edition

Selected and edited by
Thomas Bredsdorff and Anne-Marie Mai

Translated by John Irons in cooperation
with Klaus Høeck

MUSEUM TUSCULANUM PRESS ✤ UNIVERSITY OF WASHINGTON PRESS

Copenhagen   Seattle

2011

Thomas Bredsdorff and Anne-Marie Mai (eds.)
100 Danish Poems: From the Medieval Period to the Present Day

© Museum Tusculanum Press and the editors, 2011
All poems translated by John Irons in cooperation with Klaus Høeck, except Inger
Christensen's "Juninatten", p. 298, courtesy of Bloodaxe Books/Susanna Nied
Translation consultant: Karin Sanders
Cover design: Pernille Sys Hansen, Damp Design
Set in Bembo and printed by Narayana Press
ISBN 978 87 635 3128 3

This book is published with financial support from
The Danish Arts Council

STATENS
KUNSTRÅD
DANISH ARTS COUNCIL

Published in Europe by

MUSEUM TUSCULANUM PRESS
University of Copenhagen
126 Njalsgade, DK-2300 Copenhagen S, Denmark
www.mtp.dk

Published in the United States by

UNIVERSITY OF WASHINGTON PRESS
PO Box 50096, Seattle, WA 98145, USA
www.washington.edu/uwpress

Library of Congress Cataloging-in-Publication Data

100 Danish poems: from the medieval period to the present day: bilingual
edition / selected and edited by Thomas Bredsdorff and Anne-Marie Mai;
translated by John Irons in cooperation with Klaus Høeck. — 1st ed.
p. cm.
"Published in Europe by Museum Tusculanum Press, University of Copenhagen"--
T.p. verso.
Parallel text in English and Danish.
ISBN 978-0-295-99150-4 (University of Washington Press: alk. paper) —
ISBN 978-8763531283 (Museum Tusculanum Press: alk. paper)
1. Danish poetry—Translations into English. I. Bredsdorff, Thomas. II. Mai,
Anne-Marie, 1953- III. Irons, John, 1942- IV. Høeck, Klaus, 1938- V. Title: One
hundred Danish poems: from the medieval period to the present day.
PT7983.E5B74 2011
839.1'1008—dc23   2011024160

Contents

Introduction

Anne-Marie Mai

There are many places one could start when writing an introduction to poetry written in the Danish language from the medieval period to the present day. We have chosen to begin with a short verse and a small piece of music to go with it. The verse, which has been added to the last page of a medieval runic manuscript from c. AD 1300 containing the Scanian Law – an old Records of the Court – reads as follows:

> Drømde mik en drøm i nat um silki ok ærlig pæl (I dreamt a dream last night of silk and fine brocade).

This short verse, accompanied by a finely drawn music staff with notes, is the oldest secular text to have survived in northern Europe, and its location in the Records of the Court has given rise to much speculation: Did the writer jot down a few popular lines of verse for his own amusement? Or is there something in the text that refers to the content of the records? The answer remains uncertain. The words "ærlig pæl" could possibly be translated with "an honest measure", i.e. justice, and the writer's dream could possibly have to do with wealth and justice. "Silk and fine brocade", however, is the most widespread translation. No matter which interpretation one decides to accept, it is obvious that the line of verse has a pleasing and prominent position on the page. The reader cannot help noticing it and thinking that the writer must have appreciated this brief verse and wanted to pass it on to others.

The interest in using verses, writing them down and including them within a tradition is characteristic of Danish poetry. The long history of Danish poetry speaks neither of a reluctance to deal with poetry or exclusiveness; on the contrary, verses and poems seem over the centuries to have been everywhere in people's lives, from cradle to grave, in their everyday lives and on festive occasions. Danish poetry, it should be noted, has had a large, widespread appeal in society, not simply having been reserved for a wealthy, upper-class few. Certain poetic genres have been popular, others elitist, but the writing of verses in general has since the Middle Ages been known and used in all walks of life. And poetry and song are closely knit in a Danish context, something that still applies in recent ages, where quite a number of classics of modern poetry from the 19th and 20th centuries are song-texts that are still well known. Even though new lyric poetry is not consistently set to music to the same extent as, for example, in the poetry-loving country Chile, it is nevertheless worth noting that many of the poems in this anthology can be sung – this also applies to modern poems by Thøger Larsen and Johannes V. Jensen.

Danish poetry has often dealt with the big questions of existence: life, death, love, hope and faith, and in this respect it does not differ from either Nordic or international poetry. But Danish poems are strongly influenced by the particular timbre of the language, formed by the contours of the landscape, the life-rhythm of modern small towns, and they are also full of impressions from the light Northern summer nights, the autumn gales and the long, dark winter months. The profound existential searching and the open, free way of talking between the sexes, between young and old, beat strongly in Danish poetry.

The hundred Danish poems in the present anthology will, it is to be hoped, give an impression of the many poetic qualities to be found in Danish lyric poetry in various historical periods.

A thread running through the history of Danish literature

The anthology opens with two ballads, that of Ebbe Skammelsøn, which can be classified as a ballad of chivalry, and that of the maid in the guise of a bird, which belongs to the ballads of magic. The two ballads have come down to us in handwritten ballad books of the nobility from the 16th century. The old ballads have survived to the present day via hand-written books, pamphlets, printed books – resulting from the invention of the art of printing – and, not least, an oral tradition with the writing down of ballads provided by informants, something that particularly took place in the 19th century. The ballads would seem to have been the work of individual poets from a fairly high social environment, belonging to a common European genre, the universe of which probably has its origins in 13th-century northern France, i.e. the French troubadour tradition. Even so, the ballads also have antique and Norse sources. In addition, the ballad books of the nobility record the fact that the writing down of the ballads/songs in Denmark began relatively early compared with other European countries, and that the works have been a very important part of Renaissance culture.

Quite simply, the ballads run like a long thread through the history of Danish literature. They point to the medieval world by virtue of their

Norse sources; they were a subject of interest for both the court and the nobility during the Renaissance and were part of the struggle between the old aristocracy and the Crown as regards the writing of history. The ballads were important in the old aristocracy's self-fashioning of their high birth, genealogy and high culture, while the Crown used them in order to emphasise its own historical power. The ballads, however, have also had a popular appeal and a wide dissemination via pamphlets and the oral tradition. After the Renaissance, many of the ballads became part of popular culture and literature.

In the 19th century, the ballads became a source of inspiration for the ideas of German-inspired Romantic poetry concerning the connection between language, people, history and nation. For the Romantic poets, the ballads – along with Norse literature – were a gold mine, out of which it was possible to forge both strong national-romantic constructions about Denmark the mother country, as in Oehlenschläger's poetry, and golden ideas concerning the past and future of an enlightened people and their mother tongue, as in Grundtvig's poetry.

In modern and modernist poetry and the poetics of the 20th century, the ballad tradition became a literary impulse for depth-psychological thematics and symbolism, although this is characteristically enough a feature more of its prose than its poetry. Even so, the language of the ballad does provide a sounding board for such poets as Tove Ditlevsen, Erik Knudsen and Pia Juul.

In the 21st century, ballads are still being used and interpreted: Rock bands and jazz musicians are recording new versions of the old ballads. It is also interesting to note how present-day rap poetry, just like the ballads, uses a four-beat line and a varying number of unaccentuated syllables, together with fixed poetic figures of speech.

The ways of literary history are often extremely unfathomable, and it is quite thought-provoking to see that the metre of the ballad has returned to Danish literature via American underground culture. The old themes of the ballads – revenge, crime, boasting matches, involvement in the relation between the sexes and being outlawed from the community – also recur, even though there is undeniably a long way in terms of cultural history from the maidens of the ballads with their beautiful tresses and lily-white hands to the "ho's" of the rappers. Despite this, the women of the old ballads are more than a match for their younger sisters when it comes to their thirst for revenge and their violent nature.

Poetry and faith

One of the most remarkable stories in Danish literature is that of the life and works of King Christian IV's daughter Leonora Christina. Her principal work *Jammers Minde* (A Memory of Lament), completed at the end of the 17th century, tells of her many years of imprisonment in the Blue Tower oubliette, accused of participating in the high treason committed by her husband. The work was miraculously preserved by her family, but did not reach a wider audience until the mid-19th century, at a time when Denmark, after a disastrous defeat in 1864 at the hands of Prussia, was thirsting for evidence of Danish cultural values. Through her work, Leonora Christina wanted to demonstrate her innocence and her spiritual strength, and she succeeded to such an extent that posterity has often accepted her interpretation of her story to be the whole truth. As Hans Christian Andersen wrote in one of his tales, she became one of the hearts in the nation's coat of arms. Present-day historians agree, however, that Leonora Christina was far from being as innocent of treason against the Danish king as she herself claimed. But what she has lost in historical credibility she has gained in literary reputation: Many literary historians are now of the opinion that her *Jammers Minde* is a major work of European stature, inspired by French, German, English and Italian novel-writing and confessional literature. In it, she tells in both prose and verse, and with considerable humour, of her tribulations and survival strategies. A number of spiritual songs are part of the work, one of which is included in the present anthology. In the tower, she wrote poetry in order to keep up her spirits and to confirm the covenant she feels she has entered into with God. We meet a self-aware, believing speaker that talks to herself and with God, portraying the struggle she has in finding her direction in a world picture based on the contrasts between good and evil, life on earth and the life beyond, the secular and the spiritual, frailty and strength, the transient and the eternal.

One of the contemporary poets that Leonora Christina set great store by was the clergyman and hymn-writer Thomas Kingo, with whom she had contact during her incarceration and by whom she was later visited when, after her release, she lived in Maribo. They shared a conception of the importance of faith for human self-esteem and the experience of the sudden vicissitudes of human existence. In both their writing the speaker features strongly, although in Kingo this speaker is a general one with which anybody can identify, whereas in Leonora Christina's spiritual songs we meet a personal, confessional speaker. Even so, they both confront this speaker with the contradictions of life and develop an elegant poetry that is capable of using the Danish language to write durable, singable verse. With Kingo's poetry, the long process of converting Latin rhyme schemes into Danish-language poetry – introduced by Anders Arrebo's major work *Hexaëmeron* (published in 1661) – was finally completed. And in Leonora Christina's *Jammers Minde* we find expressive spiritual songs in a beautiful and intimate Danish language, woven into a text where High German, Low German, French and Danish are alternately used in a both trenchantly ironic and good-humoured characterisation of people at court and in prison.

Kingo was the first Danish poet to write about the light Northern summer nights – "dend deylig Sommer-nat saa dage-blanded er" (the lovely summer night is so mixed with day) is how he puts it. This short, finely sensitive line is to be found early on in an otherwise dramatic and formidable occasional poem about Christian V's naval battle against Sweden off Öland in 1676, where the rest of the poem booms bombastically and majestically with "savage din".

In Kingo's hymn-writing, references to nature are often connected with death and decay. Nature appears in the form of hay, bones and worms, representing mortality and evil. But nature can also be used metaphorically to refer to resurrection and the life beyond. This is particularly true of the gleaming sunrise, with Kingo telling his soul – poetically and with a good grasp of Luther's theology – that God will preserve "the flower petal of the body".

Kingo's hymn-writing for the Danish church from the end of the 17th century marks the culmination of the major task following the introduction of the Reformation in 1536 of establishing a corpus of hymns in the Danish language. But Kingo is not merely a master of hymn-writing, whose texts are still in use and valued for their poetic qualities both inside and outside church circles. His occasional and pastoral poems also represent a pinnacle of Danish and Nordic poetic writing. In his pastoral poems, Kingo writes delightful lines about being in love, with the warmest kisses and embraces to his chosen one. But the Funen squire Jens Steen Sehested goes much further in his poems when it comes to erotic outspokenness. In the present anthology, Sehested is represented by a merry masturbation sonnet from 1690.

The ghastly conditions of the poor at Odense Infirmary are captured by Kingo in the keenest physical details in his long rhyming petition to

Christian V, where the reader hears about the poor sick creatures that are unable to chew their own food, are full of sores and abscesses, are in the process of coughing up their own lungs or in their madness grunt like pigs and strike themselves till they start bleeding.

Kingo's poetry has a practical function, with the poet making use of his knowledge and skills within theology and poetry in order to make his words expressive and appealing to high monarchs and officials as well as believing congregations. In the present anthology, Kingo is represented by two hymns that are still well known and in use in Denmark.

Less than fifty years after the publication of a Danish hymnal dominated by Kingo's hymns, Hans Adolph Brorson renewed the tradition for hymn-writing and spiritual songs in Denmark. In the 1730s, Brorson began to publish his booklets with Christmas hymns, followed in 1739 by his main work *Troens rare Klenodie* (The Rare Jewel of the Faith), which consists of both original and translated hymns that could be sung to popular secular dance tunes of the time and were written in a fervent poetry that makes Danish a language of feelings.

Brorson belonged to the large circle of young theologians who had experienced German Pietism as a new, powerful and fruitful spirituality, and who were in contact with the Pietist environments in Halle and Herrnhut. It was from here that they received ideas and became familiar with hymns that were now circulated in a Danish context. In the various Pietist persuasions, spiritual songs were absolutely vital. To sing was a way in which the believer could express his or her innermost feelings, and in the song itself the singer's body and soul both serve Jesus.

While Kingo's theology and art were underpinned by the idea of the contrast between the heavenly and the earthly and of human life being split between the infinite and the finite, the central feature of Brorson's hymn-writing was the internalisation of belief and personal conversion. Kingo's version of the imperative of faith is found in such lines as "Far, Verden, far vel, / Jeg keedis nu længer at være din Træl" (Farewell, world, farewell, / As thrall here I'm weary and no more will dwell). Brorson's version, on the other hand, is contained in such lines as "Ach søger de nædrige Stæder, / I Støvet for Frælseren græder, / Saa faar I vor JEsum i Tale / Thi Roserne voxer i Dale" (Oh, seek what is low and in keeping, / In dust for your Saviour be weeping, / Then you will our Jesus be knowing, / For roses in valleys are growing).

The collection of songs in *Troens Rare Klenodie* is compiled in such a way that the drama of faith, with doubt, conversion, penance and victory, is experienced and lived through in the seven sections of the work: "Faith's Feast of Joy", "Faith's Grounding", "The Means of Faith", "The Fruit of Faith", "Faith's Battle and Victory", "Faith's Glory" and "The Conclusion of Faith". Here we do not follow the church year, as is the case with Kingo's hymnal, but the various phases and themes of religious life. Man experiences both danger "where I walk" and walking with Jesus, the angels and God himself. The scholarly joy of old Arrebo at God's creation becomes in Brorson a personal wonder and ecstasy. The hymns "Up! Everything That God Has Made" and "The Fairest of Roses" included in the present anthology contain a number of images that convey the immensity of the divine world and man's incapacity to express himself in language and to comprehend. Brorson's *Klenodie* was especially intended for devotional use outside the church – at the vicarage, in the home and for private use. This new spirituality spread as a result of the popular Schleswig Pietist revival movement, with many missionaries from German religious circles gaining a foothold in the church, with even the court espousing Pietism and creating its own particular version: State Pietism. But this form of Pietism and the radical Moravians soon clashed. From an absolutist society's point of view, radical Pietism made believers far too independent, self-affirming and autonomous, and the authorities imposed prohibitions and punishments for those making contact with the Moravian missionaries.

Like Kingo, Brorson eventually became a bishop. But his time as bishop in Ribe was not without conflicts and problems. Brorson had to balance between radical Pietism, which the absolutist state had made illegal, but with which he himself sympathised, and the old Lutheran orthodoxy, which was popular among the clergy. Brorson experienced a violent religious crisis during his years in Ribe, fearing that he would simply end up in hell. His posthumous poems in *Svane-Sang* (Swan Song, 1765) allow the conversation between Jesus and the soul to pass through fear and doubt in a poetry that is full of melodiousness and linguistic mastery. One can see, taste, smell, hear, feel and experience in a poetry where time is but "a grain of salt". The believer has but "a little time" before "gaining all", and the poetry foreshadows what is to come, as it winds into constantly new and enchanting visions and times – "a first fruits" where man is aware of the spirit and the coming kingdom of heaven in his heart, here and now, as in the religious song "Her vil ties, her vil bies" (Be Silent Now and Bide Your Time). Contemporaries passing by Brorson's home, Taarnborg, in the 1740s heard him in the evenings playing his lute and singing his songs and hymns together with his family.

The poetry of faith is further renewed in the 19th century in N.F.S. Grundtvig's major *Sang-Værk* (Song Opus) for the Danish church. While Kingo's *Aandelige Sjungekoor* is organised around the contrast between earthly inconstancy and divine constancy, and Brorson's *Klenodie* is based on phases and experiences in religious life, Grundtvig's *Sang-Værk* is based on the course of religious history. It includes hymns from the various historical churches that Grundtvig felt had been the most important in the history of Christianity: the Hebrew, the Greek, the Roman, the English, the German and the Danish-Nordic churches. Grundtvig imagined that during precisely his age the Danish-Nordic church was ushering in a decisive religious renewal of Christianity. He meticulously compiled his *Sang-Værk* in such a way that it used texts from all six churches. The hymnal has the large world-historical perspective as its pivotal idea, although the work is of course conceived as bearing witness to the spiritual power of the sixth church, and it is here that Grundtvig's own hymn-writing marks a clear watershed. He was particularly pleased that he had drawn attention to the fact that all mother tongues and mythologies would be of importance for Christianity. He also expected a seventh church to arise that would be the final one before Christ's second coming. In the work he decided that this future church would be located by the Ganges, i.e. in India.

Grundtvig begins his song-book for the Danish church with a long prologue. Here he uses an extract from his own poetry-writing – "New Year's Morning" from 1824 – which depicts his own profound religious crisis. This is followed by 146 hymns about the universal church (the Holy Catholic Church of the creed), many of which he wrote himself, then 28 Christmas hymns, 117 Easter hymns and 73 Whitsun hymns. The hymns are organised in such a way that they are modelled on the six churches, and Grundtvig concludes with 7 original hymns, making a total of 401. In connection with Grundtvig's 50th anniversary as a clergyman in 1861, he received a large sum of money for a collected edition of his *Sang-Værk*, which comprised no less than 1,600 hymns.

The three hymns that represent Grundtvig in this anthology are still in use and they show both his view of images – which he placed so much emphasis on in the hymns – and his ideas about "folkelighed" (roughly designating an inclusive sense of community based on what is popular, egalitarian, enlightened, unassuming) and the mother tongue, which he made his point of departure for a violent confrontation with the rationalist theology of the late 18th century and the soul-destroying grind of the authoritarian grammar schools.

The hymn "The Bright Blessed Day with Joy We See" is from a time when Grundtvig was in a violent conflict with the church authorities. The hymn was intended to be used in connection with Whitsun in 1826 and the millennium celebration of the introduction of Christianity to Denmark. Grundtvig wanted to defy the ban imposed by the church authorities on unauthorised hymns being sung at church festivals. He had planned for the hymn, which was his own version of Hans Thomissøn's day-song from 1569, to be sung in Vor Frelsers Kirke (The Church of Our Saviour) in Copenhagen. But the bishop regarded it as completely unsuitable and in bad taste, because Grundtvig compared eternal life in the hereafter with life on earth. Particularly scandalous was the last verse with the line "We'll journey then to our fatherland" (Saa reise vi til vort Fædre-Land), where the word "saa" can both mean "then" as well as "likewise". This means that the hymn ends by saying: If only heaven will be just as good as life on earth at its very best! This was simply too much for the authorities. When the hymn is sung nowadays, "saa" is taken to mean "then, after this" – which gives it a different and less controversial meaning than Grundtvig's original one. After the furore about the hymn, Grundtvig was obliged in protest to tender his resignation, and for a long time he was subject to censorship and without a post. In general, his hymn-writing gave rise to many controversies, criticism and opposition. Many people regarded his theology and philosophy as being completely woolly and his imagery as being muddled, mystical and self-glorifying.

Another slightly younger renewer of hymn-writing, B.S. Ingemann, has also caused the theologians problems. Ingemann's romantic-visionary universe with transmigration of souls and lucifer-like angels of light do not accord all that well with Lutheran theology. On the other hand, his universe has served as an extremely powerful source of inspiration for Danish poets of the 20th century, especially Michael Strunge, Søren Ulrik Thomsen and Dan Turèll. The last-named quite simply fainted the first time he sang one of Ingemann's poems at morning assembly in school. Ingemann's religious poetry for children's homes became the epitome of poetry that is both sublime and conciliatory, in which the world is presented as radiant and beautiful, even for the lonely, exposed child. Institutional Christian poetry on Danish soil culminates in Grundtvig and Ingemann.

Faith and doubt continue to be prominent themes in Danish poetry in the 20th century as well, with a great many hymns that resemble those of Grundtvig and Ingemann being written in the hymn genre. But new potential and meanings are also wrested out of the language of hymns in very recent experimental poetry, such as that of Simon Grotrian.

Man in nature

One of the poets whom Grundtvig boundlessly admired and whom Ingemann had in his incontestable top hundred of Danish poets was Johannes Ewald. His poetry not only represents a high-point in Danish-language poetry of the 18th century; it also marks a turning-point in the history of national literature: Ewald was the first Dane to live and work exclusively as a poet, and his work was primarily interested in a range of modern themes concerning the autonomous individual's feeling of both pleasure and fear, the sublime experience of nature and Norse mythology as an inexhaustible source of modern poetry. Ewald was inspired by contemporary English, French and German poetry. Especially important was his meeting with the German poet F.G. Klopstock, who had been invited to Denmark in 1751 with promises of a considerable royal pension.

Klopstock's favourite genre was the ode – and it also became Ewald's. Here the poet could engage in new worldly subjects, reinterpret religious themes and cultivate his love of language and its cadences. The poet was to strive to make poetry into a movement of the soul and to stir the heart completely. For that reason, outer trappings, boring and predictable rhythms and enforced rhymes were to be avoided. Form and content were to merge completely, so that the power of the poetry itself could emerge and convey itself to the reader.

The poet should admittedly imitate the masters of Antiquity, but only so as to acquire genius himself. The odes of Horace and Pindar were also on the lips of European poets. Odes were being written in the mother tongue in England, France and Germany as early as the 17th century. In Denmark, Anders Bording was one of the most industrious verse-writers and the originator of odes in the strict forms of literary poetry that were to be used in musical presentation. The new ode of the 18th century was different – it was not to be sung but read. The individual reader was simply to look at the ode whenever he wanted to, to experience and cultivate it for his own undivided pleasure. It was no longer necessary to have a large company of guests, musicians and singers present to be able to experience poetry. The ode turned individual reading into something quite special, and the members of the newly established Det smagende Selskab (The Society of Taste) were ardent supporters of the new odes being written and they assiduously sought to further Ewald's career. Ewald himself tells of how he met "the great Klopstock" around 1768, and Klopstock's presence in Denmark bears witness to the close relations that Danish poetry acquired with German literature and thought in the 18th and 19th century.

The absolutist society of the time made use of a number of languages: Danish and German were governmental languages, while French was used at court, and Latin was the academic language of the university. But the Danish language was making good progress in poetry, on the stage and in the new debating periodicals.

Klopstock set great store by Ewald and even taught himself some rudimentary Danish in order to be able to read Ewald's first attempts. The emotional power and the very movement of Klopstock's ode accorded extremely well with Ewald's ambition and desire as a poet also to explore complex feelings and conflicting thoughts, although he in fact rarely followed Klopstock when it came to creating completely new verse forms and metres for his odes. His most famous ode, "The Delights of Rungsted" (1775), which is included in the present anthology, is still – formally speaking – closer to the slightly older song-poetry than to Klopstock's odes, which are decidedly conceived to be read aloud or silently.

In "The Delights of Rungsted", the poetic speaker is presented as the centre of divine creation. Indeed, the poet is himself the authority that produces the divine dimensions in the world of nature and creates experiences and emotions in his listener. The ode is constructed in such a way that the verses evoke the murmuring fall of the streams in the first section of the ode, the fall only ceasing when Ewald mentions his own poet's breast and depicts how the sounds and sights of the place fill him with inspiration: "Where Rungsted encloses delights pure and chaste: / There did the muse fill my breast."

The conclusion of the ode has proved a mystery for literary research. Who is the "sweet friend" the poet addresses and asks if she has enjoyed the poem? Biographical research has guessed that it might be Ewald's mother or his early love Arendse, whom Ewald often returns to in his poetry. But speculation has also been rife in suggesting that she might possibly be a new sweetheart in Rungsted whom Ewald had fallen in love with. The closest research can get is when it claims that the most important thing one can say about her is that Ewald includes a listener in his poem and asks her what her experience of the poem is. For the first time, the reader has here become the authority of modern poetry.

If one compares Ambrosius Stub's spring aria "The Tiresome Winter Now Is Gone" from the 1740s (published in 1771), which is also included in the present anthology, with Ewald's Rungsted ode, one can see a connection between the two: The poetic speaker plays an important role in the portrayal of nature and is explicitly included in both poems. But it is also evident that something else is taking place in Ewald than in Stub. Stub's aria about the coming of spring ends with a hope that God will remember the poet and makes sure that a heavenly spring is in the offing for him. For a modern reader, the ending is startling: After the long depiction of the pleasures of nature, where all creatures are propagating with great delight, the poet introduces his hope that he will escape from earthly life! For Stub, however, the glory of nature refers to a greater divine glory that the poet is awaiting. In the Rungsted ode it is the reader and not God who appears at the end of the poem as a figure that is crucial for the poet and his experiencing of nature. This exit does not mean that Ewald relinquishes his belief in God, something that the poem "When I Was Ill", also included in the anthology, reminds one of. But the relation of the believer to God is undergoing change, and human self-reliance is increasing.

Self-awareness in Ewald's poetry caused him to deal with the strong powers of the soul, its fires and desires that can consume everything. In Ewald, the spirit that God and humanity share is, however, more important than the soul. And Ewald does not relinquish this spiritual self-awareness, not even in his last hours in 1781, when he writes "To arms, hero of Calvary!" and the dying poet hands his saved soul over to God "On its now unmade clay", i.e. its aged, dying body.

While the German colony around Klopstock cultivated the odes of Antiquity and used the genre to cause emotions and language to intertwine, in Det norske Selskab (The Norwegian Society, founded in 1774 in Copenhagen) members stuck to French classicism and with great glee made fun of the German "seraphic odes" – the word "seraph", meaning a wingèd spiritual creature, was in fact imported into Danish by Klopstock. In Det norske Selskab, Johan Herman Wessel was one of the leading poets, and he made use of eminent rhymes and punchlines to make fun of himself and the pathetic, sensitive poetry of his age. His small verses have a biting ironic gesture and an amusing nonsense that attempts to whet the reader's sense of enlightened humour and reason.

In the period after Ewald, the ode genre was used by Jens Baggesen –

with Schack Staffeldt and Ingemann also making later use of it. The break made by Romantic poetry with a fixed system of genres, its cultivation of an all-inclusive, universal poetry, did, however, mean that the ode was abandoned as something that was far too regular, and it is characteristic that Staffeldt did not provide his major Romantic poems, e.g. "The One" (*Digte*, 1808), with any indication as to genre. The universal poetry of Romanticism distanced itself from the aesthetics of rules – and even the genre where poetry had actually broken free of them lost its significance in a Danish context.

Unlike in Danish poetry, the ode was still extremely important in the major works of Romantic English poetry. The main works of Coleridge, Shelley and Keats are odes, and via English Romanticism the ode enjoyed a new lease of life in 20th-century literature – especially in American and Spanish poetry in both the modern and the postmodern periods. The songs of Walt Whitman's *Leaves of Grass* (1855), a major modern work of American literature, are often referred to as odes, and the most important poets of Spanish-language literature – Garcia Lorca and Pablo Neruda – often make use of the genre. Pablo Neruda's *Elementary Odes* (1954-59) contains sensitive, thought-provoking poetry about things as banal and down-to-earth and divinely pleasurable as tomatoes, wine, artichokes, tuna fish, salt and lemons! The beat poet Allen Ginsberg also chose to use the ode genre in a major critical poem from 1978 about plutonium pollution. The ode resurfaces in Danish literature during the 1970s, in the period after modernism, and among those who use it are such poets as Benny Andersen, Henrik Nordbrandt and Klaus Høeck. With a touch of irony and sharp poetic reflection, the ode is used here in order to approach the major issues of human life.

Benny Andersen uses the ode to write ironically about death; Klaus Høeck writes about existential conditions in his odes – addressing not the soul as in Ewald, but the body: stomach, nose, heart, genitalia and brain; Nordbrandt uses the ode to enable his verse to wind its way through an erotic universe of lurking absence.

The great moment

Like Ewald, Jens Baggesen strove in his poetry to establish a personal moment in time – an instant when the speaker gains power over time, or when the personal experience of the speaker becomes more intense. This emerging theme concerning time and the speaker is a modern one. The new rationalist science and philosophy of the 17th century had already made time and space the most important parameters for a human understanding of the world. A traditional experience and thinking of place gave way to the great abstractions of time and space. One can notice the new impulses in the way poetry begins to focus on the moment as an instant in passing time. But the poetry also points out that the moment, paradoxically enough, first really exists for a person when it is past. Only when the moment has disappeared does one recall its greatness. The birth of the moment is its death, as Ewald emphasises. But a sublime moment of time, in which joy and dread or fear are present at one and the same time, can, however, open up in the sound and form of poetry.

Jens Baggesen, who wrote poetry in both Danish and German, circles round this moment in his major European work, the travel diary *Labyrinten* (1792-93). The moment accentuates itself in the winding course of his journey and it is quite simply a time-related form of experience that characterises the speaker and the modern poetics that Baggesen develops in opposition to classicism.

Baggesen perceives the world via moments and enters time and art with his personality via the moment. The time of the moment accentuates the presence of the speaker and turns the journey into a series of turning-points, where something new takes form: a new experience, a new realisation, a new mood or a new emotion. In his travel diary this aesthetics of the moment comes to a climax when the poet has climbed to the top of the cathedral in Strasbourg and completely loses all sense of time. His preoccupation with the moment also makes that which has disappeared the subject of fascination, as in his poem "When I Was Young" (1785), which is included in the present anthology. Here Baggesen depicts his childhood and enjoys letting his tears roll at all the memories of how small and pious he was. In the poem it is in fact the fine, emotional tears that become the most important thing for the poet: The memory of childhood itself is only an excuse to shed sweet tears.

In the first decades of the 19th century, Jens Baggesen had a difficult, conflict-ridden relationship with a new generation of poets around Adam Oehlenschläger. Baggesen admired the young Oehlenschläger, but later became very critical of his Goethe-inspired dramas and spent a lot of effort criticising and debating his poetry with its supporters. They viewed Oehlenschläger as an impeccable national icon that should not be exposed to any form of criticism.

When very young, Oehlenschläger had gained important impulses in his poetry from German idealist philosophy, which Heinrich Steffens had introduced in his Copenhagen lectures in 1802. His lectures dealt with the spiritual development and unity of nature and history, and it was evident that German Romantic idealism was emancipatory thought. New conceptions were formed of God, the world and humanity, as – developing further the idealism of Antiquity – the world of ideas was seen as being the real and essential one as opposed to the outer, material world. The new Romantic idealism took up the challenge after the Enlightenment philosopher Immanuel Kant's critical discussion of reason and the boundaries of knowledge, and his definition of the possibilities of aesthetics to symbolise the world of phenomena. Kant had refuted that man was able to ultimately prove anything about himself and the world by referring to a Creator or reason as the final instance. But this theft of a sure basis for thought also opened up possibilities for a new freedom in thought and poetry.

Steffens was very enthusiastic about the German idealist philosopher Schelling's idea that the absolute, universal spirit could be used as a unifying principle in the thought process, something that joined together nature, spirit and man. In such a way of thinking, it had to be art that would complete natural philosophy, because art is always searching for the unity between man, spirit and nature. For Schelling, nature is visible spirit, while spirit is invisible nature, both of them in constant motion and in a spiritual development towards ever higher forms. It is this insight which art can realise in creative imagery. Here the artist does not imitate the outer forms of nature, but is governed by the spirit itself. Steffens was following the same line as Schelling when in his first lecture he immediately laid down that the spirit moves towards unity. The universe is ruled by a universal, infinite "Urge towards Unity" which is realised as a development of opposites and reconciliations towards higher forms. In this process, the spirit is freed from coercion.

It is doubtful if Oehlenschläger and all the other young men understood all the finesses of Steffens's lectures, but the latter's many elucidations gave rise to poetic inspiration. Oehlenschläger was not long in finishing his *Digte* (1803), which seemed to be an epoch-making work with its programme poems, dramatic poetry, ballads and poems about what poetry is all about. He used genres, metres and themes in an innovative way. The three sections of the collection – romances, combinations and Midsummer Play – formed stimulating and varying poetic patterns.

The great programme poem was "The Gold Horns", which unmis-takably revealed the the poet's objective: "The Gold Horns" was a sharp critique of an erudite culture and a society that was spiritually completely extinct, where people have no sense of history, myth and art. For genera-tions of readers, "The Gold Horns" has been the incarnation of Danish Romanticism. At the beginning of the 21st century, the picture is less clear-cut, and more poems and poets must be taken into consideration when one talks about Romanticism on Danish soil. But for most of the 20th century, "The Gold Horns" was the core text of Romanticism, read and known by generations of Danish schoolchildren.

Oehlenschläger's poem was a poetically fascinating interpretation of the find of the two Gallehus horns – the "gleaming pair from days of yore" that had turned up in 1639 and 1734 respectively in a field near Møgeltønder. The horns were stolen from the king's collection of curios and melted down in 1802 – in a Copenhagen locality close to where Oehlenschläger lived, incidentally. The thief was apprehended in 1803.

In Oehlenschläger's interpretation, the mysterious horns had brought both "times most olden" and "miracles from outside time" into the pres-ent, promising the beginning of a radiant new age. The present was, however, unable to understand this mysterious sacred relic which had to come from the gods themselves. All people saw was the magnificence and preciousness of the horns, not their spiritual and mysterious powers, and the hope of a spiritual renewal disappeared when the gods took the horns back once more. (The more profane fate of the horns was unknown when Oehlenschläger wrote his poem.)

Oehlenschläger wanted to show by means of his poem that the horns' stamp of eternity can, in the right hands and with the right recipients, create new times that are linked back to the very oldest ones. The reader is witness to a grand movement through the ages, from the time and space of the present to those of the gods, delving into history at various indicated points.

The free movement of the poem through various times expresses the longing for the divine and the eternal, showing in practice the possibilities for the poem to liberate itself from time's restricting fetters. Steffens had emphasised that when a poet sings, an endless poetic imagery spellbinds the listener and dissolves the boundaries of time. In "The Gold Horns", Oehlenschläger tried to use such a liberating, new figurative language and to make the gold horns into a living Romantic symbol.

The tension between ages that can be experienced in "The Gold Horns" was characteristic of Oehlenschläger's Romantic poetry in general. In *Digte* (1803) he included both a historical past and a mythical olden age, the present and even eternity itself. But the present is always seen as representing a decline in relation to both historical time and mythical time.

While Oehlenschläger was busy writing poems after meeting Steffens, another poet, Schack Staffeldt, was busy after Oehlenschläger's debut publishing his own poems. He tried to overtake the young genius on the inside by claiming that all the poems in his *Digte* (1804) had been written before Oehlenschläger's. Staffeldt's manipulation with time and dates of writing reveal something of the importance the Romantic period attached to the poet's originality and the idea of being the first person to introduce something new. Staffeldt's deceit made him look extremely suspect and this meant that for a long while he was seen as only a peripheral figure when later generations formed their ideas about Danish Romanticism. Posterity has often portrayed Oehlenschläger as the young man who went on to have a fine, although perhaps a somewhat complacent, cultural career, while Staffeldt is seen as the poet who, having stopped writing, ended his days in a boring post as an official in Schleswig.

Both Oehlenschläger and Staffeldt had a German family background. This was problematic, as the late 18th-century patriotic love of king and country in connection with the Napoleonic Wars was replaced by a cultivation of the excellence of the Danish as opposed to the German nation. Oehlenschläger did a great deal to underline that as a child he did not understand a word when his parents spoke German to him. Apparently, it was extremely important for him to show that his mother tongue was Danish. He even amused himself by writing to his fiancée in German when expressing the wish that a litter of kittens should be put down. For he believed that the true-blood Danish kittens did not understand German and therefore would not suspect anything!

Staffeldt's German mother tongue, however, proved yet another stumbling-block for how he wanted to be perceived by others – as a Danish poet. Time and time again, people complained that his language was heavy and long-winded, influenced by German. But part of the story also is that Staffeldt was later rehabilitated as the great Romantic poet of Danish literature when the literary critic Georg Brandes presented some of his poetry in a major essay in 1882.

While Oehlenschläger's poetry develops in the direction of a search for harmony and the idyllic, the poet in Staffeldt's work is torn apart by his longing to experience spiritual nature and his physical existence in a life on earth that almost resembles a wilderness. Staffeldt's poems mainly deal with loss and discord and only at rare moments express an experiencing of the spiritual dimension. Only via imagination, empathy and poetic suggestion is the speaker able to gaze into a mythological universe and meet his lost spiritual self, as in the poem "Initiation" (1804), which is included in the present anthology.

In Staffeldt one finds the idea of a spiritual all-Nature and the painful initiation into it of the poet – a thought he shares with both German Romantics such as Novalis and a kindred-spirit in Sweden, the poet Erik Johan Stagnelius, who repeatedly deals with poetic visions of a dead nature and his unquenchable longing to be liberated from it.

Romantic generations

In the generation of poets after Oehlenschläger and Staffeldt, it was in particular Carsten Hauch who tried to maintain the problematics of human cognition that had featured in the Romantic period. As a scientist and poet, Hauch fought hard to hold onto the Romantic visions and to avoid ending up in a conflict where faith and knowledge excluded each other. In his poem "Death's Genius" (1839), included in this anthology, the poet fantasises about death's unknown country, which he makes into a world that is far richer and more alive than life itself. Even though the poet can fill his poems with great visions and beautiful images, it is as if emptiness and nothingness spread out over life, death and the poem. Romantic imagination is still able to express itself magnificently – but it proffers no redemption.

Hauch sought to continue the line from Staffeldt and Stagnelius, whose conception of the second nature acquired its counterpart in Nordic literature in a strong, Goethe-inspired poetry, the key concepts of which are Bildung, harmony and spiritual growth. As early as in his lectures on Ewald in 1810 and 1811, Oehlenschläger saw Goethe's poetry as a counterpart to what he called Ewald's emotional bombast. From his point of view, Ewald is what Schiller calls a sentimental poet, who abandons himself completely to his emotions. Opposed to this, a naive poet becomes adult when he becomes interested not only in himself but also in his fellow human beings, real life, and his spiritual task. This poetic mode of thought caused Oehlenschläger to distance himself from a Romantic poetry about man who is divided in his longing for infinite, spiritual nature. Instead, he concentrated on using Norse mythology in a modern tragic poetry and a national humanist dramatic poetry.

In Danish poetry it is possible to distinguish in literary history between an early and a later Romanticism. For the former, the cardinal date is 1803, with Oehlenschläger's debut. This Romantic poetry was a German-inspired universal Romanticism, with Oehlenschläger, Staffeldt and Grundtvig as its main figures. Later Romanticism – the second and third generations of Romantics – cultivated a poetry influenced by Schiller, Goethe and Hegel and the concept of Bildung. Its main representatives are the mature Oehlenschläger and Johan Ludvig Heiberg, who became the leading arbiter of taste in an emerging modern literary culture, with periodicals, reviews and literary feuds. Heiberg introduced the German philosopher Hegel to Denmark and actually formulated a dialectic philosophy of art before the master himself. In Heiberg's system, speculative comedy, which he himself had invented – inspired by French and Spanish drama – was made the highest form of art. Heiberg is represented in the present anthology by "Barcarole" (1829), which was inspired both by Italian gondolier music and Goethe's "Über allen Gipfeln…" (1780). It is included in his comedy *Prindsesse Isabella eller De tre Aftner ved Hoffet* (Princess Isabella or The Three Evenings at Court), where the beautiful but also dangerous moonlight reveals the longings and heartaches of the characters. "Barcarole" is sung at the end of the comedy, where Isabella in fact asks to be spared any more melancholy barcaroles – she wants to have joyful songs to celebrate her coming wedding. The comedy was a resounding fiasco and no one remembers it nowadays, but "Barcarole" is still a well-known, popular song.

A national-Romantic poetry also culminated with the second and third generations of Romantics, to which many writers contributed, inspired not least by the many dramatic events of the Napoleonic Wars, which ended with Denmark going bankrupt and having to cede Norway, which then came under Swedish suzerainty. National Romanticism is strongly represented in both prose and poetry, but with the second- and third-generation Romantics there were also a number of clashes in the 1820s and 1830s between an amenable Biedermeier poetry and a reflective Romanticism. Many poets found themselves pulled in both directions, poets such as Emil Aarestrup, St. St. Blicher and Hans Christian Andersen.

Aarestrup allows pleasure to take the place in his poetry of Romantic reflection and a longing for eternity. Precisely the certainty of cessation, disappearance, destruction and death intensifies the moment, the brief encounter, the hour of delight or the erotic situation. Aarestrup's poems display refined word-painting, and when the poet focuses on the moment, the body gains a physicality in the world of the poem rather than becoming Romantic, ethereal dream material. The body is referred to as it actually is, something physical, and the poem can therefore be what it actually is – a work of art, an aesthetic form. The Romantic idea of art's images of the sacred and the eternal dissolve in favour of a conception of the work of art as art and pleasure. In Aarestrup, Romantic symbolism is replaced by a seductively fragmented, slightly ragged formation of images, where parts of the body indicate the desired physical whole. The eye is caught and lingers on lips, forehead, eyes, hands, locks of hair and fingers. Aarestrup is interested in fleeting time: "We only have time once", he writes. We must therefore make haste to experience the poem, the gentle pressure of fingers, the moment and eroticism's secret realm of freedom that can open out at a mere glimpse in the midst of a highly respectable living room. Aarestrup's poems spin a particular erotic-linguistic logic via his choice of words and rhymes: "Stræbe" (to strive) rhymes with "Læbe" (lip), "Bryst" (breast) with "Lyst" (delight), "Glød" (glow) with "Skød" (lap).

It was a later period of literary history writing which, inspired by art history, began to call the new harmony-seeking literature "Biedermeier literature". The name itself comes from a naive schoolteacher who was parodied in a popular German comic magazine in the 1850s. In German, "Bieder" means "respectable, good-natured, ingenuous, honest", and Biedermeier literature was interested in portraying its literary characters and their environment with an amenable, poetic and harmonious touch. The world of the family and the home was placed at the centre, as, for example, Hans Christian Andersen does in "That Ancient Tree, Don't Let It Fall", included in this anthology. Here, the otherwise eager traveller Andersen states that "one does but travel to return". It is, however, just as fearfully difficult to translate Andersen's small poems about home and family into another language as it is his poems about his native land. The texts become too banal and lack poetic tension. Perhaps the distance the present has to the texts and their own subtle play on sounds of language and rhythms cannot be translated. Andersen's lyrical poetry is, generally speaking, to be placed within Biedermeier literature and national Romanticism. But as a writer of tales and a prose-writer he belongs, together with Blicher and Kierkegaard, to a radical European Romanticism which renews the sensitive poetry about longing, absence, division and passion, found especially in Danish poetry in the works of Ewald and Staffeldt.

In this anthology, Blicher is represented by poems from his main poetic work, *Trækfuglene. Naturkoncert* (Birds of Passage. Nature Concert, 1838), where he lets the birds themselves speak, chirp and sing about their nature, their life-conditions and their distinctive characteristics. The personification is reversed in the introductory prelude, where it is the poet who uses the bird of passage as an image of himself, his problematic life and his poetry. The poem is an extension of Ewald's poetry and is sentimental, in the 18th-century meaning of the word: personal and sensitive – but precisely not nostalgic. The individual poems with bird portraits also refer back to the personifying poems of the 18th century, but with Blicher the birds are seen and described as small studies in nature. The poems are not didactic poems or fables – instead they form a nature concert, where the birds are interesting as natural phenomena, whose lives and goings-on the speakers interpret, mirror themselves in, amuse themselves over, or simply experience.

Later poetry has often returned to sensitive poetry and the themes and forms of Romanticism. Per Højholt wrote bird poems from the mid-1960s onwards that are clearly comments on Blicher's nature concert. In the late 1950s, Erik Knudsen wrote about Staffeldt's wild Romanticism in a poem included in this anthology. Peter Laugesen, via adaptations of Oehlenschläger's plays in the 1990s, has rediscovered a poet so down-graded in recent years. And the generation of poets that had its debut around 1980 have made frequent references to sensitive poetry and radical Romanticism. Michael Strunge combined inspirations from Hans Christian Andersen's tales, Grundtvig's hymns and Oehlenschläger's poems with loans and quotations from rock poetry by David Bowie and Jim Morrison and the surrealism of the 1930s. As a poet, Søren Ulrik Thomsen has been interested in Ingemann's hymns along with American minimalist sculpture and French psycho-semiotics, while Bo Green Jensen mainly uses English Romanticism and the Pre-Raphaelites as his poetic treasure trove. Pia Tafdrup, on the other hand, has been interested in later symbolist and modernist poetry by Sophus Claussen as well as Inger Christensen and such European poets as Rilke and Celan.

The modern breakthrough

In the 19th century, time and space had become boundaries that poetry hoped and believed it could transcend. A second nature and a golden age, or a new realm of freedom, was to be engendered in the poetry's sacred images of the eternal, thereby healing the division of knowledge and the limitations of earthly life.

The experiencing of the powers and limits of the imagination made the sublime, eternal moment when time and space seemed to merge into each other a new subject for poetic longing. But the brief glimpse of the moment could end up pointing out the paradox, the loss, the disappearance and the destruction as well as a desire for new moments and ever more new experiences to take their place.

Danish poetry also started in a fascinated and melancholy way to depict moments that allowed modern realities to emerge. In Hauch, the absence of romantic visions lurks, although the world of Romanticism is also filled once again and carried out in the form of beautifully polished, sensitive writing by such poets as Ludvig Holstein and Viggo Stuckenberg. In the present anthology, the two poets are represented by modern poems about a wounding, divisive love and the experiencing of the advent of spring. Holstein's poem "How Fine It Is Today" (1895) gained new popularity when it was recorded in 1973 by one of the leading artists of Danish rock music, Kim Larsen.

In the latter half of the 19th century, however, a number of young poets succeeded in expressing a new interpretation of existence and longing in their poetic universe. This applies, for example, to J.P. Jacobsen in the poem "Forest Rain" (1869). Here, readers are not to think of Oehlenschläger's vision of finding a divine nature in the smallest drop of water, but simply to experience a "terrible" rain that drenches the entire forest. There is more eroticism than divinity about Jacobsen's poem. Holger Drachmann also renews the poetic inventory of Romanticism, breathing new life into an exotic-erotic universe in his obsessive poem "Sakuntala" (1879), which fetches motifs from a world of Indian legends.

Both Drachmann and Jacobsen spearheaded the modern breakthrough in Danish literature announced by the critic and literary figure Georg Brandes. In 1871, with dazzling eloquence, he had argued that Danish literature now had to break free of its soulfulness and uninspired spiritual life. There was really a need to open up to new European impulses, and Brandes expected more of Drachmann and Jacobsen than erotic poems about dark forests and distant Indian kingdoms. Brandes was in favour of literature dealing with everyday life, and he believed that the major Romantic currents of European literature had never really manifested themselves in Denmark. So his ideas about modern longings for freedom were to a great extent a communicating and updating of a European Romantic programme about radical spiritual freedom. Civic rights and a critique of Christianity were at the heart of his view of human nature. He placed his trust in a new kind of novel that took up problematic issues – for Brandes, poetry was not the most important literary genre, even though he was among those who rediscovered Staffeldt, who represented something quite different from Oehlenschläger's national Romanticism.

Around the year 1870, works began to appear in Denmark that distanced themselves from the Romantic world of ideas and aesthetics. A new longing for freedom emerged, combined with the hope of reaching the same mental and artistic level as the outside modern world. The world opened up, also for present-day dreams and for new depths, as had been claimed by the poet-philosopher Friedrich Nietzsche, who was one of numerous thinkers and writers discovered by Brandes. The modern breakthrough came about in a literary awareness of the new realities of the urban world and the cultural opportunities they might offer.

The Nordic community of culture, which the Romantic Age had cultivated and which had culminated around the time of the first Schleswig war (1848-51), became a reality once more at the time of the modern breakthrough in the form of lively, critical exchanges, friendships and animosities between authors and critics in Norway, Sweden, Finland and Denmark.

Nordic writers and artists met in Copenhagen, Berlin and Paris on educational journeys, or in a more or less voluntary exile, such as Herman Bang and the Swede August Strindberg. Younger literary travellers were also on their way around Europe at the end of the 19th century. Sophus Claussen travelled to Paris in 1892, where he wrote his first main work *Antonius i Paris* (Antonius in Paris, 1896) about his meeting with the metropolis. Letters, poems and essays were all included in it, in a conflict between romantic longings and dreams and the new types of experiences found in the big city. Claussen's book was an extension of travel letters he had published in the daily newspaper *Politiken*. The relation between the Romantic and new types of experience is dealt with in many ways, also in the portrayal of the meeting between the *alter ego* of the writer, Antonius, and the leading Symbolist poet, Paul Verlaine. The meeting takes place on a mild, misty January evening, where the gas lamps cause the world to lose its familiar contours and one seems to be able to mirror oneself in the unknown.

For Claussen, Paul Verlaine is both a wise man of Antiquity, a genius of Romanticism, a Paris proletarian and a completely new poetic myth. A dreaming, experiencing and modern literature that stands on the threshold between two centuries was on the point of finding its forms and genres in Sophus Claussen's poetic universe. The poem "Creation", included in the present anthology, hesitatingly and doubtfully asks about the world of Romanticism and its divine glory. But the poet also finds a vitalistic life-force within himself. And the poetic creation is linked to the poet's courage to adhere to this force and passion.

Sophus Claussen stands poised between the 19th and the 20th centuries. His poetry retains a line back to the world of the Romantics, but his experiencing of the modern loss of tradition and the idea of a new life-force and passion as a vortex in existence represents a vitalism that is also present in other younger poets from the beginning of the 20th century.

The poets Johannes V. Jensen, Jeppe Aakjær and Thøger Larsen, all included in the present anthology, are leading lights in the new Nordic literature that emerged in the wake of the modern breakthrough. When Georg Brandes himself, at the beginning of the 20th century, took stock of contemporary literature, he particularly stressed that these poets were part of a modern, variegated literature. Even though Brandes was initially critical of Johannes V. Jensen, he regarded him as being a leading figure who possessed what Brandes refers to as a raw but colourful narrative ability. Brandes was clearly more interested in Jensen's prose than his poetry. But in Johannes V. Jensen, the transitions between prose and poetry are often extremely fluid. Texts that were first published as short prose and small newspaper articles are included as poems in the landmark collection *Digte 1906*, which also contains translations of poems by Johannes V. Jensen's great example, Walt Whitman.

With Johannes V. Jensen's poetry we gain a Danish contribution to an international poetic modernism, and Johannes V. Jensen is one of a total of three Danish writers to have received the Nobel Prize in literature (1944). Jensen's poetry can be characterised as modernist, because he quite demonstratively chooses to work with a completely new poetic vocabulary and a more experimental form. And the modernist label is also apposite for many of Jensen's poems, because they deal with an experience where the poet undergoes a violent confrontation between body and consciousness and between reality and fiction, and renounces a Christian interpretation of existence. In a Danish context, the concept of modernism – in the wake of Brandes's critique of literature – has often been linked with an explicit rejection of a Christian creed. And this definitely applies to Johannes V. Jensen, who was an avid supporter of Darwinism.

One recent form of literary criticism, however, points out that a number of poets in the 20th century combine a Christian interpretation of existence and a modernist poetics of fragmentation. This is the case, for example, with Ole Sarvig, included in the present anthology.

Johannes V. Jensen's modernism derives partly from a Darwinist view of nature and humanity and partly from a modern experiencing of restlessness and a loss of *locus* and tradition, something that is already indicated in the introductory poem of *Digte 1906*. Here the fiddler, i.e. the poet, asks for shelter, explaining that he has come from far away and is on his way to "far off". The abstract definition of time and space in modern life predominates over the old common people's sense of place – a theme that is also treated in other texts. The speaker in Jensen's poetry is at the mercy of the shredding-systems of his own mind and its conflicting, fragmented thoughts. Various realities and consciousnesses are constantly being confronted with each other within the poet. *Digte 1906* has to do with the modern dislocated and godless poet who lives with a both painful and wonderful experience of freedom and an insatiable desire.

Such a theme can be seen in the poem "On Memphis Station", included in the present anthology. Here the American station town entices one with happiness, fair maidens, and citizenship. But the American urban world frightens the modern traveller, who does not want to find any redeeming city or island that can still his longing, dreaming and restlessness. Jensen sees himself as a kind of Columbus, who supplies a sort of poetics of restlessness. With Johannes V. Jensen's poetry a new everyday vocabulary enters poetry, something that provides a springboard for later modernists, in particular Klaus Rifbjerg, who made his debut as a poet in 1956 and soon made his mark within many genres.

Jensen works with dislocation as a modernist theme, and in his poetry he reflects on the coming into existence of a new world, the civilised steppe, which eradicates the contrasts between town and country and between peasant and the modern culture that Jensen himself grew up in as the son of a veterinary surgeon from Farsø in North Jutland. The civilised steppe paves the way for a global sentiment that Jensen feels he experiences both in North Jutland and on his many journeys to America and the Orient.

Such a global sentiment – or what we nowadays would call globalisation – also fascinates Thøger Larsen. He expresses the idea of the connection between one's domicile and the wide new world in a different, but also extremely striking way. In a letter to Sophus Claussen he writes that the feeling one has for one's native home, which is so important for him, is an exceedingly old sentiment: Sanskrit *kshâm*, Greek *cosmos*, and Norse *heimr*, according to Thøger Larsen, mean both home and world. And this idea is a recurrent theme in his poetry, where his home region in Jutland is seen as part of a restless and mobile world. The seasons and work form changing rhythms in his oeuvre, relating to the tension between man's temporality and the stars' eternity. A vitalist conception of the strong Eros-force that leads the human cycle into both oblivion and eternity gains a vibrant, fluid language in Thøger Larsen's poetry. Because of this, many of his poems have also become well-loved Danish songs.

Thøger Larsen's first published collection, *Jord* (Earth, 1904), is organised in such a way that it begins with a general praising of "Mother Earth", after which it moves on through anthems to the sun and weather and meetings with mythological figures to an outside world that is increasingly experienced through the senses. The major poem "Pan" is placed towards the end, where the poet gazes into the infinity of the cosmos and senses a life-force or an "eternal I" above, below and in the soil and the stars. The collection concludes with the poem "Midday", which is included in this anthology. Here, the still, hot summer day stretches out into the light and makes the outside world visible, audible and perceptible. Many of Thøger Larsen's poems use a traditional poetic vocabulary, but the experience of the speaker and the outside world expresses a modern, erotic conception of existence.

It is evident in the work of Aakjær, Larsen and Jensen how the poems dissolve the national base that national Romanticism had created and allow a new Danish landscape with its own history to take shape. In Aakjær's poems from the present anthology the reader gazes into the familiar, domestic world, but at the same time it is a gaze out into the distance, and the noise of the wild geese on Walpurgis Night reminds the speaker of a longing and the cosmos where the speaker and the home belong.

In Aakjær, the stars are the orientation point in all life-situations, and they retain the speaker's outward longing, great dreams and thoughts. Aakjær always makes careful use of the natural rhythms of the language and the sounds of the outside world. There are lots of tiny sounds of trickling and chirping in Aakjær, but there is also the song between the stars that opens the small world out towards something vastly larger.

Johannes V. Jensen, Thøger Larsen and Jeppe Aakjær, in their various ways, all see the world begin; and "the modern and new" is precisely to be found in the Jutland hills that open out – for better or worse – onto the great wide world, the new life and an infinite cosmos. The native soil the poems circle around lie at the hub of the world.

Modern and modernist positions

20th-century Danish poetry gets its inspiration from the whole world, and there are connections and interfaces between various different positions. It is characteristic of Danish poetry at the turn of the 20th century, however, that it was only sporadically part of avant-garde, experimental poetry.

One of the leading critics and poets at the beginning of the century, Otto Gelsted, was sharply critical of international expressionism, preferring a cubist-inspired poetry. Gelsted himself mastered such a modern landscape poetry in, for example, the poem "September", included in the present anthology. The poem seeks to open up the reader's senses to the beautiful fertility of the cultivated agricultural landscape and its meaningful cycle. Gelsted emphasised the forming, enlightening potential of art, and viewed avant-garde experiments with considerable scepticism. Certain expressionist and surrealist impulses did, however, gain a certain foothold in modern Danish poetry and in the new periodicals of the early 20th century. Tom Kristensen, for example, wrote the expressionist novel *Hærværk* (Havoc, 1930), from which the poem "Angst" in the present anthology has been taken. However, Kristensen soon decided to shift his poetry in towards the centre, and his poem "It Is Knud Who Is Dead", dedicated to the Greenland explorer Knud Rasmussen, shows this aspect of his work. Surrealist inspiration is present in the poems of Jens August Schade, but the two poems that represent him in the present anthology show in particular that Schade was also an amusing, ingenious verse-writer who used the poem to draw the outline of modes of urban existence, often with a touch of fantasy and erotic imagination. An echo of surrealism can also be sensed in Bodil Bech's poem "Half-asleep" (1934) from the same period. Here, unknown colours, sounds and movements from the subconscious enter an otherwise known and familiar urban world and make it dangerous and fascinating. Hulda Lütken, her contemporary, portrays the loss of a fairytale, liberating erotic world in her poem "What Have You Done With Your Blue Look?" (1934). Typical of Hulda Lütken is that she alternates between love-poetry, which passionately addresses a you-figure, and poems and texts that seek to find poetic language for a time-bound angst and for the many exterior and interior threats that ravage the world of the speaker.

Painting became an important impulse for a number of the poets of the 1920s and 1930s. Gustaf Munch-Petersen, whose poetry is based on surrealism, was himself an artist, and some of his best poems almost have the feel of being ekphrases of pictures that have not been painted and that the reader does not know, but which nevertheless enter his word-painting. This applies not least to the small poem with a Bornholm motif included in the present anthology. Like Bodil Bech, Gustaf Munch-Petersen stayed with his family for a while on Bornholm, but he chose to volunteer in the Spanish civil war in 1937, and was killed on the battlefield the following year.

The young, insistent tone that also characterises his poetry can be felt in the poem "a lucky day", where God himself nonchalantly hands the poet a brand new tie, and world fame is just around the corner. Gustaf Munch-Petersen did not, however, experience any major success as a poet. His mother went around buying up his poetry collections at Copenhagen bookshops, so that he could at least experience some sales of his publications. But Munch-Petersen's death in Spain made him known, and a number of literary experts discovered his poetry. Morten Nielsen, who lost his life in the Danish Resistance during the Second World War, was, in contrast, already admired by his own generation. Present-day readers, too, notice immediately the vital sense and awareness of death that is condensed in his poetry. This can perhaps even be sensed by the reader without having any knowledge of his tragic death. Morten Nielsen's poems are perfectly able to speak for themselves, and both he and Gustaf Munch-Petersen have been important figures for generations of young poets and readers in the 20th century.

Morten Nielsen, along with Erik Knudsen, belonged to a circle of young poets and friends that in the 1940s centred around The Young Artists' Club and the periodical *Vild Hvede* (Wild Wheat), which still exists as a publication (but has changed its name to *Hvedekorn*), where

Danish poets often make their debut. Tove Ditlevsen was a comet in the young circle of the 1940s. She married the editor of the periodical, Viggo F. Møller, and had a secret affair with another of the young poets, Piet Hein. Both Tove Ditlevsen and Piet Hein soon acquired their own distinctive poetic voices. Piet Hein allowed poetry, art and architecture to synergise and was to become famous both for his Grooks and his superellipse, which has been marketed in many versions. The Grook poems were small, sharp pieces of wisdom with connections to both an English and a Nordic tradition of small verses and aphorisms. Piet Hein himself claimed that he had invented the word Grook as a term for these special verses, which are often accompanied by a drawing. Many of Hein's Grooks have become well-known idioms in Danish, and they are a source of inspiration for speeches given at everything from weddings to funerals. The characteristic feature of a Grook is that it has a philosophical point to it, and that it combines opposing emotions and moods in one and the same apt expression.

Tove Ditlevsen, unlike Piet Hein, did not have any particular educational background when she made her debut in 1939. Even as a schoolgirl from the working-class Vesterbro district of Copenhagen, she had been deeply interested in hymns and poems and undauntedly set about becoming a poet. Ditlevsen's marriage to Viggo F. Møller gave her social opportunities for realising her dream, and she became one of the most loved and widely read of Danish poets. For the mature Tove Ditlevsen, Rilke was a special model, and the poems that represent her in the present anthology show how she is both able to use a traditional, rhyming lyric form and modern free verse in portraying the emotional life of the child and the grown woman respectively.

Tove Ditlevsen's traditionalism had its counterpart among a number of the young poets from the war years who, inspired by Swedish and French poetry, worked with modern poetic forms to suit the times. After the end of the war in 1945, many of them longed to slip away from Denmark and see the world that had survived. This applied to Paul la Cour as well as Erik Knudsen and Halfdan Rasmussen. Their poems were at that time reactions to the cultural crisis that followed after the war, and their poetry was characterised by scepticism, spiritual seeking and pathos. Both Erik Knudsen and Halfdan Rasmussen also found other poetic timbres than the pathetic-critical. Halfdan Rasmussen is now best known for his verses written for children and their parents. In the present anthology, he is represented by a poem from 1952 that shows at one and the same time his unobtrusive, self-ironic and uproarious sense of humour. Halfdan Rasmussen's custom of curiously and playfully working with language was continued later by Benny Andersen, who in the 1970s wrote his major work *Svantes viser* (Svante's Songs), which today is part of the Danish treasure trove of songs. "Just think, to be remembered for the line 'And the coffee's on its way'," Benny Andersen has once remarked. And precisely the telling nature of this line says, without a doubt, a great deal about both Danish readers and Danish poetry. For it has never maintained a pathetic tone of voice for any length of time, and has incidentally also made it something of a speciality in the 20th century to place poetic pathos in perspective with a quick play on words, a self-ironic gesture or a reference to everyday life.

Various types of modernism

The modern and modernist poets of the 20th century have also created platforms for themselves by publishing periodicals. Among the most important of recent times have been *Heretica* (1948-53), which gathered a first post-war group of modernist writers, *Vindrosen* (1954-73), where young critics and writers especially in the 1950s and 1960s renewed modernism, the avant-garde periodical *ta'* (1967-68) and *Sidegaden* (1981-84), which became the forum for a new punk-inspired poetry, art and music.

In his memoirs, Thorkild Bjørnvig tells of how the circle of writers behind *Heretica* eagerly discussed what the name of their new periodical was to be. As Bjørnvig saw it, the creed of the periodical was to promote aesthetic recognition of modern, unknown man. He and Bjørn Poulsen worked for a long time on the manifesto, but they found it extremely difficult to agree, and the manifesto ended up being completely omitted for the first issue of the periodical. Instead, there followed various programmatic articles by the individual *Heretica* poets.

Bjørnvig's interpretation of the many ifs and uncertainties concerning the periodical gives an impression of the spread and disagreements in attitudes and thoughts among the young poets. *Heretica* has often been critically and negatively presented in Danish literary history writing, being conceived as a monolith that ascribed the poem a world-redeeming role and trying to throw in the lonely poet and the rural mind-set as a last reserve in the battle against the cultural crisis.

Recent literary research has a more nuanced view of the periodical and emphasises its international orientation, its ambition to present poems by Nordic and European writers and its attempt to promote a new modernist poetry. The young poets of *Heretica* definitely did not agree on any unequivocal definition of modernism, but the concept was, however, embraced by some of the leading figures of the circle.

In Ole Sarvig's work on modern art, *Krisens Billedbog* (The Picture Book of Crisis, 1950), modernism had been used as a term for the various more or less ominous effects that the modern loss of reality had had in art and literature. Sarvig defined modernism as a movement in art, starting with impressionism — as the tendency where the loss of reality, the supremacy of things and the disappearing of the human figure really got under way.

A similar view of the crisis in modern art and literature had been formulated by Bjørn Poulsen in *Heretica* in 1949. Here, he wrote that modern literature was being threatened by the intellect and the force of thought and had to cultivate the symbol in order to conquer its loss of belief and its isolation in relation to what is universally human. The poetic symbol is seen as an emergency solution for the poet, by means of which he can insert his experiencing of reality into the poem. The symbol is the quickest detour to one's fellow man.

The poet Paul la Cour, who published the first chapters of his immensely influential poetics *Fragmenter af en Dagbog* (Fragments of a Diary, 1948) in *Heretica*, used the concept of modernist poetry about poetry that approached the creative layers of the individual via imagery. He dates modernist poetry back to Hölderlin, Novalis, Baudelaire and French surrealism, mentioning Sophus Claussen as the first Danish poet whose work shows modernist traits.

In the present anthology, Ole Sarvig is represented by poems from 1943 that encapsulate the experiences of ominous waiting and hope for salvation that was the point of departure for the young Hereticans. The first of Thorkild Bjørnvig's poems in the present anthology, "September", comes from his debut collection *Stjærnen bag Gavlen* (The Star behind the Gable, 1947) and it shows precisely his idea that poetry can gain a state of balance and rest. On the other hand, the poem "The Grebe", from the collection *Figur og Ild* (Figure and Fire, 1959) is a first expression of the ecological struggle and resistance to the destruction of nature by industrialism that Bjørnvig so actively involved himself in later on in his work.

The last year of the periodical was edited by the youngest of the Hereticans, Frank Jæger, who made his debut in 1948. He was admired and fêted for his poetic imagination and bright simplicity. In the present anthology he is represented by poems that express the dark, pessimistic side of his poetry, so different from the cheerful tone of the first poems for which he became known. In "Sidenius in Esbjerg" (1959) and "After the Storm" (1976), a harrowing experience of nothingness cannot be kept away from the poet's imaginative easy-going nature. Jæger was subject to harsh criticism by the young modernists of the 1960s, who felt that his poetry was too safe; however, as with Ole Sarvig, Jæger was rediscovered by the young poets of the 1980s.

Another poet whose importance was also stressed in the 1980s is Tove Meyer, who is included in this anthology with the autumn poem "A Stranger in the Big City's Autumn" (1961). Tove Meyer – who was the same age as Munch-Petersen – is difficult to place in relation to Danish modernism. Like Bodil Bech and Hulda Lütken, she was interested in the expressive modernism of the Swedish-Finnish writer Edith Södergran, but her lyrical musicality was and remained her own, and her poems contain a profound experiencing of something that is mysteriously wordless and horrifying, that exists but is inexpressible. Throughout her life, Tove Meyer struggled with serious mental problems and committed suicide in 1972, a few years after she had published some of her most important poems.

In 1950, several of the *Heretica* poets decided to join the periodical *Dialog*, which – with *Heretica* in mind – turned against the scepticism and cultural pessimism which was on the way – as they wrote – "to drifting over into the metaphysical". This circle of writers felt that there was a need for a new inclusiveness and freedom in the debate.

Poets and critics who had communist sympathies gained a considerable influence over *Dialog*, and this soon led to many articles on Marxism, socialist realism and Soviet art. There were also, however, articles of a different and less ideologically unshakable mould, and introductions to African poetry and American literary criticism added an international perspective long overdue in the Danish debate. Ivan Malinowski, along with Erik Knudsen, took part in the activities to do with *Dialog*. Malinowski now appears to us as one of the most important modernist poets in a Danish context; his image formations are complex and move in the depths, with the potential and flowering of poetic metaphors. Malinowski's range is internationally wide – including Swedish, Spanish and American poetry – and his poems, together with jazz, rock poetry and American beat poetry, were vitally inspiring for writers making their debut in the 1960s, e.g.

Dan Turèll. Malinowski is represented in the present anthology by two poems from his debut collection *Galgenfrist* (Short Respite, 1958).

Ivan Malinowski participated in a major, crucial debate on the concept of modernism that took place at the art museum Louisiana in 1961. After an international avant-garde exhibition, "Movement in Art", that caused quite a scandal, the museum invited people to take part in a discussion on modernism and published a series of contributions in its periodical, *Louisiana-Revy* (2 and 3/1962). Ivan Malinowski here stated that he felt confused that a debate should at all be necessary – without any scruples whatsoever, he regarded modernism as being a complex of various traditions from such figures as Marcel Duchamp and Samuel Beckett, which anyone in the present ought to be able to choose or discard freely.

But in 1961 the concept of modernism had in fact been overtaken by a young generation of poets and critics that used the term programmatically and critically against the representatives of an older generation they wanted to distance themselves from. The central poet of this new circle was Klaus Rifbjerg, who made his debut as early as 1956. His poetry represented a turning towards modern realities and a living, spoken language, and together with the critic Torben Brostrøm and the writer Villy Sørensen he gave the concept of modernism a far broader content in the periodical *Vindrosen* than it had ever had for those of the *Heretica* circle.

In this new punch-packing version, modernism simply became an attitude to art determined by the present age, an attempt to penetrate and dig down into the human and to create corresponding poetry. Modernism was here no longer an escape route to the essential and spiritual or a sign of a crisis in art that had to be overcome – on the contrary. Modernism became a term for a lively, experimental literature that wanted to take up modern experiences and attitudes and criticise alienation in society and family. From having been a poetic term for crisis, modernism became a label for an experimental, linguistic conquest of reality.

The modernist poem often takes the form of a both angst- and pleasure-filled confrontation with a fragmented outside world. A provocative or surprising cluster of metaphors is arranged in ever more complex allegories of modernity, as is the case in Klaus Rifbjerg's "Refshale Island" (1960), included in the present anthology. The modernist poets are fond of changes of angle and the personification of modern objects. Children and the body are often a lyrical topic, and through a poetic confrontation with the contents of a repressed consciousness modernism seeks to promote the reader's awareness of modernity and the reader's critical stance.

In addition to "Refshale Island" – a poem from his epoch-making collection *Konfrontation* (1960) – Klaus Rifbjerg is also represented in the present anthology by poems from collections later in the 1960s. The poems display an appetite for grappling with all of existence, something that has typified his writing throughout his career, and the desire to feel the various movements of both the body and the psyche, a common thread that runs through the poems. Rifbjerg's writing has been inspired by Swedish, American and British poetry – especially Whitman, Eliot and Hemingway, and in a Danish context there are strong connections between the modernism of Rifbjerg, Johannes V. Jensen and Tom Kristensen. For a number of reasons, Klaus Rifbjerg has a quite special status in Danish literature.

His writing has at times been rebuked and criticised and has been perceived as the incarnation of brazen, incomprehensible poetry out to criticise society, something that various populist forces would like to have done away with. In connection with the reorganisation of The Danish Arts Foundation in 1964, Klaus Rifbjerg was one of the targets for the opponents of state aid to artists. But his authorship also has a special status because Rifbjerg for what is now more than half a century has produced an annual literary publication (with only one exception) and in that way constantly taken the intellectual temperature of the language and the nation.

The break away from modernism

Modernism in poetry culminated in the first half of the 1960s, with publications by Rifbjerg, Jess Ørnsbo, Jørgen Sonne, Cecil Bødker and Uffe Harder. But from the mid-1960s onwards, a number of new literary positions were taken up. Certain slightly older writers, especially Per Højholt and Inger Christensen, renewed their poetry while a whole series of young writers across genres and text-types have sought new paths.

The most important Danish poets and artists of the mid-1960s shared the feeling that the national mono-culture was seriously beginning to crumble. But rather than busy themselves with this loss, they focused on a "now" which was found to be expressed in music, film, poetry and art.

What those of the mid-1960s artistic reorientation had in common was their breaking away from modernism and its cultural-radical criticism of popular culture, its Freudian-tinted ideas of personal development and its cultivation of a condensed, special artistic language that was rich in images. The poet Hans-Jørgen Nielsen, who in this anthology is represented by poems from 1980, was during the period around the publication of the periodical *ta'* a unifying figure for the young poets. In a memoir essay he tells of how it was almost unheard of for him as a young intellectual in the 1950s to love jazz music, the sentimental radio programme Giro 413, the hard-hitting journalism of the newspaper *Ekstra Bladet* and American strip cartoons.

The break away from modernism is hard to sum up with a single concept, but it is characterised by the nature of literature being form, i.e. an aesthetic encounter between the reader, the writer and the world is constantly thematised and pinned down in a wide range of different types of texts. Everything from documentary poetry, political poetry to confessional literature, beat poetry, minimalism, system poetry, postmodernism and functional literature is all part of this poetic reorientation. So it is possible to call the break away from modernism a formal breakthrough, where one finds a new contemporaneity between various literary currents, a dialogue with literary traditions, experiments with genres from many traditions, as for example the Japanese haiku, and various attempts to include the reader in the poetic formation of meaning. It was a question of a new dialogue between the popular and the avant-garde, along with attempts to use time quite concretely in poetry and to turn the body into a medium in the work of art.

A unifying feature of the many tendencies in the break away from modernism is the attempt to make poetry relational and dialogical; and it is possible to draw many parallels between the Danish break away from modernism and contemporary reorientations in both European and American poetry: from the new open French poetic workshop OuLiPo to German concrete poetry, Italian postmodernism and American beat poetry.

A couple of the older poets also help paint the portrait of the break away from modernism: Per Højholt, who as a very young man had made his debut in *Heretica* with solemn poems, and Inger Christensen, who had written high-modernist poetry. Around the mid-1960s, they renewed their poetry, inspired by international avant-gardism and system poetry. In the present anthology, Højholt is represented by poems from an important book of the 1960s, *Min hånd 66* (My Hand 66), and by a poem from the first volume of a series of practice books that he started to publish in 1977. Højholt became a poet of poets and literary theorists in Danish literature who helped to introduce French poetry, the theory of aesthetics, avant-garde thought and poetics to a Danish context.

But he himself was to enjoy a great popular breakthrough with his parodies *Gittes monologer*, which started to appear in 1981. During that period, Højholt travelled all over Denmark in his 4WD and entertained people with texts that gave rise to the liberating laughter that Højholt had cultivated in his avant-gardist texts and shows back in the mid-1960s.

Inger Christensen is represented in the present anthology by a poem from the poem cycle *Alfabet* (1981). She is perhaps most famous for her sonnet cycle *Sommerfugledalen* (The Valley of the Butterflies, 1991), which has commanded great international attention, and she is among the few Danish poets who have publicly been broached as a possible candidate for the Nobel Prize in literature. The cycle made Inger Christensen a celebrated poet in Austria and Germany, where audiences flocked to hear her mass-like intonation of the beautiful sonnets, in which the butterflies become icons for the soul and death.

The Valley of the Butterflies is a traditional sonnet cycle that adheres to the well-known rules for the genre, and it is thought-provoking that Inger Christensen, after previous experiments with the sonnet by others, chooses to use the genre in a completely traditional way. Inger Christensen was more in tune with tendencies in the break away from modernism when she experimented with system poetry and mathematics in the so-cially critical poem "Det" (It, 1969), which gained the status of a poetic manifestation of the youth revolution.

Jørgen Leth started out as a modernist poet in the wake of the Rif-bjerg generation early in the 1960s. He was also a music, film and drama reviewer and he soon came into contact with the experimental artists who visited Copenhagen and participated in the many activities con-nected with the avant-garde Eks-Skolen (formed in 1961), where artists such as Per Kirkeby and Bjørn Nørgaard had found each other.

Jørgen Leth's poems indicated an important tendency in the new poetry: The young poets included popular literature and culture in their poetry – everything that the Rifbjerg generation, because of its cultural-radical mind-set, had gone out of its way to criticise. Leth wrote poems about competitive cycling and helped show that all kinds of themes and subjects could be dealt with in poetry. There were no themes or forms or uses of language that one could call historically ill-timed or unsuitable.

It was also characteristic that many of the new writers, like Jørgen Leth, moved freely between various artistic genres. Leth used the same Warhol-inspired method in both poetry and art. Andy Warhol's films *Empire State Building* (1964) and *Chelsea Girls* (1966), where time was used as a concrete part of the work of art, were eye-openers for young authors. In the present anthology, Jørgen Leth is represented by a poem from his later work, "Fucking" (2000), where the erotic world of experience is still important, and where the body is used as a poetic medium for a sexual language. In connection with the publication of Leth's autobiographies (2005-07), his personal sexual relations have been the subject of violent debate and indignation.

Even though the writers appeared somewhat sporadically and separately in public, it was obvious in both poetry and prose that many of them had been inspired by American poetry, jazz, blues, rock music, films and art. Impulses also came from French structuralist and poststructuralist philosophy, Polish avant-gardist theatre, Swedish, Norwegian, Finnish and German avant-garde poetry as well as Japanese haiku poetry.

Danish poetry became a part of a creative circulation between USA and Europe and the East, where American artists brought European and oriental sources of inspiration to USA and vice versa. From the mid-1960s and up to the present, it is becoming increasingly obvious that the authors have their positions in a global artistic context where many new and old sources of inspiration intersect.

One of the central figures for the young people of the mid-1960s who conveyed precisely this global artistic context was the American poet Ezra Pound. As far back as the Rifbjerg generation, there was a growing interest in Pound. The modernists in particular read Pound in order to grasp the experience of a divided, fragmented world where shards of mythology, past and present poetry are whirled into one huge composition. Pound's poetry was here therefore interpreted as a modern sign of this fragmentation.

The generation of the mid-1960s, however, read Pound's work in a completely different way. It was enthusiastic about Pound because his poetry actually did constitute a whole, a flickering montage that included all kinds of art, various times and various experiences – and made them all contemporaneous. Pound's *Cantos* (1915-62) were now interpreted as the exact opposite of loss and fragmentation. Pound's poetry was felt to be important because he included all everyday language and everything in the outside world.

Both Dan Turèll, Peter Laugesen and Klaus Høeck embraced the *Cantos* to such an extent that they themselves tried to construct large composite, citing, experimental texts that directly referred to Pound. Pound's famous dictum "Make It New" was the translation of a sentence by the Chinese philosopher Confucius, and Pound's point was that poets should embrace literary history and renew it by writing poems, quoting and making every use of the material.

The authors of the mid-1960s embraced these ideas, their major sources of inspiration also including the American poets Charles Olson, Jack Kerouac, William S. Burroughs and Allen Ginsberg as well as the rock poets Bob Dylan, Lou Reed and John Lennon.

In the present anthology, Klaus Høeck is represented by a sequence from the large systematic and encyclopaedic work *Hjem* (Home, 1985), where the poet, basing himself on the formulae for the Danish subsoil, constructs along three tracks (culture, nature and spirit) a huge poetic edifice which he finally allows to disintegrate once more. Here, the work experiments with the old tradition of creation poetry, first practised in a Danish context by the 13th-century Latinist Anders Sunesen, and later by the champion of Danish literary poetry Anders Arrebo. Høeck's sequence about the nine roses has been taken from the culture track, the section "Nurseries. Cultivated Flowers", and it assumes the form of a ritual for love between the sexes. It is typical that both the highest and the most profane subjects and themes are played out in the fugal composition of the work. Here one meets everything from wild flowers to tin cans with pigs' hearts in a creamy sauce, art museums and refuse dumps. Høeck's method is derived from cybernetic ecology that does not discard or discharge excessive language-scraps and syllables, but works all of them into a huge poetic universe where the reader will personally have to decide where to start reading. This language ecology allows, among other things, the Lord's Prayer to re-emerge as a prayer to "our fatheress / you who are in the heavening". Høeck's cybernetic super-forms have made him one of the most productive poets in Danish literature so far.

Peter Laugesen is represented by a long piece from the collection *Kultur* (1990), where, among other things, one can notice the influence of the American poet Charles Olson, who emphasised that the poet is to work on the poem via "composition by field" and address the reader with a form of "projected verses". Reader and poet are to listen to the poem as a field of energy out of which various types of meaning flow. The poet is to keep hold of the smallest parts of the poem, its syllables and its oral quality and use his own breathing and writing rhythm when working with the language, and find the special poetic energy in his voice and in his writing. The poem is not, however, to cultivate the poet's personality, psyche or subjectivity – it is a question of getting the poem to create an open field. Such poetics runs counter to both a modernist and a symbolist view of poetry, which seeks to close or complete the poem. Patterns of speech, the clattering and chattering of the typewriter and the body's living feeling are a breath in Laugesen's poetry. In the sequence "What I Want to Write About" the poet is borne off by his own stream of language and allows his thoughts to be distracted so as to get into contact with the small words that are kicked out of the language when in politics and criticism big words and letters are used about what is traditionally defined as being important in life. But the poet is not interested in all that has already become names. He wants to reach the words and the stratum in language that almost does not mean anything. The poet wants to grasp the images of the body when they become words and the words of the body when they become images, as it says at the end of the poem with a chiasmus that is typical of Peter Laugesen. There is a reference to Easter in the middle of the poem that can also be interpreted as an attempt to get words to rise again from the hackneyed, reductive use of language in society. Laugesen often performs his poems together with musicians, creating collages of sound and rhythm in his poems.

Dan Turèll is represented by the poem "To Be Beat" (1971), the motto of which has been taken from one of the youngest poets of the beat generation, Gregory Corso. The poem shows how beat poetry, like the improvisation, repetition and variation of jazz and bebop, becomes a poetics for a feeling of life where New York and Gl. Kongevej, a street in Copenhagen, are immediately connected with each other. In his poetry, Turèll has a keen sense of sound patterns and structures, and both he himself and other musicians have set his texts to music. (Turèll in fact performed together with Allen Ginsberg during the latter's visit to Denmark in 1983, when Ginsberg – together with his partner, the poet Peter Orlovsky, and a musician – sang and recited texts.) The poem "To Be Beat" itself becomes a piece of beat music in its own tempo and also with references to oriental Zen philosophy and Buddhism, which Dan Turèll subscribed to. His major work *Karma Cowboy* (1974) combines in the very title Eastern philosophy and American icons from films and comic strips. Dan Turèll worked with a whole series of different genres and let them interact in a large textual universe of newspaper columns, crime stories, montages and books of poetry. Turèll was a weekly columnist for the daily newspaper *Politiken*, and even though his columns are strongly time-related, they are still worth reading, as for example is the journalism of his model, Herman Bang. Turèll's spoken language rhetoric was also a literary genre – even the most banal statements became poetic texts when he started to speak – and a series of radio and TV recordings with Turèll still stand as literary manifestations.

The mid-1960s witnessed the emergence of a completely different kind of poet than Dan Turèll – Henrik Nordbrandt. He made his debut in 1966 and, unlike many of his contemporaries, he was completely repelled by both beat poetry and rock poetry. He found inspiration to a far greater extent in Greek, Arabic and Chinese poetry. When still only a young man he left Denmark, whose mental and physical climate he found in every way depressing, and for long periods of his life as a professional writer he has lived in the Mediterranean countries. He has also mediated and introduced their recent culture and poetry to Denmark.

Nordbrandt works with a central-lyrical modernism where departure and arrival, travel and restlessness are important themes. He has a special ability to get poetic images to unfold and surprise one rather than to enclose a completed meaning. Instead, the reader of the poem constantly follows new facets of the imagery. When one reads poems by Henrik Nordbrandt, there are always new stories that come into being, new arabesques that have to be pursued or an enigmatic absence that the poem is heading towards. At the same time, the poet often gathers the complex meanings together in a surprising paradox, when absence is suddenly and completely replaced by a sensory presence. Henrik Nordbrandt is represented in the present anthology by poems from 1966 and 1985, both of which demonstrate aspects of the poetics of paradox and image he often works with.

Like Henrik Nordbrandt, Marianne Larsen chose studies at university that included languages only few people mastered – in her case Chinese. And like Nordbrandt, she has translated poems: While he translates from Turkish, among other languages, she has translated from Chinese.

Marianne Larsen made her debut in 1971, and in her writing – like that of Peter Laugesen and Klaus Høeck – she combines an advanced awareness of language and writing with a committed critique of society. In the present anthology she is represented by the poem "snow white" (1974), which deals with the female role and gender in a way that challenges all its readers and cannot simply be relegated to the unshakable feminist confessions that were so popular in Denmark during the 1970s. Marianne Larsen always challenges language and set opinions.

Johannes L. Madsen, who can be placed in the early break away from modernism, mainly worked with concrete poetry, which has played an important role in poetry since the mid-1960s – also in Marianne Larsen's poetry. Madsen's small oeuvre has been rediscovered by new poets of both the 1980s and 1990s. His collected poems were published as a result of this interest in 2003. Madsen's works include a number of surrealist, concrete poems such as "spilt out sputtering with acid" (1969), which is included in the present anthology. The poem is a rhythmical, musical and figurative composition, a kind of rap text, but with a different rhythm than that of rap. Johannes L. Madsen's poems sometimes take the form of long discharges of words; the images formed in the poems become so concrete and distorted that they start to form a kind of painting that burns its way into the reader's retinas. One notices a wild passion and a will to complete the line that is reminiscent of Johannes Ewald and his statement that he chewed scores of his pens to pieces when struggling with his lines. This has perhaps something to do with the fact that Madsen, like Ewald, often writes about what poetry is and can do when the poet's imagination is so strong that it almost bowls the poem over.

Variegated poetry

In the period from the mid-1960s to the present, Danish poetry has spread out in many directions, working with new genres and media. Poetry can fortunately not be streamlined, even though many readers and critics alike are sceptical about what is variegated and experimental as well as in terms of the new media that literature is also starting to use or is being used by. The first Danish-language websites for new poetry had already opened by the late 1990s. The website www.afsnitp.dk experimented early on with poetry and art, since when a number of Danish-language websites for new poetry have come into being. Here, crossovers between poetry, music and art are often tried out, but digitalisation does not, however, mean that the book will disappear as one of the strongest mediums for poetry. The latest publications of poetry also show that the book itself is an aesthetic and poetic form of expression.

Several of the new poets who emerged in the late 1970s and the early 1980s have been extremely successful, also internationally – first and foremost Pia Tafdrup. The lines of connection between the poets of the last decades of the 20th century and the poets of the mid-1960s are, however, extremely clear. Pia Tafdrup used Per Højholt as a guide in connection with her first poetic attempts, and has since liked to perform publicly with readings together with Inger Christensen. Søren Ulrik Thomsen, for his part, immediately established a cooperation with Jørgen Leth when he was asked to take part in a film about his authorship, and he has referred to Højholt, Christensen, Nordbrandt and Høeck as sources of inspiration. F.P. Jac became part of the group of poets who called themselves "Bandet nul", which also included Asger Schnack and Klaus Høeck. This group got Per Højholt, Inger Christensen and Michael Strunge to contribute to their publications as special guest stars.

In the present anthology, Pia Tafdrup is represented by the poem "June Dream" (1998), which shows how she takes the experiences of the body as her point of departure and is able to develop an imagery that becomes autonomous, so that the poem both deals with something quite concrete and also reaches out towards many-facetted meanings about the actual coming into existence of the poem. This whole issue to do with the nature of writing poetry is something she has also dealt with in detail in *Over vandet går jeg* (I Walk on the Water, 1991), where she also discusses inspiration she has gained from international high-modernism and Danish symbolism. F.P. Jac is represented by a sequence from his main work *Misfat* (1980), which deals with the artist as a vulnerable and critical bohemian, a figure that he diligently cultivated in his public self-staging. The poets who made their debut in the 1980s turned against the Marxist literary criticism of the 1970s, which liked to see the poet as a cultural worker among others. Jac insisted on living out the conception of the poet who, drunk on booze, language and art, is constantly at odds with society. Søren Ulrik Thomsen distanced himself from Jac's cultivation of the bohemian, but retained the name of poet as a precise expression of what he was professionally striving for. Thomsen did not wish to see himself as a writer who enters the social debate, but as a poet who each time has to start from scratch with words and language.

Søren Ulrik Thomsen developed these ideas in *Mit lys brænder* (My Light Is Burning, 1985), where he also discussed sources of inspiration in art and sculpture. His poems often remind the reader of sculptures – one can move around them and admire their composition. This also applies to the poems included in the present anthology. The poem "Dentist, Grave. Wedding Ring" is dedicated to Michael Strunge, who committed suicide in 1986. Here the *memento mori* that is often a part of Søren Ulrik Thomsen's poetry has become quite explicit.

Michael Strunge himself is represented in the anthology by the early poem "Speed of Life" (1978), which many readers – like the poem "The Machinery of Night" (1981) – saw as programme poems for a no-future-punk-generation. The poem "19 June" (1984) marks the conclusion of Strunge's young, visionary poetry. His last publication, *Verdenssøn* (Son of the World, 1985), was characterised by violent criticism and parodies of visionary poetry and by intense attempts to find new modes of poetic expression. The musician Nikolaj Nørlund set a number of these poems to music in his 1996 release *Navnløs* (Nameless), which captured the desperation that typifies *Verdenssøn*. Michael Strunge's collected poetry was published for the first time in 1993. This large black, one-volume work was an enormous sales success and spurred on the publication of collected poetry editions by other contemporary Danish poets.

The most recent poets included in the present anthology were born in the 1960s, which brought so much that was new into Danish litera-ture. Pia Juul's poetry exists in a special field between spoken language and figurative language and is related to the British-American poetry in the tradition of Emily Dickinson and Sylvia Plath. A Danish source of inspiration is Agnes Henningsen, who in her memoirs from the early 20th century created a language of emancipation, full of subtleties and with alternating overplayed and underplayed points. In the present anthology, Pia Juul is represented by a piece of erotic rhetoric, where the seduction is both kittenish and raw. Juul's poetic voice is here – as always – clear and clearly new.

Simon Grotrian keeps the line open to both Ewald and Grundtvig. He works with a surrealist religious poetry that is certainly all that Otto Gelsted hated and warned so strongly against at the beginning of the 20th century. Simon Grotrian has in recent years also tried to renew old Danish hymn-writing. He does things that are unexpected and surprising, as he writes hymns that simply make the reader laugh out loud.

Naja Marie Aidt concludes the anthology with a poem from her collection *Alting blinker* (Everything Blinks, 2009), which is set in New York. Aidt's poetry often depicts different ages in life and their worlds of experience, and while she further develops motifs from Tove Ditlevsen's writing, it is also clear that she is living and writing in a completely dif-ferent (and globalised) age to Ditlevsen. She writes both prose and poetry and has the capacity to let the genres inspire each other. In the poems from New York, the writer is confronted both with her love of her own language and her anxiety about finding a fixed location and permanent home. Everything blinks in the post-postmodern world around her, where the female speaker flits between many kinds of cultural and personal possibilities, but where she also – as a Danish speaker, a daughter and a mother – has chosen a basis for her life and its many suspended meanings.

Vulgarity, tension-breaking laughter, high pathos, profound seriousness and erotic rhetoric – all of these are very much alive in Danish poetry.

Translation by John Irons

100 Danish Poems

Ebbe Skammelsøn

Skammel bor i Ty,
både rig og øvert kåd;
så høviske haver han sønner fem,
de to for's ilde ad.
Fordi træder Ebbe Skammelsøn
så mangen sti vild.

Ebbe han tjener i konningens gård
både for guld og fæ;
Peder hans broder lader bygge et skib,
han rejser op sejletræ.

Midt udi den gården
der aksler han sin skind;
og så går han i højeloft
for jomfru Lucelille ind.

"Hil sidder I, jomfru Lucelille,
I syr hr. Ebbe klæ'r;
hr. Ebbe tjener i konningens gård,
han spotter eder og hæder."

Det svared jomfru Lucelille,
og svared hun for sig:
"Han spotter ingen stolt jomfru,
end halve sider mig."

"Står op, jomfru Lucelille,
I giver mig eders tro!
Det vil jeg for sandingen sige,
det Ebbe døde i fjor."

Svared det jomfru Lucelille,
og svared hun for sig:
"Halve mere skade får I deraf,
end jeg venter mig."

MEDIEVAL BALLADS

Ebbe Skammelsøn

Skammel lives in Ty
both rich and mighty glad,
so courtly the five sons he has –
the end two met was bad.
So outlawed must Ebbe Skammelsøn
                    tread tracks far from home.

Ebbe he serves at the king's high court
for gold and kine serves he;
Peder his brother he has a ship built,
its mast a straight tall tree.

And out there in the courtyard
he ups and shoulders his skin;
and then Maid Lucelille's
high loft he enters in.

"Hail Maid Lucelille, sit you here
and sew Knight Ebbe fine frocks;
Knight Ebbe serves at the king's high court
You and your honour he mocks."

That answered Maid Lucelille,
and answered full and free:
"He never does mock a maiden proud,
far less does he mock me."

"Rise up, Maid Lucelille,
And pledge yourself my wife!
In truth I now do tell you:
That Ebbe last year lost his life."

Answered that Maid Lucelille,
and answered full and free:
"Half more the hurt of it you'll have
than lies in wait for me."

"Hør I det, jomfru Lucelille,
giver Peder eders tro!
Det vil jeg for sandingen sige,
det Ebbe døde i fjor."

Drukke de det fæstensøl
og end den samme nat;
brylluppet end før månedsdag,
de rådte det iså brat.

Det var Ebbe Skammelsøn,
han vågned om midjenat;
og siger han sin næste svend
af sin drøm så brat.

"Mig tott', at min stenstue
stod al i lysen lue!
der brændt' inde min kære moder
og så min skønne jomfru."

"Det I tott', eders stenstue
stod al i røden glød:
det er: Peder, eders broder,
har bryllup med eders fæstemø."

Det var Ebbe Skammelsøn,
han ind for kongen gik;
beder han sig orlov,
så bradelig han det fik.

Det var Ebbe Skammelsøn,
han kom ridendes i by:
"Hve'n er dette møgle folk,
her er samlet af ny?"

Svared det den lille mø
alt i sin kjortel rød:
"Det er Peder, eders broder,
har bryllup med eders fæstemø."

"Hear you me, Maid Lucelille,
And pledge yourself Peder's wife!
In truth I now do tell you:
That Ebbe last year lost his life."

In beer they plighted both their troth
even in that same night:
the wedding they fixed for that day month
as quickly as they might.

It was Ebbe Skammelsøn,
at midnight he awoke;
turned to the man right next to him,
of his sudden dream he spoke:

"I thought I saw my stone chamber
ablaze unto the skies!
my mother dear consumed within,
my maiden fair likewise."

"What you thought was your stone chamber,
its gleam spread far and wide:
'Tis Peder your own brother
who's made your love his bride."

It was Ebbe Skammelsøn,
he went to see the king;
begged for leave of absence,
was directly granted him.

It was Ebbe Skammelsøn,
came riding into town:
"Who then are these people
now gathered all around?"

Answered him the young maiden
dressed in her kirtle red:
"'Tis Peder, your own brother,
who now your love has wed."

Det var Ebbe Skammelsøn,
ban ville af gården ride;
hans moder og hans søster' to
de bad ham holde og bie.

"Hør I det, kære moder,
I lader mig nu ride!
og bier jeg i aften,
I træder det, me'n I leve."

Den ene sin søster gav han guldbrase i bryst,
den anden guldringen af hand;
det havde han jomfru Lucelille agtet,
han tjente i fremmed land.

Hans fader bad hannem i salen gå,
sidde af de øverste bænke;
hans moder fik ham kande i hånd,
bad ham gå at skænke.

Skænkte han den brune mjød
og så den klare vin;
hver tid han til bruden så,
da randt ham tår å kind.

Mælte det de fruer
alt å de øverste bænke:
"Hvi mon Ebbe Skammelsøn
så sørgendes gå at skænke?"

"I æder og I drikker
mjød og klaren vin!
Alt få I andet at tale
end om sorrigen min."

Sildig om den aften,
rimen han faldt å;
og det da var den unge brud,
hun skulle til sengen gå.

It was Ebbe Skammelsøn,
who from the place would ride,
his mother and his sisters two
they bade him wait and bide.

"Oh hear me, my dear mother
Allow me now to ride!
were I to bide this evening,
You'd rue it all your life."

One sister he gave a fine golden brooch,
the other a ring for her hand;
for Maid Lucelille he'd had it wrought,
when serving in foreign land.

His father bade him sit at the bench
placed highest in the hall:
his mother placed a jug in his hand,
and bade him pour for them all.

He poured for all the golden mead
and then the wine full clear;
each time he glimpsed the lovely bride,
his eye it shed a tear.

The ladies at the topmost bench
they spoke in disbelief:
"Why does Ebbe Skammelsøn
pour wine while in such grief?"

"You eat and drink, my ladies,
both mead and cool clear wine!
Soon there'll be else to speak of
than the sorrow that is mine."

That evening late when dew did fall
and all had drunk and fed,
the time came for the fair young bride
to seek her wedding bed.

Ledte de den unge brud
alt til sit brudehus;
for går Ebbe Skammelsøn,
han bær for hender blus.

Ledte han den unge brud
alt ad den højeloftsbro:
"Og drages eder det til minde,
I gav mig eders tro?"

"Al den tro, jeg eder gav,
den haver Peder, eders broder;
al' de dage, jeg må leve,
jeg vil eder være for moder."

Det svared Ebbe Skammelsøn,
hannem randt tår å kind:
"Jeg havde agtet eder til hustru
og ikke til moder min.

Høre I, jomfru Lucelille,
I rømmer med mig af land!
Jeg vil slå Peder, min broder, ihjel
og lide for eder den tvang!"

"Slår I Peder, eders broder, ihjel,
og siden skal I mig miste;
så må I sørge eder selv ihjel
som vilden fugl å kviste."

Det var Ebbe Skammelsøn,
han sit sværd uddrog;
det var Lucelille,
han til jorden vog.

Så tog han det blodige sværd
alt under sin skarlagenskind;
så gik han i stenstuen
for Peder, sin broder, ind.

They all led the fair young bride
to where her bed was made:
before went Ebbe Skammelsøn,
his torch did light the way.

Along the gallery he led
the bride, though he was loath:
"And do you happen to recall
To me you did plight your troth?"

"All I ever pledged to you,
Has Peder now, your brother;
all the days I yet may live
I'll be to you as a mother."

Then answered Ebbe Skammelsøn,
the tears ran down his cheek:
"It was as wife I you would wed,
and I no mother seek.

Hark you, Maid Lucelille,
With me now flee the land!
my brother Peder I will slay
and that hard fate withstand!"

"If brother Peder you do slay,
I'm lost to you for ever;
Then you must grieve yourself to death
as a bird astray must shiver."

It was Ebbe Skammelsøn,
sword from sheath did draw;
it was Lucelille
he cut down to the floor.

His bloody sword he then did hide
beneath his purple skin;
he entered the stone chamber
where Peder his brother was in.

"Hør du, Peder Skammelsøn,
og du tøver alt for længe!
Det er alt en sejerstund,
si'n bruden gik til senge.

Hør du, Peder Skammelsøn,
du far alt med leg!
Bruden sidder i brudeseng,
bier dig efter bleg."

"Hør du, Ebbe Skammelsøn,
og kære broder min;
jeg lover dig i denne nat
at sove hos bruden min!"

Det var Ebbe Skammelsøn,
han sit sværd uddrog;
det var Peder Skammelsøn,
han til jorden vog.

Hans fader misted hans venstre fod,
hans moder sin højre hånd;
fordi træder Ebbe Skammelsøn
så vidt i fremmede land.
Fordi træder Ebbe Skammelsøn
så mangen sti vild.

"Hark you, Peder Skammelsøn
the time too fast has fled!
A full hour by the clock has passed
since the bride went to her bed.

Hark you, Peder Skammelsøn
all does you avail!
The bride sits in the bridal bed,
and waits for you so pale."

"Hark you, Ebbe Skammelsøn,
dear brother by my side;
I promise you this selfsame night
to sleep with my fair bride!"

It was Ebbe Skammelsøn,
sword from sheath did draw;
It was Peder Skammelsøn
he cut down to the floor.

His father parted with his left foot,
his mother her right hand;
So outlawed must Ebbe Skammelsøn
steer clear now of this land:
So outlawed must Ebbe Skammelsøn
tread tracks far from home.

Jomfruen i fugleham

Jeg ved vel, hvor en skov hun stander,
hun står foruden under fjord;
der gror inde de fejreste træ,
som nogen mand haver hørt.
Så vinder en svend sin jomfru.

Der gror inde de fejreste træ,
som man kalder silje og linde;
der spiller inde de ærlige dyr,
som man kalder hjorte og hinder.

Der spiller inde både hjorte og hinde
og andre dyr så skønne;
der synger så lidel en nattergal
udi en lind så grøn.

Det spurgte Nilaus Erlandsøn,
[som dyren' er vant at bede],
han lader sin ganger med det røde guld sko,
og did rider han at lede.

Did red Nilaus Erlandsøn,
så såre da mon han lange;
der var han i dage tre,
han kunne ikke fuglen fange.

Så sætte han snaren på alle de træ,
som fuglen var vante at være;
den fugl blev i sin' øjen snar,
han måtte hende dog ombære.

Han sætte snaren på alle de stier,
som fuglen' var vant at gange;
den fugl var i sin' øjen så snar,
han kunne hende ikke fange.

The Maid in the Guise of a Bird

I know where there lies a forest,
far out at the edge of the fjord;
therein there grow the fairest of trees
that ever a man has heard.
So does a man gain his maiden.

Therein there grow the fairest of trees,
that one calls wood-willow and lime.
therein there play the noblest of beasts
that one calls the hart and the hind.

Therein there play both the hart and the hind
and other beasts pleasing to see;
there sings so tiny a nightingale
up in a lime so green.

Of this learned Nilaus Erlandsøn.
[a hunting man known for his skill],
he had his steed shod with shoes of red gold,
and yonder he rode for a kill.

Yonder did ride Nilaus Erlandsøn,
so deep-felt was his rapture;
there he stayed for three whole days,
but never the bird did he capture.

Then traps he did set on all of the trees
the bird would choose to alight on;
the bird it grew so keen of eye
the net he never could tighten.

Then traps he did set on all of the paths
the bird would walk on by nature;
the bird it was so keen of eye
he never was able to catch her.

Han tog øksen i sin hånd,
han ville det træ neder fælde;
der kom den mand, der skoven åtte,
han skød sin skaft imellem.

"Hugger du neder min fæ'rne skove,
og gør du mig den vælde:
jeg lover dig, Nilaus Erlandsøn,
så dyrt skalt du det gælde."

Det da mælte den skønne jomfru,
hun stod på højen tinde:
"Ungersvend, vilt du lyde mit råd,
da skalt du fuglen vinde.

Hør du, favren ungersvend,
og vilt du lyde mit råd:
du får ikke af vilden fugl,
uden du haver tammen brad."

Han skar braden af sin bryst,
han hængte det på lindekvist;
hun flagred' med sin' vinger, hun lod vel om,
fuld ondt var braden at miste.

Det da var den lidel nattergal,
hun fik det blodige brad;
så blev hun til skønneste jomfru,
der måtte på jorden gå.

Jomfruen under linden stod
i silkesærk hint røde;
ridderen tog hende udi sin arm,
de klaged hverandre deres nød.

Ridderen tog hende i sin arm,
klapped hende ved hviden kind:
"Sig mig, allerkæreste min,
hvem voldte sorrig din?"

He took his axe up in his hand,
he would the tree have felled;
the man who owned the forest came,
his spear between he held.

"If you chop down my forefathers' trees
and do me such a wrong:
I promise you, Nilaus Erlandsøn,
you'll rue the day ere long."

Then came the voice of the fair maid,
up from the top of the tree:
"Young man, should you heed my advice,
Then yours the bird shall be.

Hark you well, you handsome man,
and heed you my advice:
without tame flesh you shall not catch
the wild bird in a trice."

He cut the tame flesh from his breast,
he hung it from a branch of lime;
she flapped her wings, it pleased her well,
to gain such flesh lost no time.

It was the tiny nightingale
the tame bloody flesh she soon found;
then she became the loveliest maid
that ever had trod the ground.

The maiden under the lime tree stood
in silken shift of red;
the knight he took her by the arm,
their woes to each other they said.

The knight he took her on his arm,
her lily-white cheek he did stroke:
"Oh tell me, dearest to my heart,
who then did such sorrow provoke?"

"Jeg sad over min faders bord,
jeg legte med roser og liljer;
min stedmoder kom der gangendes fram,
det var ikke med henders minde.

Så skabte hun mig til en lidel nattergal,
bad mig ad skoven flyve;
min' syv møer i ulvelige,
bad, de skulde fuglen rive."

Jomfruen under linden stod,
slog ud sit favre hår;
der kom løbendes henders tjenestemøer,
i ulvelige de var.

Nu haver Nilaus Erlandsøn
forvunden båd' angest og harm;
nu sover han så gladelig
udi den jomfru henders arm.
Så vinder en svend sin jomfru.

"At my father's table I did sit,
with roses and lilies did play;
my stepmother came into the room,
who wanted to have me away.

She made a small nightingale out of me
and told me to fly to the wood:
my seven maids into wolves were all turned,
told to tear the bird if they could."

The maiden under the lime tree stood,
tossed her fine golden hair;
out ran her seven maids to her,
as wolves they were all still ensnared.

Now has Nilaus Erlandsøn
defeated all fear and all harm;
now without a single care
he sleeps on his maiden's arm.
So does a man gain his maiden.

LEONORA CHRISTINA ULFELDT (1621-1698)

Guds goedhed imod mig at ihuekomme

Op op, min Siæl oc Sinde,
Guds Goedhed til att minde,
   Som ræcker dig sin Haand,
Som Byrden med mig bærer,
Som mig sin Wille lærer,
   Oc selffwer lindrer miine Baand.

Mit Hiærte, glæm ded icke,
Huad udi Mørcken Kircke
   Nii dage ieg udstoed,
Hwad Angist, Sorrig, Qwide,
Hwad Spott, oc stanck ieg liide,
   Da styrckede Gud Sind oc Moed.

Betenck min stoere Trængsel,
Mit lange haarde Fengsel,
   Min Iammers Elffte Aar.
Ey ey saa ded bedrøffwer;
Gud er den som dig prøffwer,
   Han kiender best hwad du formaar.

Hid. Santz, Fornufft og Læmmer,
Indhellig sammen stæmmer
   Guds Goedhed winde kand,
Som Eder haffwer sparet,
Fra Kranckelse bewaret
   I denne min forfalden Stand.

Mig Wanded gick til Tænder
Aff Sorrig wringtis Hænder
   Ieg snobblet, dog ey falt.
Thi Herren var min Støtte,
Min Foed selff monne fløtte,
   Loff være dig O! Mæctig *Alt.*

LEONORA CHRISTINA ULFELDT (1621-1698)

To Remember God's Goodness towards Me

Up, up, my mind and soul
God's goodness to recall
   who reaches me His hand,
who shares with me life's loads,
who me His will unfolds
   Himself does soothe my chafing bonds.

Do not forget, my heart,
how in a church so dark
   for nine whole days I pined,
what fear I suffered, pain,
what agonies, disdain.
   Then God did strengthen heart and mind.

Recall my great distress,
My prison's endlessness,
   my woes' eleventh year.
Not so that it should grieve;
God's trials have no reprieve,
   for He knows best what you can bear.

Here, reason, sense and limbs,
Join in a common hymn:
   God's goodness can prevail;
He's offered you His ease,
preserved you from disease
   in this poor state so weak and frail.

In weeping all but drowned,
hands wrung in grief profound,
   I stumbled, but fell not;
the Lord support did prove,
my own foot I could move,
   thanks be to Thee, almighty God.

Tack skee dig, Naadsens Kille;
Att du mig Ræffse wille,
   Saa Mild oc Faderlig;
I Nød warst dog til Stede,
Mit Hierte Suck tilrede,
   Der Macten wille knuuse mig.

Gud, for dig ieg needfalder;
See til mig i min Alder
   Som stunder nu fast til,
Aff Aaget mig udspende,
Giør paa min Træl snart Ende,
   Dog ey hwad ieg, men hwad du wilt.

(1674)

I praise Thee, mercy's seat,
for chastisement so sweet,
 so fatherly and mild.
Close by in time of need
my sighing heart to heed
 when power would crush this earthly child.

God, at Thy feet I fall:
My span of years recall,
 whose course is almost run.
Release me from my yoke,
My thralldom now revoke.
 Though not my will but Thine be done.

(1674)

THOMAS KINGO (1634-1703)

Keed af Verden, og kier ad Himmelen

Far, Verden, far vel,
Jeg keedis nu længer at være din Træl,
De Byrder, som du mig har bylted oppaa,
Dem hvister jeg fra mig og vil dem forsmaa,
Jeg river mig løß, og jeg keedis nu ved
    Forfængelighed,
    Forfængelighed.

Hvad er det dog alt
Som Verden opsminker med fauer Gestalt?
Det er jo kun Skygger og skinnende Glar,
Det er jo kun Bobler og skrattende Kar,
Det er jo kun Ise-skrog, Skarn og Fortred,
    Forfængelighed,
    Forfængelighed.

Hvad er mine Aar,
Som smugende svinder og snigende gaar?
Hvad er min Bekymring? mit Tanke-fuld Sind?
Min Sorrig? min Glæde? mit Hovedis Spind?
Hvad er mit Arbeyde? min Møye? min Sved?
    Forfængelighed,
    Forfængelighed.

O Riigdom og Guld,
Du Jorderiigs Afgud i skinnende Muld,
Du est dog af Verdens bedragelig Ting,
Som voxer, aftager og vexlis omkring,
Du est dog, i høyeste Mercke og Meed,
    Forfængelighed,
    Forfængelighed.

THOMAS KINGO (1634-1703)

Weary of the World, and With Heaven Most Dear

Farewell, world, farewell
As thrall here I'm weary and no more will dwell,
The manifold burdens that on me have lain,
I wrest them now from me and do them disdain,
I wrench myself free, though am wearied withal:
'Tis vanity all,
'Tis vanity all.

And what everywhere
Does this world embellish with visage so fair?
'Tis all merely shadows and baubles of glass,
'Tis all merely bubbles and clattering brass,
'Tis all but thin ice, filth and mischief withal:
'Tis vanity all,
'Tis vanity all.

My years what are they?
That furtively dwindle and sidle away?
And what are my worries? My thought-troubled mind?
My joy or my sorrow? My fancies so blind?
And what do my work, moil and toil all recall?
'Tis vanity all,
'Tis vanity all.

Oh riches and gold,
You false earthly idol so bright to behold,
You are though among the deceits the world brings
That wax, wane and alter with all other things.
You are but vain glory whate'er may befall:
'Tis vanity all,
'Tis vanity all.

Ach, Ære, hvad er?
Hvad er dine Kroner og Krandse du bær?
Misundelse sidder dig altjd paa Ryg,
Du hemmelig stødis og sielden est tryg!
Du ofte der snubler, hvor andre de gleed,
    Forfængelighed,
    Forfængelighed.

Ach, Yndist og Gunst,
Du hastig opførte og faldende Dunst,
Du konstig opblæsere, hvegende Vind,
Som tusind har Øyen og dog løber blind,
Hvad est du naar mand dig ved Soolen hâr seed?
    Forfængelighed,
    Forfængelighed.

Ach, Venskab og Troo,
Som alt efter Lykken veedst Fløyet at snoo!
Du smukke Bedragere, heldige Skalk,
Som skuffer saa ofte i Drøfvelsens Kalk
Du est, som og jeg af Forfarenhed veed,
    Forfængelighed,
    Forfængelighed.

Ach, kiødelig Lyst,
Som mangen med dødelig Læber hâr kyst,
Dit fengende Tynder, din flyvende Gnist,
Hâr mangen i ævige Luer henhvist,
Din Skaal synis Hunning, men Drikken er leed
    Forfængelighed,
    Forfængelighed.

Saa far da, far vel,
Du skalt nu ey lenger bedrage min Siæl,
Bedragelig Verden jeg takker dig af,
Og synker dig ned i Forglemmelsens Grav,
Jeg lengis at bøde min Sorrig og Nød
    I Abrahams Skiød,
    I Abrahams Skiød.

Ah, honour— 'tis what?
Your crowns and your laurels proclaim what you're not,
And envy consumes you and sits on your back,
You lack peace of mind and are prone to attack!
You stumble where others contrive not to fall:
 'Tis vanity all,
 'Tis vanity all.

Ah, favour and grace
That mist-like enfold us are gone without trace.
You fickle inflator that puffs up the mind,
You thousand-eyed creature that e'en so are blind,
When viewed 'gainst the sun one can see that you pall:
 'Tis vanity all,
 'Tis vanity all.

Ah, friendship and trust,
That knows how to veer vanes to bliss with every gust!
You handsome deceiver, you fortunate pup,
That fails us so often in sorrow's deep cup
You say what experience has us recall:
 'Tis vanity all,
 'Tis vanity all.

Ah, joys of the flesh
That many have fatally snared in their mesh,
You quick-burning tinder, you spark on the wind,
Have sown flames eternal for those that have sinned,
Your cup seems like honey, the drink though is gall:
 'Tis vanity all,
 'Tis vanity all.

Farewell, then, farewell
No more your deceits shall my soul now compel,
Oh world of delusion, I now you dismiss,
Consign to oblivion's deepest abyss,
My grief and affliction no more me shall chafe:
 With Abraham safe,
 With Abraham safe.

Der skal mine Aar
Begyndis i Ævigheds deylige Vaaer,
Der skal ikke Dagen ved Solen opgry,
Ey Maanen tilmaale mig Næde og Ny,
Men JEsus er Solen, hvis Straaler er strød
    I Abrahams Skiød,
    I Abrahams Skiød.

Min Rigdom og Guld
Skal være af idel Bestandighed fuld,
Dend skal ikke Tyven bestiele mig da,
Dend skal ey Spitzfindighed skakre mig fra,
Min Rigdom er frj for ald Jorderigs Stød
    I Abrahams Skiød,
    I Abrahams Skiød.

Jeg Ære skal faa
Fra Thronen min JEsus hand sidder oppaa,
Mig Kronen skal givis med Herlighed fyldt,
Med Blodet af Lammet alt over forgyldt,
Dend faar jeg, om Satan end selv det fortrød,
    I Abrahams Skiød,
    I Abrahams Skiød.

Med Yndist jeg skal
Fremskinne blant Englenis hellige Tall,
Misundeligt Øye mig ikke skal see,
GUds Ansigt mig altid i Øyne skal lee,
Der skal jeg bespotte dend avindsyg Død
    I Abrahams Skiød,
    I Abrahams Skiød.

Der hâr jeg en Ven,
Min JEsus, som elsker og elskis igien,
Mit Øye der seer ham saadan som hand er,
Hand Kierligheds Himmel-bluss stedse frembær,
Ved Aanden staar Kierlighed ævig i Glød
    I Abrahams Skiød,
    I Abrahams Skiød.

There all of my years
Will start in eternity's spring without tears,
My days will not dawn with the rise of the sun,
Nor moon's wax or wane tell when night has begun,
My sun is Lord Jesus with rays like gold staves:
　　With Abraham safe,
　　With Abraham safe.

My riches and gold
Will always be mine both to have and to hold,
No robber can ever deprive me of them,
No bartering cause me to part with one gem,
I never will find myself left as a waif:
　　With Abraham safe,
　　With Abraham safe.

My honour is won
From that throne my Jesus is sitting upon,
A crown filled with glory for me is in store,
With blood of the lamb it is gilt ever more,
'Tis mine though the devil me gladly would strafe:
　　With Abraham safe,
　　With Abraham safe.

With grace I will shine
As one of the angelic host so divine,
No envious eye shall my face ever see,
God's countenance gaze ever-smiling on me,
There will I pour scorn on death's envious grave:
　　With Abraham safe,
　　With Abraham safe.

There I have a friend,
My Jesus who loves me I love without end,
My eye will regard him unclouded and fair,
The heavenly torch of his love proffered there,
In spirit Love's blaze I eternal may crave:
　　With Abraham safe,
　　With Abraham safe.

Min Lyst og min Fryd
Forfriskis ved Engle-basuner og Lyd,
Men GUd er ald Lysten for mig og for dem!
Far op da, min Siæl, og ald Verden forglem!
Mens glem ey at Lysten er ævig og sød
  I Abrahams Skiød,
  I Abrahams Skiød.

(1681)

My rapture and joy
Are quickened when angels their trumpets employ,
But God is all joy both for me and their kind!
Rejoice then, my soul, all the world leave behind!
Mind well on your heart God his joy will engrave:
With Abraham safe,
With Abraham safe.

(1681)

Hver har sin Skæbne

Sorrig og Glæde de vandre tilhaabe,
   Lykke, Ulykke de ganger paa Rad,
Medgang og Modgang hin anden anraabe,
   Soelskin og Skyer de følgis og ad!
      Jorderiigs Guld
      Er prægtig Muld,
Himlen er Ene af Salighed fuld.

Kroner og Scepter i Demant-spill lege,
   Leeg er dog ikke dend kongelig Dragt!
Tusinde Byrder i Kronerne hvege,
   Tusindfold Omhu i Scepterets Magt!
      Kongernis Boe
      Er skiøn Uroe!
Himlen allene giør salig og froe!

Alle Ting hâr sin foranderlig Lykke!
   Alle kand finde sin Sorrig i Barm!
Tiit ere Bryst, under dyrebar Smykke,
   Fulde af Sorrig og hemmelig Harm!
      Alle hâr sit,
      Stort eller Lit!
Himlen allene for Sorgen er qvit!

Velde og Vijßdom og timelig Ære,
   Styrke og Ungdom i blomstrende Aar,
Høyt over andre kand Hovedet bære,
   Falder dog af og i Tjden forgaar!
      Alle Ting maa
      Enden opnaa,
Himmelens Salighed Ene skal staa!

To Each His Destiny

Sorrow and joy hand in hand go together,
    Fortune, misfortune as neighbours do dwell,
Luck and adversity call to each other
    Sunshine and clouds are companions as well!
        Earth's brightest gold
        Is but fine mould,
Heaven alone is where bliss can unfold.

Gold crown and sceptre they sparkle and glitter,
    Glitter is not, though, what royal robes imply!
Thousands of burdens a crown's weight embitter,
    Thousandfold cares in a sceptre's power lie!
        Life for a king
        Unrest will bring!
Heaven alone can give bliss without sting!

Everything's fortune is waxing and waning!
    Everyone finds his own grief in his heart!
Often a breast, though bejewelled, is complaining,
    Weighed down by woe and by rage torn apart!
        Trials we have all,
        Some large, some small!
Heaven alone is where cares cannot gall!

Wisdom, dominion and temporal glory,
    Vigour and youth in the years of our prime,
Hold their head high, but the end of the story
    Is that they perish when ravished by time!
        All things must end
        None can contend
Heavenly bliss can alone all transcend!

Deyligste Roser hâr stindeste Toorne,
　　Skiønneste Blomster sin tærende Gift,
Under en Rosen-kind Hiertet kand foorne,
　　For dog at Skæbnen saa sælsom er skift!
　　　　I Vaade-vand
　　　　Flyder vort Land,
　　Himlen hâr Ene Lyksaligheds Stand.

Vel da! saa vil jeg mig aldrig bemøye
　　Om ikke Verden gaar efter min Agt!
Ingen Bekymring skal kunde mig bøye,
　　Intet skal giøre mit Hierte forsagt!
　　　　Sorrig skal døe,
　　　　Lystigheds Frøe
　　Blomstris paa Himle-Lyksaligheds Øe!

Angist skal aule en varende Glæde,
　　Qvide skal vinde sin Tott udaf Teen!
Armod skal prydis i rjgeste Klæde,
　　Svaghed skal reysis paa sundeste Been!
　　　　Avind skal staa
　　　　Fengsled i Vraae,
　　Himlen kand Ene alt dette formaa!

Lad da min Lod og min Lykke kun falde
　　Hvordan min GUd og min HErre hand vill,
Lad ikkun Avind udøse sin Galde,
　　Lad kun og Verden fulddrive sit Spill!
　　　　Tjdernis Bom
　　　　Bliver dog tom,
　　Himlen skal kiøre al tingest her-om!

(1681)

Fairest of roses have sharp thorns aquiver,
    Loveliest flowers their poisonous sap,
'Neath rosy cheeks can a heart always wither,
    Strange how a destiny each does enwrap!
        As storm-tossed boat,
        Our land's afloat,
Heaven alone all sweet bliss does promote.

Well then! No worry shall me overpower
    Should the world not do as I'd have prevail!
No tribulation shall cause me to cower
    Nothing shall cause my heart ever to fail!
        Sorrow shall die,
        Joy's seeds on high
On heaven's isle of pure bliss multiply.

Fear shall give rise to a joy that's enduring,
    Agony's distaff from tufts spin fine thread!
Poverty rich robes shall make most alluring,
    Weakness on sound legs shall rise from his bed!
        Envy shall stand
        Cornered, unmanned,
Heaven alone all of this can command!

Let then my fate and my fortune be fashioned
    As does my LORD and my MASTER desire,
Let no spite reign, nor no envious passion,
    Let but the world do as it would conspire!
        Time's loom will stare
        Empty and bare,
Heaven will weave all that is to be there!

(1681)

JENS STEEN SEHESTED (ca. 1640–ca. 1697)

Sonnet

Naar Jeg gienvordighed og tiden vil fordrifve,
    Da gaar Jeg til min skat, som mig til rede staar,
    Den under Jeg en pladtz imellem been og laar.
Min bomuld-bløde haand veed redskabet at stifve,
Som mig til ønsch behag en hiertens lyst kand gifve
    Med tagten op og need, saa lenge Jeg formaar
    At nyde saadan lyst, endtil der springer haar,
Som nesten hver gang skeer, da lader Jeg det blifve,
    Thi det som før var stifft paa min udvalde skat
    Er da formeget brugt, afmegtig, mat og slat,
Det henger slunken ned, endtil med mine finger
    Og krammen Jeg det giør tilbørlig stind og stif,
Da giør Jeg mig, som før, til min forlysters tvinger,
    See her min hiertens lyst, see her min tids fordrif.

(ca. 1690)

JENS STEEN SEHESTED (c. 1640–c. 1697)

Sonnet

When I would banish hardship or am at my leisure,
    I seek the treasure out that readily will rise,
    Whose seat I do not grudge between my legs and thighs.
My cotton-gentle hand this tool brings to full measure
That can fulfil my each desire and heart-felt pleasure
    With up and downward motion for as long as I
    Can sample such delight, until the gasping sigh
That nearly always comes, at which I leave my treasure,
    For what was once so stiff about my chosen one
    Is overused, enfeebled, limp and now quite done,
It dangles flabbily till I with fingers firm
    And squeezing duly make it stiff beyond compare,
And o'er my pleasurer dominion reaffirm,
    See here my heart's delight, see here my pastime fair.

(c. 1690)

HANS ADOLPH BRORSON (1694-1764)

DEn yndigste Rose er funden

DEn yndigste Rose er funden
Blant stiveste Torne oprunden,
    Vor JEsus den deyligste Pode
    Blant syndige Mennisker grode.

Alt siden vi tabte dend Ære,
GUds Billedes Frugter at bære,
    Var Verden forvildet og øde,
    Vi alle i Synden bortdøde.

Som Tidsler ey mere kand due,
End kastes i brændende Lue,
    Saa tiente ey Verden til andet,
    End vorde ved ilden forbandet.

Da lod GUD en Rose opskyde,
Og Sæden omsider frembryde,
    At rense og gandske forsøde
    Vor Vextes fordervede Grøde.

Saa blomstrer GUds Kircke med Ære,
Og yndige Frugter kand bære.
    Thi JEsus dends Grøde opliver,
    Og Vædske i Vexterne giver.

Ald Verden nu burde sig fryde,
Med Psalmer mangfoldig udbryde,
    Men mange har aldrig fornommen,
    At Rosen i Verden er kommen.

Forhærdede Tidsel-Gemøtter,
Saa stive, som Torne og Støtter,
    Hvi holde I Eder saa rancke
    I Stoltheds fordervede Tancke.

HANS ADOLPH BRORSON (1694-1764)

The Fairest of Roses

Now found is the fairest of roses
Its beauty midst thorns it discloses,
    Our Jesus this offshoot and dower
    Midst us human sinners did flower.

Since lost is the glory of bearing
The fruit of God's image, uncaring
    The world has seemed, barren and wasted,
    We all by our sins death have tasted.

As thistles to nought can aspire
Than all be consigned to the fire,
    So too was the world fit for burning
    And cursed with no hope of returning.

Then God let a rose thrive and flower.
Its seed He did further empower
    To cleanse and to sweeten entirely
    The yield that was ruined so direly.

Now God's Church its glory is wearing,
The finest of fruits can be bearing,
    For Jesus its yield is reviving,
    The plants with new sap are all thriving.

The whole world with joy should be singing,
The air with glad psalms should be ringing,
    But many are deaf to the telling:
    The rose in the world has its dwelling.

You thistle-minds, hardened and sickly,
As statues so stiff, thorns so prickly,
    Why stand you there tall and unblinking
    In pride's so depraved way of thinking?

Ach søger de nædrige Stæder,
I Støvet for Frælseren græder,
Saa faar I vor JEsum i Tale,
Thi Roserne voxer i Dale.

Nu, JEsu, Du stetze skal være
Min Smykke, min Rose og Ære,
Du gandske mit Hierte betager,
Din Sødhed jeg finder og smager.

Min Rose mig smykker og pryder,
Min Rose mig glæder og fryder;
De giftige Lyster Hand døder,
Og Kaarset saa liflig forsøder.

Lad Verden mig alting betage,
Lad Tornene rive og nage,
Lad Hiertet kun daane og briste,
Min Rose jeg aldrig vil miste.

(1732)

Oh, seek what is low and in keeping,
In dust for your Saviour be weeping,
    Then you will our Jesus be knowing,
    For roses in valleys are growing.

You, Jesus, will be beyond measure
My rose and my glory, my treasure,
    My heart you have captured completely,
    Your sweetness does nourish and feed me.

My rose is my jewel and my treasure,
My rose is my joy and my pleasure;
    My poisonous lusts you have beaten,
    The cross you deliciously sweeten.

Let this cruel world seek to ensnare me,
Let thorns try to scratch, rend and tear me,
    Let life from my poor heart be taken,
    My rose will remain unforsaken.

(1732)

Op! all den ting, som Gud har gjort

Op! all den ting, som Gud har giort,
Hans herlighed at prise,
Det mindste han har skabt, er stort,
Og kand hans magt bevise.

Gik alle konger frem i rad,
I deres magt og vælde,
De mægted' ey det mindste blad,
At sætte paa en nælde.

Ja! alle englers store kraft,
Som himle-scepter føre,
Har ingen tiid den evne haft
Det mindste støv at giøre.

Det mindste græs jeg undrer paa,
I skove og i dale,
Hvor skulde jeg den viisdom faae,
Om det kun ret at tale?

Hvad vil jeg da begynde, naar
Jeg lidet giennemkiger,
Hvor mange folk der gik og gaaer,
I alle verdens riger.

Hvad skal jeg sige, naar jeg seer,
At alle skove vrimle,
De mange fugle-spring, der skeer
Op under herrens himle?

Hvad skal jeg sige, naar jeg gaar
Blant blomsterne i enge,
Naar fugle-sangen sammen slaaer
Som tusind harpe-strenge?

Up! Everything That God Has Made

Up! Everything that God has made,
His glory now be praising,
The smallest creature too is great,
And proves his might amazing.

Though earth's great kings came forward, clad
In all their might and mettle,
The smallest leaf they could not add
To but a single nettle.

Yea! all the angels with their power,
Like sceptres in high station,
Have never caused at any hour
A speck of dust's creation.

The smallest blade in vale or wood
No wonder can excel it,
Where should I wisdom gain and could
Find ample words to tell it?

What should I do now when my mind
Is slow in comprehending
How great the host of humankind
Their earthly way are wending.

What shall I utter, when I see
The woods with life abounding,
The many birds that leap with glee
Beneath the heaven's rounding?

What shall I utter, when I walk
Among the meadow's flowers,
When all the birds in song do talk
Like thousand harp-string showers?

Hvad skal jeg sige, naar mit sind
I havets dybe grunde
Kun dog saa lit kand kige ind,
Og seer saa mange munde?

Hvad skal jeg sige, naar jeg vil,
Saa høyt jeg kand opkige,
Og vende alle tanker til
Det blanke solens rige?

Hvad skal jeg sige, naar jeg seer,
Hvor stierne-flokken blinker,
Hvor mildt enhver imod mig leer,
Og op til himlen vinker?

Hvad skal jeg sige, naar jeg op
Til Gud i aanden farer!
Og seer den store kiempe-trop
Af blide engle-skarer?

Hvad skal jeg sige? mine ord
Vil ikke meget sige;
O GUd! hvad er din viisdom stoer;
Din godhed, kraft og rige;

Alt det, som haver aande, skal
Vor skabere begegne,
Hans lov skal fylde bierg og dal,
Og alle verdens egne.

O! priser Gud paa denne jord,
Hver som har sands og tunge,
Og all den deel, i himlen boer,
Vor skabers lov skal siunge.

Slaaer alle folk paa denne jord
Med fryde-tone sammen,
Halleluja! vor Gud er stoer
Og himlen svare amen.

(1739)

What shall I utter, when my mind
Down on the sea's bed merely
So little in its depths can find
And many mouths see clearly?

What shall I utter, when I yearn
To gaze at heaven rightly,
And all my thoughts will upwards turn
To where the sun reigns brightly?

What shall I utter, when I see
How hosts of stars are gleaming,
How mildly each smiles down at me,
And I return their beaming?

What shall I utter, when I soar
In spirit to my Maker?
And see th'angelic hosts in awe
Stand mustered by the acre?

What shall I utter? All I say
Says nothing and seems mindless;
Oh God! Your wisdom rules alway,
As do your power and kindness.

All that's imbued with spirit shall
Our Maker soon be meeting.
His praise shall sound in hill and vale,
This earthly world completing.

Oh! Praise the Lord all those below
With voice and senses willing,
And all who dwell above now show
Our Maker's praise in singing.

Let all below with one accord
Join joyfully in winging
Their Hallelujah! Great our Lord—
Amen the heav'ns are ringing.

(1739)

AMBROSIUS STUB (1705-1758)

Du deylig Rosen-Knop

Du deylig Rosen-Knop!
Lad mig dig ret betragte!
Hver Mand maae dig jo agte,
  Naturen har nedlagt
  Hos dig al Konst og Pragt;
De fiine farved' Blade,
Os i Uvished lade,
  Om ey en ziirlig Dragt
  Indtager meer end Pragt;
De Blade giør saa mange,
Smaa Labyrinthers Gange,
  Og dufte Luften op;
  Du deylig Rosen-Knop!

Men ak! du visnede,
I gaar saae jeg med Glæde
Dig paa dit Torne-Sæde;
  Jeg brød dig af, men see!
  I Dag du visnede;
Din friske Farve svinder;
Dit matte Rødt mig minder,
  Din Herlighed forgaaer;
  Din Skiønhed Ende faaer;
Naturens Mesterstykke;
Ach, hvor er nu dit Smykke?
  I Gaar du blomstrede,
  I Dag du visnede.

Kom, Phillis! kom og see,
Min Rose paa dig kalder;
Din Skiønhed eengang falder;
  Kom, Phillis, kom og see!
  Betragt dit Billede!
Alt hvad man deyligt finder,

You Rosebud Sweet and Fair

You rosebud sweet and fair!
Close to, let me inspect you!
Each man must needs respect you,
    In you all nature's art
    And splendour dwell apart;
Each petal's coloured feather
Leaves us uncertain whether
    Apparel neat and trim
    Says more than splendour's whim:
A maze where coloured petals –
In paths where each unsettles –
    Add fragrance to the air;
    You rosebud sweet and fair!

Today, alas, you're gone,
But yesterday with pleasure
I viewed your thorn-borne treasure;
    I plucked you, whereupon
    Today, alas, you're gone.
Your bright shades fade and pall
Your dull red tells me all
    Your glory is but brief
    Your beauty held in fief;
You jewel of nature's crown,
Where now is your fine gown?
    Your blossoming is done,
    Today, alas, you're gone.

Come, Phyllis, come and see
My rose does now invite you;
Your beauty won't requite you;
    Come, Phyllis, come and see!
    Your image view quite freely!
All that's a source of pleasure

De rosenrøde Kinder,
   Den Mund, den Deylighed,
   De Øynes Munterhed,
Den nette Krop og Hænder,
Som sig hvers Gunst tilvender,
   Forgaaer; kom, Phillis! see!
   Betragt dit Billede!

   Een Skiønhed evig staaer,
Som ey for Tiden falder,
Og ey for Aar og Alder;
   Men Evigheden naaer,
   Een Skiønhed evig staaer;
See, Phillis! det er Dyden,
Stræb efter den i Tiden!
   At og en deylig Aand
   Sin Bolig ligne kand;
Lev til din Skabers Ære
I Dyden hans at være!
   Naar alting da forgaaer,
   Din Skiønhed evig staaer.

Cheeks crimson beyond measure,
 That mouth, its honeyed ploy
 Those eyes, their sparkling joy
That neat body, those neat hands
That every favour do command
 Do fade; come, Phyllis, see
 Your image view quite freely!

 One beauty outlasts others —
When all else only withers —
And years and age outweathers,
 And gains eternal vales
 One beauty never fails.
Virtue, Phyllis, its name,
Seek it ere time's no claim!
 And that a spirit true
 May dwell as is its due,
Live but to praise your maker
In virtue be its taker!
 So when all else does wither,
 Your beauty lasts forever.

Den kiedsom Vinter gik sin gang

Aria

Den kiedsom Vinter gik sin gang,
Den Dag saa kort, den Nat saa lang
        Forandrer sig
        Saa lempelig;
Den barske Vind, den mørke Skye – maa flye;
    Vor Kakkelovn saa eene staaer,
    Og hver Dags Kolde syge faaer;
    Den tykke Vams, den foret Dragt
    Er alt hengt hen, og reent foragt,
Og Muffen er tillige giemt – og glemt;
    Mand frygter ey, at Snee og Slud
    Skal møde dem, som vil gaae ud;
        Thi lad os gaae
        At skue paae,
Hvor smukt Naturen sig beteer – og leer.

Ach see hvor pyntet Soelen gaaer
Med lange Straaler i sit Haar;
        Den varme Krands
        Er rette Kands
For alle Ting, som nu maa grye – paa Nye;
    Det klare, lyse Himmel Blaae
    Er værd at kaste Øye paae;
    See Fuglene i Flokke Tal
    I Luftens viide Sommer-Sal,
De holde snart hvert Øyeblik – Musik;
    De kappes daglig toe og toe
    At bygge hvor de best kan Boe,
        Her flyver een
        Jo med sin Green,
Een Anden Sankker Haar og Straae – saa smaae.

The Tiresome Winter Now Is Gone

Aria

The tiresome winter now is gone
The day so short, the night so long
    At gentle pace
    Do change their face,
Now must dark clouds and winds that bite – take flight;
The fireplace stands alone, unstacked,
And each day's cold by shakes is racked;
The fleece-lined coat and doublet warm
Are hung away and held to scorn,
The muff is likewise out of kind – and mind;
    One fears no more that snow and sleet
    On going out one then will meet;
    So let us rise
    And now apprize
How sweetly nature does beguile – and smile.

Oh see, how richly dressed the sun
With gold-tressed hair its course does run
    Its ring of fire
    Can but inspire
All things that now accrue – anew;
The blue sky up above so clear
Is worth a gaze, both far and near;
See all the birds in mighty squalls,
That fill the air's wide summer halls,
Their joy they constantly prolong – in song;
    They daily two by two compete
    To make their nesting-place complete,
    Look, past one streaks
    With twig in beak,
Another culls small hairs and straws – then soars.

Ach See! hvor tegner Marken Vel
For Bonden heele Verdens Trel,
    Hand leer fordi
    Hans Slaveri
Skal endes med sin Frugtbarhed – i Fred,
    Hist gaaer de kaade Lam i fleng
    Og spøge i den grønne Eng,
    De knæle med en Hiertens Lyst
    For Moders mælke-fulde Bryst,
De qvægnes ved den søde Taaer – de faaer.
    Hist vogter Hyrden Qvæg og Korn;
    Et Hunde-Biæl, en lyd af Horn.
        Er ald Hans Spil;
        Men hører til,
Hvor smukt den Skov ham svare maae – der paa.

Ach see et meget yndigt Syen
Paa Skovens grønne Øyenbryn,
    Den høye Top
    Skal klædes op,
Og Vaaren pynter Bøgen ud – til Brud.
    Naar Solen brender som en Glød,
    Og stikker Ild i Barm og Skiød,
    Da har mand jo bag hvert et Blad
    Abscondselfor sin Matte Rad.
Her smager Thee og et Glas Viin – fra Rhin,
    Imidlertid man faaer at see
    Et ret naturligt Assemblee,
        Hver Fugl har stemt
        Sit Instrument,
De raske Dyer vil Danse net – og let.

Ach see hvor Speyle klar og glat
Den søe dog er i Lave sat,
    Det er jo som
    At Soelen kom
Kun for at see sit Skilderie – deri,
    Den Fisk, som stak i Dynd og Skarn,
    Og slap fra Frost og Fange Garn,

Oh see! the fields are looking well
The farmer, though the whole world's thrall,
  Now smiles to see
  His slavery
Will end in their increase – in peace,
 The lambs at random play and leap,
 And frolic 'mongst the meadow's sheep,
 They kneel with joyful heart at rest
 And suckle at their mother's breast,
By every single drop refreshed – afresh.
 The shepherd there guards flock and corn;
 A dog's sharp bark, a call of horn,
  Are all his art,
  Though all in part;
How sweetly do the woods reply – nearby.

 Oh see, a sight most passing fair
 At wood's green eyelids over there
  Each tall tree crest
  Is being dressed,
And spring decks out the beech with pride – as bride.
 So when the sun burns like a torch,
 And breast and lap does almost scorch,
 Behind each leaf is refuge found
 When weary heads seek sheltered ground.
Here tea refreshes, as does wine – from Rhine,
 And meanwhile one may gaze intent
 At what is nature's parliament,
  The birds rejoice
  With well-tuned voice,
The agile beasts will nimbly dance – and prance.

 Oh see, how mirror-smooth and clear
 The lake is fashioned over here,
  It almost seems
  The sun most dreams
Of gazing at its visage fair – down there,
 The fish once caught in filth and mire
 That frost and net could not acquire,

Hand faaer nu atter Moed og Liv,
Og spøger frit i Rør og siv,
See hist, hvor stolt hans Finner gaaer – og slaaer.
Nu lirrer Frøen med sin Mund
Imod den søvnig Aften Stund,
Jeg tænker Paa
Mit Hviile-Straae
Og ender min Spadsere Gang – i Sang.

Saa er da Himmel Jord og Vand
Opmuntret ved min Skabermand,
Jeg gik omkring
Blant Tusind Ting,
Guds Forsyn spores ved Enhver – i sær.
Bekymret Siæl! saa seer du dog,
At Alting staaer, i Herrens Bog,
I hvor det gaaer, saa veed jeg grandt,
Mit Navn staaer tegnet deriblandt;
Gud kommer vist min Tarv ihu – end nu,
Hand Rammer nok den rette Tiid
Da Himlen den skal blive bliid;
Jeg tør maaskee
Vel faae at see
Min Vinter blive til en Vaar – i Aar.

Now feels the urge to live and breed
And freely sports midst rush and reed,
See here, how proudly fins now flash – and splash.
The frog now croaks its serenade
When drowsy day begins to fade,
With blade of grass
I watch time pass
And end my walk that took so long – in song.

So do the water, sky and earth
By my Creator gain rebirth,
I roamed among
World's mighty throng,
Through all God's providence did run – each one.
Oh troubled soul! Will you just look
And see all things are in His book,
Whate'er befalls, I know full well
That I among them all may dwell,
God is still mindful of my need – indeed,
He's sure to find the perfect time
When heaven's bells will peal and chime;
It could just be
I too may see
My winter will as spring appear – this year.

Gravskrift

Jeg, salig Owe Gierløv Meyer,
Begik Sottiser, som jeg pleier,
Men denne Gang begik jeg fem,
Den sidste var dog værst blandt dem;
Thi gik jeg hiem, skar ud min Strube,
Og sidder her i Helveds Grube,
Hvor nu den lede Satan eier
Mig, salig Owe Gierløv Meyer.

(1775)

Epitaph

I, the late Owe Gierløv Meyer,
Did stupid things my life entire,
Though this time I did five of them,
The last of which was quite a gem;
For I went home and cut my throat,
And here I sit, in Hell's deep moat,
Where now the devil sets on fire
Me, the late Owe Gierløv Meyer.

(1775)

Digterens Gravskrift over sig selv

Han aad og drak, var aldrig glad,
Hans Støvlehæle gik han skieve;
Han ingen Ting bestille gad,
Tilsidst han gad ei heller leve.

(1785)

The Poet's Epitaph upon Himself

He ate and drank, was never glad,
He wore his boots heels down one side;
Ambition – that he never had,
And finally just upped and died.

(1785)

JOHANNES EWALD (1743-1781)

Da jeg var syg

Beatus ille, qui procul negotiis — Horat:

Lyksalig Den, som langt fra Verdens Larm,
Er ikke riig — ey heller alt for arm
Hvis Siel kan uforstyrret tænke sig,
Og Væsenet, som den bør være lig!
Er Daarens Tilraab — Ærens tomme Skal,
Er Dynger af et glimrende Metal
Er gyldne Lænker — er en kronet Træl
Er Verden os saa vigtig, som vor Siæl?
Hvi sank din stærke Siæl afmægtig ned,
Du første Mand — dybt — til Ustadighed?
Hvi stodst du ikke stærk ved Almagts-Haand?
Hvi kom Adspredelser til Viisdoms-Aand?
Thi kun Adspredelser var Siælens Død,
Ved Vredens Røst blev Tankerne forstrød
Nu rave de forvildede omkring,
Blant gode og blant skadelige Ting.
Siel hold din Salighed! — nu har du den!
Men Støvet kalder dig fra Himmelen!
Chimæren sluger Støvet, som du saae!
Nu veedst du selv ey hvad du tænker paa!
Ak! — naar min Andagt — naar min Bøn er varm,
Naar jeg opløftet — høyt — i Naadens Arm,
Udbreder Gud — og føler himlisk Lyst,
Hvi kommer da Dorine til mit Bryst?
Og naar jeg fandt den rene Kierlighed
Den Ild, som ingen Viis tør rødme ved,
Hvi river da en Tanke af Homer
Min Siel fra den Helene, som jeg seer?
Ak! stadig var vor Tanke god og viis,
Og Sielen fandt — og blev i Paradiis!
Thi Eftertanken kiender Salighed
Den finder den men hæfter ey derved.
O Adams Barn! — o ulyksalige!
Hvi søger du da selv Adspredelse?

JOHANNES EWALD (1743-1781)

When I Was Ill

Beatus ille, qui procul negotiis – Horace:

Happy the man, who far from life's allure
Is not too rich – and likewise not too poor
Whose soul untroubled then can contemplate,
The being too that it should emulate!
Should fools' acclaim and glory's empty shell –
Should heaps of gleaming metal and their spell –
Should golden chains – a slave that has been crowned –
The world – as dear as our own soul be found?
Why did your once strong soul sink helplessly,
You first of men – deep – to inconstancy?
Why did you quail at the Almighty's hand?
Distraction your wise spirit not withstand?
For all distraction marks the soul's demise,
At anger's voice all thoughts are scattered wide
In great confusion they now reel about
Midst things both good and bad weave in and out,
Soul hold to blessedness! – 'tis yours today!
By dust you are from heaven called away!
Chimera swallows all the dust you saw!
Your own thoughts you do not know any more!
Ah! – when devotion – when my prayers are warm,
When I uplifted – high – on mercy's arm,
Spread God abroad – and feel divinely blessed,
Why does Dorine then come to my breast?
And when I found pure love in its full flush
The fire at which no wise man e'er would blush,
Why does a thought of Homer then wrench free
My soul from that fair Helen whom I see?
Ah! were our thoughts but constant, good and wise
Our soul would find – and stay in paradise!
For blessedness reflection can espy
It feels it but is not attached thereby.
Oh child of Adam! – oh unhappy one!
Why do you seek distraction you should shun?

Hvi svimler du? – See Strudelen! – og skielv!
Betænk! – hvad er saa kostbart, som du selv?
Lyksalig den, som ey den vilde Klang,
Af fulde Glas – og ey Sireners Sang
Ey Guldets Troldoms Røst – ey Klirrende
Af Mordrisk Staal, og ey Herolderne
Ey falske Venners Hvislen — Usles Graad
Kiedsommeliges Gaben – Daarers Raad
Ey stærke Fienders Brøl – ey Svages Skrig,
Berøver Gud – og Lyst — og Sands – og Sig!
Velkommen Gift, som raser i mit Bryst!
Velkomne Harm, som reent fordrev min Lyst!
Og Mangel – du som togst min sidste Ven,
Velkommen! — thi du gavst mig, Mig igien.
Som Skaberen kun henter Fryd af sig,
Og uden andres Hielp er lykkelig;
Saa skal jeg ære Ham – og føle Mig
Og glemme Roes – og Guld – og Brøl – og Skrig!

(1771)

Why are you faint? – Behold the maelstrom – quake!
Think now! – is not your precious self at stake?
Happy the man who's not by clink so gay
Of brimful glass – nor by the sirens' lay
Nor the enslaving voice of gold – nor clash
Of murd'rous steel, nor by some herald brash
Nor false friends' mocking tones – nor wretches' tears
The tedium of bores – fools' counsel's snares
Nor by foes' mighty roar – or weak men's cries,
Deprived of God – joy – sense – himself likewise!
Welcome you poison raging in my breast!
Welcome all pain that has my joy suppressed!
And lack – you who it was took my last friend,
Welcome! – since you gave me myself again.
Since my Creator only can know pure delight,
And without others' help be happy quite,
I will then honour him – my self stay nigh,
Forget all fame – and gold – each roar – and cry!

(1771)

Rungsteds Lyksaligheder. En Ode

I kiølende Skygger,
    I Mørke, som Roser udbrede;
Hvor Sangersken bygger
    Og quiddrende røber sin Rede –
    Hvor sprudlende Bække,
    Snart dysse, snart vække
Camoenernes Yndling, den følende Skiald,
    Med steds' eensrislende Fald -

Hvor Hiordene brøle,
    Mod Skovens letspringende Sønner,
Og puste, og føle
    Den Rigdom, i hvilken de stønner –
    Hvor Meyeren synger
    Blant gyldene Dynger,
Og tæller sin Skat, og opløfter sit Raab,
    Til den, som har kroned hans Haab.–

Hvor skiærtsende Bølger
    Beskvulpe den Vandrer, hvis Øye,
Snart stirrende følger
    Med Helsinges graanende Høye;
    Snart undrende haster
    Blant Skove af Master, —
Og forsker, og kiender den Fremmedes Flag,
    Og glemmer den heldende Dag.–

Hvor eensommes Liise,
    Venskabelig lindrende Slummer,
Tit bød en Louise,
    Forglemme sin kiærlige Kummer –
    Hvor Glæder tilsmiile
    Den Vandrende Hviile,
Hvor Rungsted indhegner den reeneste Lyst;
    Der fyldte Camoenen mit Bryst.–

The Delights of Rungsted. An Ode

In shadows refreshing,
    In darkness from roses now stealing;
Where busily nesting
    The songstress her home is revealing—
    Where streams whose carousing
    Now lulls, now is rousing
The Muses' best darling, the sentient bard,
    With murmurings close to the heart—

Where cattle are lowing,
    At woodland-sons' fleet gallivanting,
And breathe hard at knowing
    The plenty in which they are panting—
    Where reapers are singing,
    Midst golden stacks swinging,
And count out their treasure and let cries resound
    To him who their hope now has crowned.

Where, skittishly playing,
    Waves wash o'er the roamer, who quick-eyed
First finds his gaze straying
    At Helsinge's grey-shaded hillside
    Then wond'ringly hastens
    Through forests of masts and
Inspects, then makes out foreign flags straight away,
    Forgetting the fast-waning day.—

Where balm of the lonely,
    Sweet slumber so gently relieving,
Louise oft solely
    Could help one forget the heart's grieving—
    Where joys offer home, a
    Repose for the roamer,
Where Rungsted encloses delights pure and chaste:
    There did the muse fill my breast.

Hvor Kummer og Smerte,
    Fandt glade dit Aftryk, Du Høye,
Det ædleste Hierte,
    I hvert et medlidende Øye -
    Hvor Venlighed pryder
    De strængeste Dyder;
Der voxte min Sang; og den undrende Skov
    Gav Gienlyd af Skaberens Lov. –

Jeg saae dine Throner,
    O Almagt! – og stirrede længe –
Men hellige Toner
    Foer giennem de zittrende Strænge –
    Hvert Blad, hvor mit Øye
    Fandt Præg af den Høye,
Opflammede Siælen – da voxte min Sang! –
    Da raste den mægtige Klang!

O Verdeners Fader! –
    Saa sang jeg – Du Stærke! – Du Viise! –
Gud! – som Myriader,
    Som Himlenes Vældige priise! –
    See Støvet kan bære,
    Din Rigdom, Din Ære,
Din Godhed, o Fader! – saa sang jeg – og Fryd
    Brød Læbernes bævende Lyd. –

Lyksalige Digter,
    Som Glæden indbød til sin Hytte;
Til venlige Pligter;
    Til Friehed, som Dyder beskytte! –
    Cheruber fornemme
    Hans dristige Stemme,
Og Himle forsamles omkring ham; og Lyst
    Udbredes i Menniskets Bryst. –

Where pain and affliction,
    With joy found your imprint, Oh High One,
The pure heart's depiction
    By every compassionate eye won –
    Where friendship adds worth to
    The strictest of virtues;
There did my song grow; and the forest in awe
    Re-echoed the Great Maker's law.

I saw your thrones gleam too,
    Almighty! – my gaze all aquiver –
But tones divine passed through
    The strings with each shiver –
    Each leaf where I sighted
    The High One ignited
My soul – and exulted at which my song swelled! –
    The mighty sound could not be quelled! –

Oh all the Worlds' Father! –
    So sang I – You Strong One! – You Wise One!
God! Whom myriads are
    Now praising as do heaven's prized ones!
    See, how dust can carry
    Your plenty, your glory,
Your goodness, oh Father! – so sang I – and joy
    My lips' quaking sound did employ. –

O poet most blissful,
    That gladness bade come to his dwelling;
To duties most cheerful,
    To freedom, through virtues compelling! –
    All cherubs while winging
    His bold voice hear ringing,
And heavens are gathered around him; and joy
    Unfolds in man's breast, ne'er to cloy.

Men Du, som allene
   Fremkaldte den Lyst af min Smerte,
Siig! – Kan min Camoene
   Udbrede sin Fryd i dit Hierte? –
   O siig mig, Veninde! –
   Kan Sangens Gudinde,
Med smeltende Toner belønne det Skiød,
   Hvoraf min Lyksalighed flød? –

(1775)

But you, you alone drew
    From anguish such joy beyond measure
Say! – has my muse power to
    Unfold in your heart greatest pleasure?
    O sweet friend, recite me! –
    Can song's goddess lightly
With soft-melting notes the lap then reward
    That me such delight did afford? –

(1775)

Johannes Ewalds sidste poetiske Følelser
nogle Timer før hans Død

Udrust dig, Helt fra Golgatha!
　　Løft høit dit røde Skiold;
Thi Synd og Skrek – du seer det ja –
　　Angriber mig med Vold.

Udstræk dit Glavind i din Harm
　　Mod dem, som trodse dig!
Nedstyrt dem med en vældig Arm
　　Fra Lyset – og fra mig.

Da skal jeg, sikker ved din Haand,
　　Ei frygte Døden meer;
Men offre dig min frelste Aand
　　Paa dens nedbrudte Leer.

　　　––––––––––––––––––

O Herre! forund mig Liise og Roe;
　　Men revser du mig med Smerte,
Da lær mig at taale – at bede – og troe,
　　Og JESUS opfylde mit Hierte.

(1781)

Johannes Ewald's Last Poetic Sentiments
Some Hours Prior to His Death

To arms, hero of Calvary!
   Lift high your bright-red shield;
For sin and dread – as you can see –
   By force would have me yield.

In righteous ire your sword outstretch
   'Gainst those who you defy!
Hurl from the light – and me, poor wretch –
   Such foes before I die.

Safe in your hand I then will view
   My death without dismay;
And my saved spirit offer you
   On its now unmade clay.

Oh Lord! rest and relief vouchsafe;
   Though if you would chastise me,
Teach me endurance – prayer – and faith,
   Let my heart CHRIST suffice me.

(1781)

JENS BAGGESEN (1764-1826)

Da jeg var lille

Der var en Tid, da jeg var meget lille,
Min hele Krop var kun en Alen lang;
Sødt, naar jeg denne tænker, Taarer trille,
Og derfor tænker jeg den mangen Gang.

Jeg spøged i min ømme Moders Arme,
Og sad til Hest paa bedste Faders Knæ,
Og kiendte Frygt og Grublen, Sorg og Harme,
Saa lidt som Penge, Græsk, og Galathe.

Da syntes mig, vor Jord var meget mindre,
Men og tillige meget mindre slem;
Da saae jeg Stiernerne som Prikker tindre,
Og ønskte Vinger for at fange dem.

Da saae jeg Maanen ned bag Høyen glide,
Og tænkte: gid jeg var paa Høyen der!
Saa kunde jeg dog rigtig faae at vide
Hvoraf, hvor stor, hvor rund, hvor kiøn den er!

Da saae jeg undrende Guds Sol at dale
Mod Vesten ned i Havets gyldne Skiød,
Og dog om Morgnen, tidlig atter male
Den hele Himmelegn i Østen rød.

Og tænkte paa den naadige Gud Fader,
Som skabte mig, og denne smukke Sol,
Og alle disse Nattens Perlerader,
Som krandse Himmelbuen Pol til Pol.

Med barnlig Andagt bad min unge Læbe
Den Bøn, min fromme Moder lærte mig:
O gode Gud! o lad mig altid stræbe,
At vorde viis, og god, og lyde dig!

JENS BAGGESEN (1764-1826)

When I Was Small

There was a time when I was very small
A mere two feet was all I measured then;
And, when I think of this, tears sweetly fall,
So I think of it time and time again.

In tender mother's arms in play I grew
And on dear father's knee to ride I'd seek,
Of fear and brooding, grief and wrath I knew
As little as of gold and ancient Greek.

The earth much smaller then to me did seem
But at the same time much less evil too:
Then did I see the stars like bright dots gleam,
And wished for wings to seize them as I flew.

I saw the moon then slide behind the hill,
And thought: If only I were standing there!
Then I can really find out if I will
Of what it is – how big, how round, how fair!

I saw the sun then in amazement dive
Into the sea's gold lap far in the West
And yet at early dawn once more contrive
To have the Eastern sky in crimson dressed.

And of my Heav'nly Father did I think
Who me and this fine sun created whole,
And all these nighttime pearls on their great string
That span the starry vault from pole to pole.

With reverential lips did I repeat
The prayer my pious mother had me say:
O gracious God! Oh let me always seek
To be both wise and good, and You obey!

125

Saa bad jeg for min Fader, for min Moder,
Og for min Søster, og den hele Bye;
Og for Kong Christian, og for den Stodder,
Som gik mig krum og sukkende forbi.

De svandt, de svandt de Barndoms blide Dage!
Min Rolighed, min Fryd med dem svandt hen;
Jeg kun Erindringen har nu tilbage:
Gud lad mig aldrig, aldrig tabe den!

(1801)

I prayed then for my father and my mother,
And for my sister and for all the town;
And for King Christian, and for the poor beggar
Who passed me by, deep sighing and bent down.

All gone, all gone, my childhood's golden lustre!
My peace of mind, my joy with them are gone;
The memory of them is all that I can muster:
May I, please God, ne'er lose what once so shone!

(1801)

SCHACK STAFFELDT (1769-1826)

Indvielsen

Jeg sad paa Pynten ved Sundets Bred,
    Himlene smilte,
Og saae med Længsel i Dybet ned,
    Bølgerne hvilte,
Da hælded' Solen til Havets Bryst
Og rundtom rødnede Luft og Kyst.

Og brat fra Skyerne Strengeleeg
    Anelsen vakte,
I Aftenrøde Musen nedsteeg,
    Harpen mig rakte,
Og raskt et brændende Kys mig gav,
Nedsynkende i det luende Hav.

Da rundt en anden Natur der blev,
    Vindene talte;
Fra Skyer, som blege for Maanen hendrev,
    Aanderne kaldte,
Et Hierte slog varmt og kiærligt i Alt,
I Alt mig vinked' min egen Gestalt.

Dog blev fra nu for Tanke og Trang
    Jorden et Fængsel;
Vel lindrer ved Anelse, Drøm og Sang
    Hiertet sin Længsel,
Dog brænder mig Kysset, jeg kiender ei Fred
Førend jeg drager Himlene ned!

(1804)

SCHACK STAFFELDT (1769–1826)

Initiation

I sat far out on the sound's still shore,
    The skies were smiling;
And filled with longing I gazed down o'er
    The waves beguiling.
The sun slipped into the sea's embrace,
The coast and sky joined in blushing grace.

With sweet foreboding a harp I heard,
    The clouds now rending;
The muse descended, in sunlight girt,
    Her lyre extending.
She sealed my lips with kiss of fire
And sank down into her shimmering pyre.

Then all around me the world was new:
    The winds spoke softly;
From pale clouds drifting before the moon
    Called spirits lofty;
In all creation a loving heart beat,
My own reflection in all did I meet.

Since then the earth each thought and desire
    Does now imprison;
Though dreams ease longing, as do song's lyre
    And premonition,
The kiss consumes me, no peace can see birth
Before the skies I bring down to earth!

(1804)

Det Eene

Alt det Skjønne forgaaer, fordi at ei Aanden skal nøjes
    I sin fornedrede Stand: stedse skal Længslerne her
Brænde i Menneskets Barm, liig Lampen i natlige Fængsel,
    Der i Mørke og Mulm Mærke paa Himmelens Lys.
Menneske! ei hvad du har, men hvad du savner og attraaer,
    Det er din kostbarste Skat, det er din ypperste Værd,
Thi det Herlige kun ved Savn du kan dig tilegne:
    Nøje er Menneskets Fald, Længsel dets højeste Flugt.
Alt det Skjønne forgaaer, Symbolernes Verden omskiftes
    Og i andre Tegn taler det Eene sig ud.
Grav i Verdenens Aarbog: der ligger Seklernes Rader,
    Som henskyllede Lag, Aandernes Bundfald og Spor.
Kloden er selv en Ruin, og som Skimlen paa smuldrende Muure,
    Af dens brustne Granit spirer den seenere Vaar.
Ikkun et Eeneste er, mens Tiderne dale og stige,
    Ikkun et Eeneste var, er og skal være som før:
Det er det evige Liv, som liig Blodet fra Hjertet, udflyder
    Gjennem den heele Natur, hen og tilbage igjen;
Saa forkynder sig Sjælen i stedse omskiftede Miner,
    I utallige Træk varig den samme og een.
Derfor *det* kun er til, hvori sig det Eene opholder,
    Kun Ideen, som Skjold, værger Forgjængelsen af:
I dit Levnets Kunstværk Ideen du derfor fremstille,
    Stemme dig op til din Art, Arten er evig som Gud,
Ellers gaaer du til Grund, som Boblen brister paa Havet:
    Havet er, dog hvor er Boblen, dets farvede Barn?
Men hvis Ideen udfylder dit dybe, betydende Levnet,
    Da er udødelig du, Gud er i dig, du i Gud.
Sjeldne Naturer nu fra Tiden Issen unddrage,
    Biergtoppe liig, som sees høit over Vandflodens Speil.
Anderledes det var, og anderledes det bliver,
    Fremtid Gjentagelsen er af den forbigangne Tid.
Ja! der var fordum et Old, da Naturen barnligt udtrykked'
    I det troeste Præg Faderens evige Træk,
Da den, liig rødmende Frugt, end ikke fra Stammen sig skilled'
    Og i det vovede Fald fri, men forgjængelig blev.
End den *gyldne* Sphære bag Fortids Formørkelse ruller,

The One

All that is beautiful dies, that the spirit shall gain no contentment
    In its debased human state: longings shall thus here below
Man's bosom forever consume, like the lamp in a dark night-time dungeon,
    Which, at the dread dead of night, a mark on the light of the sky.
Man! it is not what you own, but what you long for and crave for,
    This is your treasure most dear, this is your value most high,
The glorious you can but own by suffering great deprivation:
    Man's fall is stricture, longing its heavenmost flight.
All that is beautiful dies, the world of symbols knows change,
    And in different signs the One expresses itself.
Delve in the world's annals: there centuries lie in succession,
    Like strata washed ashore, deposit and trace of the spirit.
The globe itself is a ruin, and, like mould that now crumbles on walls,
    Out of the granite's great rifts sprouts what will later be spring.
One single thing can stand firm through the rise and the fall of the ages,
    One single thing ever was, is and will be as before:
Eternal life is its name, which, like blood from the heart, flows
    Through all nature, flows outwards and later returns;
So too the soul shows itself, its mien always changing
    Its features uncountable, constantly one and the same.
Therefore *this* only exists, in which the One can reside,
    The idea only, as shield, repels all that passes away.
In your life's work of art this is why you present the idea,
    Attune to your own nature, that nature eternal as God,
You are otherwise lost, like bubbles that burst on the sea:
    The sea still remains, but its bubble, its bright-coloured child?
Should though the idea transfuse your deep, significant life,
    You are immortal – in God as God is in you.
Exceptional natures withdraw now their summit from time,
    Like mountain peaks, seen far beyond the flood's surface.
Of old it was otherwise, otherwise will it be later,
    The future a mere repetition of a time long since past.
Yes! there once was an age when, childlike, all nature expressed
    With imprint most faithful the eternal traits of the father,
When as yet, like ripening fruit, it had not left the bough
    And in its bold fall become free though ephemeral.
As yet behind the eclipse of the past the *golden* sphere rolls,

Poesien den end holder i rhytmiske Baand;
Alle Længsler did sværme, liig Skibbrudne, hvilke fra Skjæret,
    Nøgne, nødlidende, see fjernt den forønskede Bugt.;
Var er det klagende Sagn, *skal være,* den jublende Spaadom,
    Sagn og Religion, Minde og længselfuldt Haab,
Tidens Poler de ere, som stedse forgjæves sig søge,
    Indtil de blive til eet der, hvor ei Tiden er meer. –
Selviske *Nutid,* som kun i Øjeblikket rodfæster,
    Verdenslivet for dig staaer i sit Vintersolstits;
Du Nødvendighed trodser og brammer med Frihedens Septer?
    Fri i dit Frafald du er, Frihed er Valget af Aag.
Viid, at Selvhed er i Naturen det rasende Oprør,
    Og den uhyre Synd Friheds gigantiske Barn;
Selvhed er Sønnens Oprør mod den, som Livet ham skjænkte,
    Ikkun *Sønnens Død* soner Forbrydelsen af. –
Saa forgaae da, Natur, liig Feberens grundløse Blændværk,
    Og helbredet fra dig, langsomt, med Tidernes Løb,
Stræbe det affødte Liv til Verdens salige Hjerte,
    Og i Eenhedens Skjød, sonet, Bevidstheden døe.

(1808)

As yet it keeps poetry still in its most rhythmical bands;
All longings swarm thither, like castaways, who from the rocks,
    Naked, in direst distress, see far off the bay that they crave.
Was is the plaintive myth, *will be* the joyous prediction,
    Myth and religion, fond memory and much desired hope,
Poles of time are they, vainly and constantly seeking each other,
    Until they melt into One, there where time is no more. –
Self-seeking *Present*, rooted but in the moment,
    World-life for you can but stand in its midwinter solstice;
Necessity you do defy and freedom's sceptre do flaunt?
    Free in defection are you, your freedom the choice of a yoke.
Know then that selfdom is raging rebellion in nature,
    And sin that is monstrous freedom's gargantuan child;
Selfdom the son's great revolt against what life him has granted,
    Only the *death of the Son* can ever atone for the crime –
So may you die, nature, like fever's groundless delusion,
    And cured from you, slowly, with passage of time,
May life that now is engendered strive for the world's blessed heart,
    And in unity's lap, atoned for, may consciousness die.

(1808)

Aftenrøden

Rose i en Vase af Lasur,
    Som af Solens Bølgegrav fremstiger,
Hvergang fra den sørgende Natur
    Hendes Ven til andre Verdner viger!

Ikkun Maanen, rødmende for dig,
    Dristig i din Purpurkalk nedskuer;
Himlens Stierner langt fra holde sig,
    Elskere med tause, dulgte Luer.

Skjønne Himmelblomst af Lys og Luft,
    Af de Reeneste en hellig Datter!
Aftnen samler Vaarens heele Duft
    Og den i din Purpurkalk indfatter.

Ak! men Natten ud fra Østen gaaer,
    Sagte sig dens Rige rundt udbreder,
Himmelrose! end du herlig staaer,
    Dog du snart de matte Blade spreder.

Roser! eders Søster er ei meer
    Græder Dug til Minderosens Minde!
Lærker! jubler, naar I atter seer
    Haabets Rose høit paa Østens Tinde!

(1808)

134

Sunset Glow

Rose held in a vase of clearest glaze
　　Up from wat'ry sunlight-grave ascending
Every time from nature's mourning gaze
　　Her close friend to other worlds is wending!

Moon's pale visage, in lone blush for you,
　　Dares observe your crimson petal cluster;
Heaven's stars maintain their distant view,
　　Lovers, though with silent, hidden lustre.

Beauteous heav'nly flower of light and air,
　　Of the purest ones a holy daughter!
Evening garners all spring's fragrance fair
　　In your crimson calyx as an altar.

Night, alas, advances from the east,
　　Its domain so stealthily diffusing;
Heav'nly rose! for eyes though still a feast,
　　You anon dull petals must be losing.

Roses! your sweet sister's life is told,
　　Weep in tribute dear your dew of mourning!
Larks! rejoice when you again behold
　　Hope's sweet rose on eastern peaks of morning!

(1808)

ADAM OEHLENSCHLÄGER (1779-1850)

Guldhornene

De higer og søger
i gamle Bøger,
i oplukte Høje
med speidende Øie,
paa Sværd og Skiolde
i muldne Volde,
paa Runestene
blandt smuldnede Bene.

Oldtids Bedrifter
anede trylle;
men i Mulm de sig hylle,
de gamle Skrifter.
Blikket stirrer,
sig Tanken forvirrer.
I Taage de famle.

"I gamle gamle
hensvundne Dage!
da det straalte i Norden,
da Himlen var paa Jorden,
giv et Glimt tilbage!"

Skyen suser,
Natten bruser,
Gravhøien sukker,
Rosen sig lukker.
De øvre Regioner
toner!
De sig møde, de sig møde,
de forklarede Høie,
kampfarvede, røde,
med Stierneglands i Øie.

ADAM OEHLENSCHLÄGER (1779-1850)

The Gold Horns

They peer in pages
of ancient sages,
on opened barrows
their gaze now narrows,
on shield and sword in
each castle ruin,
on runestone boulders
midst bones now moldered.

Old deeds exciting
cast spells if bidden;
but earth keeps hidden
the ancient writing.
Their gaze unseeing,
Thoughts wild and fleeing
In mists they're groping.

"You days of glory
lost well past hoping!
when the North shone clearly
with heaven here nearly,
may we glimpse your story!"

Clouds are rushing,
Night is hushing,
Barrows sighing
Roses shying.
The heavens' highest ceiling
pealing!
The high ones transfigured
are teeming, are teeming,
daubed red for war's rigours,
their eyes starlike gleaming.

"I som raver i blinde,
skal finde
et ældgammelt Minde,
der skal komme og svinde!
Dets gyldne Sider
skal Præget bære
af de ældste Tider.

Af det kan I lære.
Med andagtsfuld Ære
I vor Gave belønne.
Det skiønneste Skiønne,
en *Møe*
skal Helligdommen finde!"
Saa synge de og svinde.
Lufttonerne døe!

Hrymfaxe den sorte
puster og dukker
og i Havet sig begraver.
Morgenens Porte
Delling oplukker
og Skinfaxe traver
i straalende Lue
paa Himlens Bue.

Og Fuglene synge.
Dugperler bade
Blomsterblade,
som Vindene gynge.
Og med svævende Fied
en Møe hendandser
til Marken afsted.
Violer hende krandser.
Hendes Rosenkind brænder,
hun har Lilliehænder.
Let som en Hind
med muntert Sind,
hun svæver og smiler;

"You who reel and are blind
will find
a relic of bygone year
that will come and disappear!
Its sides full golden
the stamp will be wearing
of times most olden.

Its lesson's for sharing.
With reverent bearing
our gift you repay us
Of beauties the fairest,
a *maid*
will this treasure discover!"
They sing and pass over.
The airborne sounds fade.

Black Rimfaxe, fawning
his mouth flecked with lather,
plunges into the ocean.
Gates of the morning
are ope'd by day's father:
Skinfaxe in motion
with fire seems to leaven
the arch of the heavens.

The birds are all singing.
Dewdrops give showers
To petals of flowers
That breezes are swinging.
And with graceful lilt
a maiden now dances
with violet-garlands
away to the field.
Her rosy cheeks bright,
Her hands lily-white.
Light as a deer
With spirit so clear
she floats sweetly smiling;

og som hun iler
og paa Elskov grubler –
hun snubler!
og stirrer og skuer
gyldne Luer,
og rødmer og bæver
og zittrende hæver
med undrende Aand,
af sorten Muld,
med sneehvide Haand,
det røde Guld.

En sagte Torden
dundrer!
Hele Norden
undrer!

Og hen de stimle
i store Vrimle,
og grave og søge
Skatten at forøge.
Men intet Guld!
Deres Haab har bedraget
De see kun det Muld,
hvoraf de er taget.

Et Sekel svinder!!

Over Klippetinder
det atter bruser.
Stormenes Sluser
bryde med Vælde.
Over Norges Fielde
til Danmarks Dale
i Skyernes Sale,
de forklarede Gamle
sig atter samle.

Love-thoughts beguiling
her mind in a tumble
she stumbles!
and sees as she gazes
golden blazes,
and blushes and shivers
and lifts with a quiver,
amazed at the sight,
from the earth's black hold
with hands snow-white
the crimson gold.

A peal of
distant thunder!
The North's
in total wonder!

With crowds soon forming
now seething, now swarming
they dig without measure
for yet more treasure.
But no more gold!
Their hope was mistaken.
They see but black mould
from which they've been taken.

A century dies!!

O'er summits the cry
again is sounding.
With force astounding
Storm's floodgates break.
O'er Norway's peaks
to Denmark's vales
in lofty halls
once more they gather
the ancient fathers.

"For de sieldne Faae
som vor Gave forstaae,
som ei Jordlænker binde,
men hvis Siele sig hæve
til det Eviges Tinde,
som ane det Høie
i Naturens Øie,
som tilbedende bæve
for Guddommens Straaler,
i Sole, i Violer,
i det Mindste, i det Største,
som brændende tørste
efter Livets Liv,
som – o store Aand
for de svundne Tider!
see dit Guddomsblik
paa Helligdommens Sider,
for *dem* lyder atter vort Bliv!
Naturens Søn,
ukiendt i Løn,
men som sine Fædre
kraftig og stor,
dyrkende sin Jord,
ham vil vi hædre,
han skal *atter* finde!"
Saa synge de og svinde.

Hrymfaxe den sorte
puster og dukker,
og i Havet sig begraver.
Morgenens Porte
Delling oplukker,
og Skinfaxe traver
i straalende Lue,
paa Himlens Bue.

Ved lune Skov
Øxnene trække
den tunge Plov,
over sorten Dække.

"For the precious few
who our gift well knew
who no earthly chains bind
but whose souls rise up
to eternity's top
who sense what is high
in Nature's eye
who adoringly learn
divine rays to find,
in suns, violets – in all,
the great and the small
who thirsting still burn
for the Life of Life,
who – oh great spirit
of ancient times! –
see your divine gaze
on its sacred sides,
for *them* is our stay!
A son of nature,
an unknown creature,
but strong and tall
as his fathers withal,
is tilling his soil,
we will honour his toil –
he'll *once more* uncover!"
They sing and pass over.

Black Rimfaxe, fawning
his mouth flecked with lather,
plunges into the ocean.
Gates of the morning
are ope'd by day's father:
Skinfaxe in motion
with fire seems to leaven
the arch of the heavens.

By woodland brow
The oxen heave
the heavy plough
and furrows cleave.

Da standser Ploven,
og en Gysen farer
igennem Skoven.
Fugleskarer
pludselig tier.
Hellig Taushed
alt indvier.

Da klinger i Muld
det gamle Guld.

Tvende Glimt fra Oldtidsdage
funkler i de nye Tider.
Selsomt vendte de tilbage,
gaadefyldt paa røde Sider.

Mystisk Helligdom omsvæver
deres gamle Tegn og Mærker.
Guddomsglorien ombæver
Evighedens Underværker.

Hædrer dem, thi Skiebnen skalter
snart maaskee de er forsvunden.
Jesu Blod paa Herrens Alter
fylde dem, som Blod i Lunden.

Men I see kun deres Lue,
ikke det ærværdigt Høie!
Sætte dem som Pragt tilskue
for et mat nysgierrigt Øie.

Himlen sortner, Storme brage!
Visse Time du er kommen.
Hvad de gav de tog tilbage.
Evig bortsvandt Helligdommen.

(1803)

The plough seems to freeze,
and a shiver is heard
to pass through the trees.
Flocks of birds
cease to call
Holy silence
consecrates all.

The ringing of old
of ancient gold.

Gleaming pair from days of yore
in later ages dazzling.
Strangely they came as before,
on crimson sides so puzzling.

Sacred mystery enshrouds
ancient runes and signs.
A holy aura trembles round
these miracles from outside time.

Honour them, for fate can falter
soon maybe no more they'll rove.
May Christ's blood on God's high altar
fill them, as did blood the grove.

You see gleam as the whole story,
not what's venerable and high!
Only show their outer glory
to a dull indifferent eye.

Skies grow dark, the storms awaken!
Certain hour, your word is law.
What they gave has been retaken.
What was sacred is no more.

(1803)

Hvor blev I røde Roser dog

Hvor blev I røde Roser dog
Fra Ungdoms Dage glade?
I min Erindrings Psalmebog
Jeg giemmer Eders Blade.

Og skiøndt hvert Blad er guult og graat,
Som Farven af de Døde,
Den Sommerdag jeg mindes godt,
Da de var purpurrøde.

I deres fine Væv endnu
Jeg kiender hver en Aare.
Som før af Morgenduggen, nu
Den fugtes af min Taare.

(1832)

Where Are You Now, You Roses Red

Where are you now, you roses red
From days of youth so blissful?
I keep your petals long since shed
In recollection's missal.

And though each petal's dull and grey,
Its shade like those departed,
I still recall the summer day
When crimson they all started.

In their silk weave I still can view
Each vein so finely fretted.
Once moistened by the morning dew,
Now by my tears it's wetted.

(1832)

Præludium

Sig nærmer Tiden, da jeg maa væk!
　　Jeg hører Vinterens Stemme;
Thi ogsaa jeg er kun her paa Træk,
　　Og haver andensteds hjemme.

Jeg vidste længe, jeg skal herfra;
　　Det Hjertet ikke betynger,
Og derfor lige glad nu og da
　　Paa Gjennemreisen jeg synger.

Jeg skulde sjunget lidt meer maaskee —
　　Maaskee vel ogsaa lidt bedre;
Men mørke Dage jeg maatte see,
　　Og Storme rev mine Fjædre.

Jeg vilde gjerne i Guds Natur
　　Med Frihed spændt mine Vinger;
Men sidder fast i mit snævre Buur,
　　Det allevegne mig tvinger.

Jeg vilde gjerne fra høien Sky
　　Udsendt de gladere Sange;
Men blive maa jeg for Kost og Ly
　　En Stakkels gjældbunden Fange.

Tidt ligevel til en Smule Trøst
　　Jeg ud af Fængselet titter;
Og sender stundom min Vemodsrøst
　　Med Længsel gjennem mit Gitter.

Lyt og, o Vandrer! til denne Sang;
　　Lidt af din Vei du hidtræde!
Gud veed, maaskee det er sidste Gang
　　Du hører Livsfangen qvæde.

STEEN STEENSEN BLICHER (1782–1848)

Prelude

The time approaches for me to part!
   Now winter's voice is compelling;
A bird of passage, I know my heart
   In other climes has its dwelling.

I have long known that I cannot stay;
   Though this is no cause for grieving,
So free from care as I wend my way
   I sing at times before leaving.

I should at times have perhaps sung more –
   Or should perhaps have sung better;
But dark days crowded oft to the fore,
   And gales my feathers did scatter.

In God's fair world I would fain have tried
   To spread my wings out in freedom;
But I'm imprisoned on every side
   And can't escape from my thralldom.

From lofty skies would I fain have tried
   To blithely sing and not fretted;
But for my shelter and food must bide
   A jailbird poor and indebted.

At times I make the consoling choice
   To let my gaze outward wander:
And sometimes send my poor mournful voice
   Through prison bars yearning yonder.

Then listen, traveller, to this song;
   To pass this way please endeavour!
It might, God knows, not last very long
   Before this voice fades for ever.

Mig bæres for, som ret snart i Qvel
    At Gitterværket vil briste;
Thi qviddre vil jeg et ømt Farvel;
    Maaskee det bliver det sidste.

(1838)

This coming evening, I can foretell,
    May see my prison bars breaking;
For I will sing now a fond farewell,
    Perhaps my final leave-taking.

(1838)

Stæren

Eja! Velkommen du lystige Stær!
Har vi din Skjelm nu tilbage her?
Hvor har du stjaalet i Vinter din Viin?
Sidste Høst kneb du ved Mosel og Rhin.
Nu har du vist været nede ved Cap,
Og med Constantia lædsket dit Gab;
Eller som Probenreuter med Fif
Gjæstet Madeira, maaskee Tennerif.
Sikkert, af Druen begeistret, du spaaer
Om den med Længsel forventede Vaar;
Knæbbrer som Storken, og kviddrer som Svalen,
Fløjter som Droslen og Nattergalen.
Vist nok, ifald jeg det nøje tager,
Alt jo af Efterabelse smager;
Men om du gjør det kun temmelig godt,
Vil jeg dog kalde dig min Pierrot.
Er af Plastikere du ikkun Halen,
Staaer du end dybt under Originalen:
Vækker du om den Erindringer ømme,
Glæder mit Hjerte med Foraarsdrømme.
Drømme jo ere, som Hvermand veed,
Skjønnere ofte end Virkelighed.

(1838)

The Starling

Ah starling! Most welcome, you bird of good cheer!
Are we to have all your pranks again here?
Where have you stolen last winter your wine?
Last time you dined down at Mosel and Rhine,
Now you've most probably been at the Cape,
And with Constantia sampled the grape;
Or, flying salesmen, with tricks up your sleeve
Frequented Madeira, perhaps Tenerife.
By grapes enlivened, you'll maybe foretell
That spring we've yearned for and wanted so well;
Clack like the stork, chirp like swallows that wing,
Or like the thrush and the nightingale sing.
But, if I listen most carefully too,
All's imitation and never quite you;
Though you're no expert, I am even so
Willing to give you the name of Pierrot.
Though not the tail-end of copies by far
With the original you're not on par:
Yet you sweet memories of it provide,
With dreams of spring you my heart do revive.
And, as all know, a dream often can be
Lovelier than any reality.

(1838)

N.F.S. GRUNDTVIG (1783–1872)

De levendes Land

Jeg kjender et Land,
Hvor Haaret ej graaner, og Tid har ej Tand,
Hvor Solen ej brænder, og Bølgen ej slaar,
Hvor Høsten omfavner den blomstrende Vaar,
Hvor Aften og Morgen gaa altid i Dans
    Med Middagens Glans.

O, dejlige Land,
Hvor Glasset ej rinder med Taarer som Sand,
Hvor intet man savner, som Ønske er værd,
Hvor *det* ikkun fattes, som smertede her!
Hvert Menneske søger med Længsel i Bryst
    Din smilende Kyst

Forjættede Land!
Du hilses i Morgenens spejlklare Strand,
Naar Barnet mon skue din Skygge fuld skjøn
Og drømmer, du findes, hvor Skoven er grøn,
Hvor Barnet kan dele med Blomster og Siv
    Sit Smil og sit Liv.

O, flygtige Drøm
Om Evigheds-Øen i Tidernes Strøm,
Om Templet for Glæden i Taarernes Dal,
Om Halvgude-Livet i Dødninge-Sal!
Med dig fra de fleste henfarer paa Stand
    De levendes Land.

O, skuffende Drøm!
Du skinnende Boble paa Tidernes Strøm!
Forgjæves dig Skjalden, med Mund og med Pen,
Af glimrende Skygger vil skabe igjen;
Naar Skyggen er ligest, da hulke de smaa,
    Som stirre derpaa.

N.F.S. GRUNDTVIG (1783–1872)

The Land of the Living

I know of a land
Where hair does not grey, and where time's rule is banned,
Where sun does not burn, and where wave does not ring,
Where autumn embraces the blossoming spring,
Where morning and evening unceasingly dance
    In noon's brightest glance.

Oh, wonderful land,
Where glass does not run full of tear-drops as sand,
Where nothing is wanting that's worth holding dear,
Where that does not lack which so pained us back here!
With breast filled with longing we seek ever more
    Your sweet-smiling shore.

Oh, long-promised land!
We greet you in morning hour's mirror-clear strand,
When perfect your shadow the child may espy
And where woods are green dreams that there you must lie,
Where too it can share with the rushes and flowers
    Its smile and its hours.

Oh, transient dream
Of island eternal in time's rushing stream!
Of joy's sacred temple in life's vale of tears,
Of life half-divine in this hall's mortal years!
The land of the living with you melts away
    From those made of clay.

Oh, hope-dashing dream!
You glittering bubble on time's rushing stream!
In vain would the poet, with voice and with pen,
From bright-gleaming shadows create you again;
Where shadow comes closest, the small will all weep
    Who on it gaze deep.

Fortryllende Drøm
Om Evigheds-Perlen i Tidernes Strøm!
Du gjækker de arme, der søge omsonst,
Hvad Hjærtet begjærer, i Billed og Kunst,
Saa varigst de kalde, hvad sikkert forgaar
    Som Timer og Aar.

    O, Kjærligheds Aand!
Lad barnlig mig kysse din straalende Haand,
Som rækker fra Himlen til Jorderigs Muld
Og rører vort Øje med Fingre som Guld,
Saa blaalig sig hæver bag buldrende Strand
    Det dejlige Land!

    O, himmelske Navn,
Som aabner for vores din hellige Favn,
Saa Aanden usmittet kan røre ved Støv
Og levendegjøre det visnede Løv!
O, lad mig nedknæle saa dybt i mit Ler,
    At Gud mig kun ser!

    O, Vidunder-Tro,
Som slaar over Dybet den hvælvede Bro,
Der Isgangen trodser i buldrende Strand,
Fra Dødningehjem til de levendes Land!
Sid lavere hos mig, du højbaarne Gjæst!
    Det huger dig bedst.

    Letvingede Haab!
Gudbroder, gjenfødt i den hellige Daab!
For Rejserne mange til Landet bag Hav,
For Tidender gode, for Trøsten, du gav,
Lad saa mig dig takke, at Glæde jeg ser,
    Naar Haab er ej mer!

Oh, spell-binding dream
Of pearl that's eternal in time's rushing stream!
You fool those poor persons who all seek in vain
In image and art what the heart would retain,
And make them call lasting what just disappears
    Like days, months and years.

Oh, spirit of love!
Your hand let me kiss, reaching down from above
From heaven's fair skies to this earth's murky hold
And touching our eyes with its fingers of gold,
So blue-tinged there climbs behind surf-roaring strand
    The wonderful land!

Oh, heavenly name,
Whose sacred embrace does our nature enflame,
So spirit can mingle with dust without grief
And bring back to life every dead withered leaf!
Oh, deep in my clay let me fall on my knee
    So God may see me!

Oh, faith beyond bliss,
Whose high-vaulted bridge spans the gaping abyss
When drifting ice threatens in surf-roaring strand
From poor mortal dwelling to far promised land!
Come farther down to me, you high-honoured guest!
    That pleases you best.

Oh, hope fleet of wing!
Oh, brother reborn through divine christening!
For all journeys made to the land o'er the sea,
Good tidings and comfort you've lavished on me,
May I ever thank you, so joy is in store
    When hope is no more!

O, Kjærlighed selv!
Du rolige Kilde for Kræfternes Elv!
Han kalder dig Fader, som løser vort Baand,
Al Livskraft i Sjælen er Gnist af din Aand;
Dit Rige er der, hvor man Død byder Trods;
    Det kommer til os!

    Vor Fader saa huld!
Du gjærne vil trone i Templet af Muld,
Som Aanden opbygger i Midlerens Navn,
Med rygende Alter i Menneske-Favn,
Med Himmellys-Bolig af Gnisten i Løn,
    Til dig og din Søn.

    O, Kristelighed!
Du skjænker vort Hjærte, hvad Verden ej véd;
Hvad svagt vi kun skimte, mens Øjet er blaat,
Det lever dog i os, det føle vi godt;
Mit Land, siger Livet, er Himmel og Jord,
    Hvor Kjærlighed bor.

(1824)

Oh, love perfect love!
Quiet source of fierce torrents that mightily move!
He calls you his father who ransoms our plight
Your spirit all soul's vital force does ignite;
Your kingdom is there where man death does defy;
  May us it be nigh!

  Our father sublime!
You willingly reign in earth's temple of grime,
Who builds up the spirit in Jesu's sweet name,
In human embrace with an altar aflame,
With heaven-bright dwelling of faith dearly won,
  For you and your son.

  Oh, Christian faith sweet!
You grant every heart what the world cannot greet;
What barely we glimpse while our eye is still blue,
Is living within us, we know this is true;
Both heaven and earth are my land, life confides
  Where love e'er resides.

(1824)

Den signede Dag med Fryd vi seer

Den signede Dag med Fryd vi seer,
Af Havet til os opkomme;
Den lyse paa Himlen, meer og meer,
Os alle til Lyst og Fromme!
Det kiendes paa os, som Lysets Børn,
At Natten hun er nu omme!

Den signede Stund, den Midnats-Tid,
Vor Herre han lod sig føde,
Da klared det op i Øster-Lid,
Til deiligste Morgen-Røde:
Da Lyset oprandt, som Jordens Bold
Skal lysne udi og gløde!

Om levende blev hvert Træ i Skov,
Og var saa hvert Blad en Tunge,
De kunde dog ei Guds Naades Lov
Med værdelig Røst udsjunge;
Thi evig nu skinner Livets Lys,
For Gamle og saa for Unge!

Ja, havde end Maal hvert Straa i Vang,
Hver Urt udi Mark og Lunde,
Slet ikke for os den Takke-Sang
Opstemme tilgavns de kunde,
Som Dagen hør til, for Lys og Liv,
Mens tusinde Aar henrunde!

Forgiæves det er, med liden Magt,
At ville mod Bjerg opspringe,
Men Ørnen er snild, han naaer sin Agt,
Naar Veiret ham bær paa Vinge,
Og Lærken hun er en lille Fugl,
Kan lystig i Sky sig svinge!

The Bright Blessed Day With Joy We See

The bright blessed day with joy we see
Rise out of the sea at dawning;
It lightens the sky unceasingly,
Our gain and delight adorning!
As children of light we sense that soon
Dark night will give way to morning!

Our Lord chose the blessed midnight hour
To come down without our knowing,
Then clear in the east in dawn's pale bower
The sun's hues in strength were growing:
Then light filled the sky, in which the earth
Shall shimmer with inner glowing!

Were each forest tree to come alive,
And each leaf a voice be granted,
The law of God's mercy they'd contrive
In vain in words to have chanted;
Since Life's Light now shines for ever more,
In old and young firmly planted!

Yea, though every blade of grass could speak,
In meadow or field or clearing,
A thanksgiving hymn they could not seek
To sing for our human hearing,
Befitting the day, for light and life,
While eons their course are steering!

In vain would the weak man try who chose
To conquer the mountain summit,
The eagle is wily, though, and knows
The wind will not let it plummet,
And even the small blithe lark can brave
The sky and yet overcome it!

Med Sus og med Brus den stride Aa
Nedfuser fra Klippe-Tinde,
Ei mæle saa lydt de Bække smaa,
Dog risle de fort og rinde,
Saa frydelig snoe de sig fra Eng,
Op under de grønne Linde!

Saa takke vi Gud, vor Fader god,
Som Lærken i Morgen-Røde,
For Dagen, Han os oprinde lod,
For Livet, Han gav af Døde,
For Alt hvad paa Mark, i tusind Aar,
Der groed til Sjæle-Føde!

Saalænge vi see den gyldne Soel,
Og Skoven er Daners Have,
Da plante vi May i Kirke-Stol,
Og Blomster paa Fædres Grave,
Til glædelig Fest, med Liv og Lyst,
Til mindelig Pindse-Gave!

Da rinde vel og, som Bække smaa,
Fra Øine os Taarer milde.
Og Bække i Flok de giør en Aa,
Den higer mod Lysets Kilde,
Den stiger i Løn, som Hjerte-Suk,
Alt aarle, og dog end silde!

Som aldrig saa lang er nogen Dag,
At Aften er jo i Vente,
Saa haver det Lys og Solbjergs-Lag,
Som Gud udi Kirken tændte;
Men immer det dages dog paa Ny,
Hvor Hjerterne Morgen vente!

The river so brash with thund'rous noise
From crag-face comes downwards crashing
The streams down below have no such voice,
Though murmur with gentle plashing,
So gently they wind through grassy lea
Up under the lime trees splashing!

So thank we our God, our father good,
As larks in their dawn-time chorus,
For each day he gave, as so we should
For life he from death won for us,
For all that has nurtured human souls
For thousands of years before us!

As long as we see the golden day,
And woods are the Danes' own bowers,
We'll deck every pew with sprigs of may
And forefathers' graves with flowers
A wonderful feast of life and joy,
A Whitsuntide gift that's ours!

And then from our eyes will start to flow
Mild tears like a stream now thriving,
And streams join and to a river grow
That fain for Life's Source is striving
It secretly gains, like some deep sigh,
So early yet late arriving!

And no day can have so long a growth
That evening cannot be sighted,
Its light and its setting sun are both
What God in his church has lighted;
But ever again it dawns anew
For hearts who in morn delighted!

Nu sagtelig skrid, du Pindse-Dag,
Med Straaler i Krands om Tinde!
Hver Time, til Herrens Velbehag,
Som Bækken i Eng henrinde,
Saa frydelig sig den Sidste snoer
Op under de grønne Linde!

Som Guld er den aarle Morgen-Stund,
Naar Dagen opstaaer af Døde,
Dog kysser os og, med Guld i Mund,
Den liflige Aften-Røde,
Saa tindre end maa det matte Blik,
De blegnende Kinder gløde!

Saa reise vi til vort Fædre-Land,
Der ligger ei Dag i Dvale,
Der stander en Borg, saa prud og grand,
Med Gammen i gyldne Sale,
Saa frydelig der, til evig Tid,
Med Venner i Lys vi tale!

(1826)

Let day gently glide this Whitsuntide,
With haloing rays full-flashing!
The hours pleasing God as past they slide,
As meadowland stream soft-plashing,
So joyously now the last one winds,
Up under the lime trees splashing!

Like gold is the dawn just moments old,
When day from its death is rising,
Yet we too are kissed with lips of gold
By sunset so sweet-enticing,
Then every dull gaze will glint afresh,
Pale cheeks with new blush surprising!

We'll journey then to our fatherland,
Where no day lies still thereafter,
Where stands a strong castle, proud and grand,
Whose halls all resound with laughter,
And there we will talk till time is done
In light with our friends hereafter!

(1826)

Et jævnt og muntert, virksomt Liv paa Jord

Et jævnt og muntert, virksomt Liv paa Jord,
Som det, jeg vilde ei med Kongers bytte,
Opklaret Gang i ædle Fædres Spor,
Med lige Værdighed i Borg og Hytte,
Med Øiet, som det skabdes, himmelvendt.
Lysvaagent for alt Skiønt og Stort herneden,
Men, med de dybe Længsler vel bekiendt,
Kun fyldestgjort af Glands fra Evigheden;

Et saadant Liv jeg ønsked al min Æt,
Og pønsed paa med Flid at forberede,
Og naar min Sjæl blev af sin Grublen træt,
Den hviled sig ved "Fadervor" at bede.
Da følde jeg den Trøst af Sandheds Aand,
At Lykken svæver over Urtegaarden,
Naar Støvet lægges i sin Skabers Haand,
Og Alting ventes i Naturens Orden:

Kun Spiren frisk og grøn i tidlig Vaar,
Og Blomster-Floret i den varme Sommer;
Da Modenhed imøde Planten gaaer,
Og fryder med sin Frugt, naar Høsten kommer!
Om kort, om langt blev Løbebanen spændt,
Den er til Folkegavn, den er til Grøde;
Som godt begyndt er Dagen godt fuldendt,
Og lige liflig er dens Aftenrøde.

(1841)

A Simple, Cheerful Active Life on Earth

A simple, cheerful, active life on earth,
A cup I'd not exchange for monarch's chalice,
In noble forebears' tracks a path since birth,
With equal dignity in hut and palace,
With eye as when created heav'nward turned,
All beauty here and grandness keenly knowing,
Familiar though with those things deeply yearned,
Stilled only by eternity's bright glowing.

I wished for all my line just such a life,
And zealously I planned for its fruition,
And when my soul grew tired from toil and strife,
The "Lord's Prayer" was its rest and its nutrition.
Then from truth's spirit I great comfort gained,
And felt joy hover o'er each garden border,
When dust is placed in its creator's hand
And all is waited for in nature's order:

Just fresh, green buds that sprout in early spring,
And in the summer heat the flowers' profusion;
And when the plants mature and long to bring
Their harvest fruit to autumn's full conclusion!
The human span assigned is short or long,
It is for common weal, its yield is growing;
The day that started well will end as strong,
And just as sweet will be its afterglowing.

(1841)

B.S. INGEMANN (1789-1862)

I Østen stiger Solen op

I Østen stiger Solen op:
Den spreder Guld paa Sky,
Gaaer over Hav og Bjergetop,
Gaaer over Land og By.

Den kommer fra den favre Kyst,
Hvor Paradiset laae;
Den bringer Lys og Liv og Lyst
Til Store og til Smaa.

Den hilser os endnu saa smukt
Fra Edens Morgenrød,
Hvor Træet stod med evig Frugt,
Hvor Livets Væld udflød.

Den hilser os fra Livets Hjem,
Hvor størst Guds Lys oprandt
Med Stjernen over Bethlehem,
Som Østens Vise fandt.

Og med Guds Sol udgaaer fra Øst
En himmelsk Glands paa Jord,
Et Glimt fra Paradisets Kyst,
Hvor Livets Abild groer.

Og alle Stjerner neie sig,
Hvor Østens Sol gaar frem:
Den synes dem hiin Stjerne liig,
Der stod ved Bethlehem.

Du Soles Sol fra Bethlehem!
Hav Tak og Lov og Priis
For hvert et Glimt fra Lysets Hjem
Og fra dit Paradiis!

(1837)

B.S. INGEMANN (1789-1862)

The Sun That in the East Does Rise

The sun that in the East does rise
Drapes clouds with golden gown,
O'er seas and peaks it sails the skies,
O'er countryside and town.

It comes from that fair coast so bright
Where Paradise once lay;
It comes with joy and life and light
To great and small alway.

It brings to us a greeting fine
From Eden's rising dawn,
Where stood the Tree with fruit sublime,
Where Life's pure fount was born.

It greets us from Life's home afar,
Where God's light did abound
O'er Bethlehem with that bright star
The East's Wise Men once found.

And with God's sun comes from the East
A distant heavn'ly glow,
A glimpse of Paradise's coast,
Where Life's great orchards grow.

And all the stars from near and far
Bow as East's sun gains height:
It seems to them so like the star
O'er Bethlehem that night.

You sun of suns from Bethlehem!
May thanks and praises rise
For every glint from Light's true home
And from your Paradise!

(1837)

Der staaer et Slot i Vesterled

Der staaer et Slot i Vesterled,
Tækket med gyldne Skjolde;
Did gaaer hver Aften Solen ned
Bag Rosenskyernes Volde.
Det Slot blev ei med Hænder gjort:
Mageløst staaer det smykket;
Fra Jord til Himmel naaer dets Port;
Vor Herre selv det har bygget.

Fra tusind Taarne funkler Guld;
Porten skinner som Ravet;
Med Straalestøtter underfuld
Sig Borgen speiler i Havet.
Guds Sol gaaer i sit Guldslot ind,
Skinner i Purpurklæder.
I Rosensky paa Borgens Tind
Staaer Lysets Banner med Hæder.

Solenglen svinger Lysets Flag,
Vandrer til fjerne Lande;
Ham følger Liv og Lys og Dag
Bag Nattens brusende Vande.
Liig Solen farer Livet hen,
Gaaer til Forklaringskysten:
Med Glands opdukker Sol igjen
Fra Paradiset i Østen.

(1839)

A Castle Stands 'neath Western Skies

A castle stands 'neath western skies
Gold shields its roof have studded;
The evening sun behind it dies
Midst cloud banks so newly ruddied.
That castle by no hand is wrought:
Perfectly though it's gilded;
Its gate soars up to heaven's court;
Our Lord Himself did once built it.

From thousand turrets sparkles gold,
Amber its gate is gleaming;
The sea reflects its walls of old,
With pillars of sun's rays teeming.
God's sun into its castle crowds,
Purple raiment inflaming,
On battlements in rosy clouds
Light's banner's glory proclaiming.

Sun's angel waves the flag of light,
Sets off for distant quarters;
Life, light and day him follow right
Behind night's loud foaming waters.
And like the sun life seeks the coast
Full of transfiguration
Where sun the east once more will host
With paradise as its station.

(1839)

CARSTEN HAUCH (1790-1872)

Dødens Genius

O, du, som græder, vift din Taare bort!
Og du, som sørger, husk din Sorg er kort!
Thi du har Ro, naar Hiertet stille staaer,
Og Dødens Engel læger dine Saar.

Ja skiøndt i Graven falmer Fyrstens Dragt,
Og skiøndt kun Ormen der har Kongemagt,
Saa frygt dog ei, naar med et ydmygt Sind
Du ad den mørke Hvælving vandrer ind.

Thi hvad du virker i din bedste Stund,
Hvad Pigen aner i den dunkle Lund,
Hvad Orglet vækker med sin dybe Klang,
Hvad Barnet skuer i sin Drøm saa lang,

Og hvert et Ord, der skienker Livet Trøst,
Hvert ædelt Forsæt, hver uskyldig Lyst,
Hvert saligt Blund i Kiærlighedens Arm,
Hvert deiligt Billed af en Digterbarm,

Det er kun Frø, der synker i mit Skiød,
Og som du skue skal, naar du er død,
At staae, som Blomster, i en evig Krands,
Mens Gravens Bølge skienker dem sin Glands.

Thi af den Graad, der randt i Støvets Land,
Den vorder her et dybt og deiligt Vand,
Hvis Dug forfrisker mine Blomster smaa,
Hvis klare Bølger ingen Storm kan naae.

I dem fornyes hver Erindring blid,
I dem forynges selv den gamle Tid,
Derfor i dem sig bader hver en Mø,
Og sukker henrykt: Det er sødt at døe.

CARSTEN HAUCH (1790-1872)

Death's Genius

Oh you who weep, brush all your tears aside!
And you who mourn, recall grief won't abide!
For you'll know rest when your heart beats no more,
Death's angel you from all your wounds will cure.

Though in the grave a prince's robes will fade,
Though only worms royal power can parade,
Be not afraid, when with a humble mind
Through that dark portal your way is assigned.

For all your efforts in your finest hour,
What the maid senses in the murky bower,
What's woken by the organ's deep rich sound,
What child intuits in its dream profound,

And every word that offers solace here,
Each fine resolve, each joy that's pure and clear,
Each sweet repose on love's arm that one takes,
Each lovely image that a poet makes,

They are but seeds that in my lap unfold,
And that when you are dead you shall behold,
That stand as flowers in a lasting wreath,
While the grave's wave adds lustre from beneath.

For of those tears that in dust's land were shed
There form refreshing waters in their stead,
The dew of which refreshes my small flowers,
Whose clear waves no fierce storm or gale devours.

In them sweet recollection is renewed,
In them is ancient time restored to youth,
So every maiden bathes there with a sigh
Of rapture, saying: It is sweet to die.

Af Bølgens Dyb sig hæver mangen Strand,
Hvor milde Blikke vinke dig til Land,
Der sidder Elskeren sin Elskov nær,
De bedste Drømme drømmes atter her.

Og hver en Ven, for hvem din Taare randt,
Selv den, du elsked, som du hist ei fandt,
Den finder du, hvor Dødens Bølge leer,
Og hvis I vil, I skilles aldrig meer.

Og Alfer leger under Rosens Tiørn,
Det er de mindste, lykkeligste Børn,
Hvis Blik jeg slukte, før de kunde see,
Hvis Mund jeg lukte, før den kunde lee.

Og Ynglingsskarer, Oldingsskygger graae,
Og skiønne Piger, længstforglemte Smaa,
Og Helteslægter fra den svundne Tid,
Paa tusind Veie samler jeg dem hid.

Og Mænd og Qvinder, spredt fra Syd til Nord,
Uhyre Aander fra en anden Jord,
Og de, der sildigst sprang af Tidens Strøm,
De mødes her med Oldtids ældste Drøm.

Og Nattens Billeder bag Fieldets Muur,
Ufødte Fostre af en vild Natur,
Og blege Larver, uden Siælens Liv,
De flagre her, som Taager, mellem Siv.

Men hine Væsner, der ved Konst blev til,
Der hist dig syntes kun et Skyggespil,
De her, som Stierner, paa min Himmel staaer,
Og vinde Liv, hvor Jordens Pragt forgaaer.

Dog uden Ende løber Dødens Vei,
Ved fierne Verdner selv den standser ei,
I Evighedens Ring den taber sig,
Og kun dens Indgang kan jeg vise dig.

(1839)

Rising from out the depths are shores of sand,
Where gentle glances wave you to the land,
There does the lover sit right close to love,
The best dreams are redreamed as there above.

And every friend for whom you shed a tear
Even the loved one who was not found here
You will discover where death's wave smiles free,
And, if you will, you'll never parted be.

And 'neath the rose's thorns the elves all play,
The tiniest happy children – these are they,
Whose gaze I put out ere they learned to look,
Whose mouth I closed ere it with laughter shook.

And hosts of youths, ancients with shadows grey,
Babes long forgotten, girls as bright as day,
Races of heroes from a time long gone,
By countless paths I join them every one.

And men and women, spread from south to north,
Tremendous spirits from another earth,
And those who latest leapt out of time's stream,
They meet here with antiquity's first dream.

Night images behind the mountain wall,
Wild nature's unborn embryos so small,
And pallid larvae who no soul-life feeds,
They flutter here like mists among the reeds.

But those creations, which by art were made,
That here seemed but the play of light and shade,
Here in my heaven are a starry host
That gains new life, while earthly glory's lost.

Though with no sign of ending is death's way,
Not even distant worlds cause it to stay,
In eternity's ring it's lost from view,
And but its entrance can I show to you.

(1839)

JOHAN LUDVIG HEIBERG (1791-1860)

Barcarole

Natten er saa stille,
Luften er saa klar,
Duggens Perler trille,
Maanens Straaler spille
Hen ad Søens Glar.

Bølgens Melodier
Vugge Hjertet ind;
Suk og Klage tier,
Vindens Pust befrier
Det betyngte Sind.

(1829)

JOHAN LUDVIG HEIBERG (1791–1860)

Barcarole

Calm the night, unstirring,
And the air so clear
Pearls of dew uncurling,
Moonlight rays unfurling
'Cross the glassy mere.

Dulcet waves appeasing
Heart that yearns for rest,
Sighs and sorrows ceasing,
Breath of wind releasing
Mind so long oppressed.

(1829)

EMIL AARESTRUP (1800-1856)

Til en Veninde

Der er en Trolddom paa din Læbe,
Der er en Afgrund i dit Blik,
Der er i Lyden af din Stemme
En Drøms ætheriske Musik.

Der er en Klarhed paa din Pande,
Der er et Mørke i dit Haar,
Der er en Strøm af Blomsteraande
Omkring dig, hvor du staaer og gaaer.

Der er en Skat af evig Viisdom
I Smilehullet paa din Kind,
Der er en Brønd, en Sundhedskilde
For alle Hjerter, i dit Sind.

Der er en Verden i dit Indre,
En sværmerisk, chaotisk Vaar –
Som jeg umulig kan forglemme,
Som jeg tilbeder og forstaaer.

(1838)

EMIL AARESTRUP (1800–1856)

To a Female Friend

Your lips bewitch with sweet enchantment,
Your gaze reveals a deep abyss;
Your voice contains unearthly music,
A wondrous strain of dreamlike bliss.

Your forehead rises clear, untroubled,
Your hair is but a sable bower;
A wafting breath of scented blossom
Seems to attend your every hour.

The dimple in your cheek's a treasure,
An endless wisdom without art;
Your disposition the restoring
Fount and spring for every heart.

Your mind's a universe displaying
The agitated flush of spring—
One that will nevermore release me,
One that I know, whose praise I sing.

(1838)

Paamindelse

Det Blaat, som kaldes Himmelblaat,
Den Jordklump, denne Haandfuld Vand,
Det Vrøvlerie af Uforstand,
Et Par Pedanter kalde ondt og godt –

O dette jammerlige Tidsfordriv!
Det kan du gabe paa? Saa smaat
Indsuger du en Drøm, man blot
Af Dumhed falder paa at kalde Liv?

O noget andet maa der være til!
Med Tænkningen fik jeg vel ikke Hul
Paa dette Forhæng, ild i dette Kul –
Thi Tænkningen er selv et daarligt Spil –

O dersom Alexander leved nu
Han rakte mig sit Sværd – og jeg – Men see:
Der skrider Døden med sin Lee
Han veed at hugge Knuden rask itu! –

(1835)

Admonition

This blue that is called azure-blue,
This scoop of water, clump of earth,
This foolish nonsense of no worth,
Called good and evil by some pedants too –

Oh, this diversion full of vain pretence!
This you can gape at? By and by
Will you take in a dream so wry
To call it life must mean you lack all sense?

Oh, surely there is more to life than this!
By human thought I could not make a hole
In this great veil, or fire in this black coal –
For thought itself is play that goes amiss –

Oh, if that Alexander were here now,
He'd proffer me his sword – and I – But see:
There with his scythe strides death ahead of me
To slice the knot he only needs one blow! –

(1835)

HANS CHRISTIAN ANDERSEN (1805-1875)

Det gamle Træ, o lad det staa

Det gamle Træ, o lad det staae,
Indtil det døer af Ælde;
Saamange Ting det husker paa,
Hvad kan det ikke melde.
Vi det saa fuldt med Blomster saae,
De friske Grene hælde.
Det gamle Træ, o lad det staae,
Det maa I ikke fælde!

Nu vil jeg da paa Vandring gaae,
Men det kan jeg fornemme,
Man reiser ud, for hiem at naae.
Thi bedst er det dog hjemme.
Naar Træet her har Blomster paa,
Det vil min Hjemkomst melde;
Det gamle Træ, o lad det staae,
Det maae I ikke fælde!

(1851)

HANS CHRISTIAN ANDERSEN (1805–1875)

That Ancient Tree, Don't Let It Fall

That ancient tree, don't let it fall
Until old age is knelling;
So many things it can recall,
What tales it could be telling.
We once did see its blossom-haul
Each branch with fruit was swelling.
That ancient tree, don't let it fall,
You must not think of felling!

Now to be journeying I yearn
But yet the truth in part is
One does but travel to return,
For home is where one's heart is.
When this old tree stands blossom-tall,
I'm nearly home it's telling;
That ancient tree, don't let it fall,
You must not think of felling!

(1851)

HOLGER DRACHMANN (1846-1908)

Sakuntala

Jeg kunde for Længsel ej sove,
en Blomstervind
slog mig imod,
strømmed herind ad mit Vindu
som en vellugtaandende Flod;
jeg hørte de høje Palmer
suse svagt
med sød Musik;
det hvisked, ihvor jeg stod og gik:
    Sakuntala, Sakuntala.

Du evige Himalaya
med Issen højt
mod Himlens Tag,
hvi sender Du dine Kilder
at møde min Fod idag?
Hvi risler de duftende Vover
mindetungt
forbi mig hen?
hvi møder mit bævende Blik igen:
    Sakuntala, Sakuntala!

O Pige, Du sænker dit Øje
saa fugtig blødt
ind i mit Blik,
som var det i denne Time
den bindende Ring Du fik!
ak, ikke en enkelt Time,
enkelt Dag,
nej tusinde Aar
skillende mellem os begge staar:
    Sakuntala, Sakuntala!

HOLGER DRACHMANN (1846-1908)

Sakuntala

I could not sleep for longing,
a flower-wind
wafted towards me,
streaming in through my window
like a fragrance-breathing river;
I heard the tall palm trees
gently murmuring
with music sweet;
it whispered where I placed my feet:
    Sakuntala, Sakuntala.

You eternal Himalaya
with summit high
against the roof of the sky,
why do you send your springs
to meet my foot today?
Why do the scented waves
heavy with memories
purl past my feet?
why trembling does my gaze again meet:
    Sakuntala, Sakuntala!

O maiden, you lower your eye
so moist and soft
into my gazing eyes,
as if it were at this hour
you were given the ring that binds!
ah, not a single hour,
a single day,
but a thousand years
do separate us now, I fear:
    Sakuntala, Sakuntala!

Du tabte ej Ringen i Floden
Dushjántas selv
har slængt den hen,
og stemmed han end den stride Strøm,
han bringer ej Ringen igen.
Dushjántas i Palmelunden
jage vil
langs Flodens Bred;
han skyder en Antilope ned:
    Sakuntala, Sakuntala.

(1879)

You did not lose your ring in the river
Dushjántas himself
has flung it therein,
and should he not stem the swift-flowing stream,
the ring he will not bring again.
Dushjántas in the grove of palms
will hunt
along the river's slope;
he downs an antilope:
    Sakuntala, Sakuntala.

(1879)

J.P. JACOBSEN (1847-1885)

Regnvejr i Skoven

Hvilken velsignet forskrækkelig Regn,
Luften den striber med Kryds og med Tegn,
Jorden med Tusinde Strømme.
Kølige Regndraabes glimrende Bold
Slynges herned med spøgende Vold,
Splintres i Smaastænk tusinde Fold.
Draaberne skilles og sammen de smelte,
Puslingebølgerne vældigt de vælte,
Dækkende Alt med et dybdeløst Hav.
Støvede Gjerder forsvarligt det vadsker,
Træernes Kroner i Ho'det det pladsker,
Stammerne løber ad Ryggen det koldt.
Kalveknæede Piles Rad
Slikker om Mund sig saa inderlig glad
Med Tusinde spidsede Tunger.
Snerlerne drikke det dejlige Vand
Vender sig ....

(ca. 1869)

J.P. JACOBSEN (1847-1885)

Forest Rain

What blessed yet terrible rain everywhere,
With crosses and signs now streaking the air,
Earth with small streams by the thousand.
Glittering globes of refreshing, cool rain
Thud to the earth in a playful refrain,
Splintering into a thousand small specks.
Droplets that shatter then once more return,
Causing the wavelets to tumble and churn,
Covering all with a thin surface sea.
Old mildewed fences it washes down soundly
Crowns of the trees on their tops are doused roundly,
And down the spines of their trunks it runs cold.
Long rows of knock-kneed willow trees
Now lick their lips quite transported with glee
With thousands of tongues sharply pointed.
Bindweed plants drink up the water so fine
Turn as they ....

(c. 1869)

VIGGO STUCKENBERG (1863-1905)

Ingeborg

IV

Nu brister i alle de Kløfter,
    som fured og sprængte mit Sind,
    Alverdens fagreste Blomster
    for Sommerens sagte Vind.

Thi to, som elsker hinanden,
    kan volde hinanden mer' ondt
    end alle de argeste Fjender,
    som hævner sig Jorden rundt:

og to, som elsker hinanden,
    kan læge de ondeste Saar
    blot ved at se paa hinanden
    og glatte hinandens Haar.

(1901)

VIGGO STUCKENBERG (1863-1905)

Ingeborg

IV

Unfolding in all of the furrows
    that lined and burst open my mind,
    all kinds of beautiful flowers
    at summer's most gentle wind.

For two who love one another
    can torture each other far worse
    than all enemies put together
    can wreak vengeance over the earth:

And two who love one another
    can heal wounds beyond all repair
    just if they look at each other
    and smooth down each other's hair.

(1901)

LUDVIG HOLSTEIN (1864-1943)

Det er i Dag et Vejr

Det er i Dag et Vejr – et Solskinsvejr!
O, søde Vaar, saa er du atter nær!
Nu vil jeg glemme rent, at det var Vinter,
nu vil jeg gaa og købe Hyacinther
og bringe dem til en, som jeg har kær.

Hun købte af de hvide og de blaa,
hun købte af de smukkeste, hun saa.
Det er i Dag et Vejr! Og Solen skinner!
Og om mig svæver lutter lyse Minder,
dem ta'r jeg med til den, jeg tænker paa.

Og de kom svævende i Ring og Rad.
Hun gik imellem dem og var saa glad.
Det er i Dag et Solskin uden Mage!
Og jeg har Solskin nok til mange Dage,
og jeg maa kysse hvert et lille Blad.

Hun kyssede dem alle, hver især,
hun bragte dem til den, hun havde kær.
Min Ven, her kommer jeg med Hyacinther!
Min Ven, nu glemmer vi, at det var Vinter!
Det er i Dag et Vejr, et Solskinsvejr–!

(1903)

LUDVIG HOLSTEIN (1864–1943)

How Fine It Is Today

How fine it is today – a day of sun!
Oh spring so dear, once more you have begun!
Now all those winter months are gone completely,
I will buy hyacinths that smell so sweetly
and take them to the one my heart has won.

She bought some white and then she bought some blue,
she bought of those most beautiful in hue.
How fine it is today! The sun is shining!
And happy memories are me entwining,
I'll take them with me to my love so true.

And they came floating down in rings and rows.
She passed among them and her heart still glows.
It is a day of sunshine without equal!
And I have sun enough till there's a sequel,
and I must kiss each little leaf that grows.

She kissed them all, she kissed them one by one,
she took them to the one her heart had won.
My friend, look, hyacinths that smell so sweetly!
My friend, those winter months they're gone completely!
How fine it is today, a day of sun–!

(1903)

SOPHUS CLAUSSEN (1865-1931)

Se, jeg mødte paa en Gade

Se, jeg mødte paa en Gade
Døden ... aah saa skøn at se,
brune sommerlige Lokker,
en Skønjomfrus Hud, som Sne.
"Lad mig leve" bad jeg Døden
i mit unge Hjertes Vé!

"Leve blot et stille Foraar
nær din fine Jomfrusné!
Nær ved dine kyske Sider
lad mig kun et Foraar se
med de Kys, som en Veninde
bag et Forhæng godt tør se!"

Klædt i tusind søde Blonder
ligned hun en Blomstereng.
Bag sin Skal af Skønhed var hun
vinterfrossen, død og streng.
Jeg har bedt Umuligheden
rede mig en Brudeseng.

Jeg har bedt Umuligheden
om at smykke sig som Brud.

Jeg har bedt om Vaar hos Døden,
derfor skal jeg slettes ud.

(1912)

SOPHUS CLAUSSEN (1865–1931)

In the Street I Met while Walking

In the street I met while walking
Death ... a sight that pleased me so,
auburn locks that told of summer
fair maid's skin as white as snow.
"Let me live" I Death requested
in my young heart's pangs of woe!

"Live for just a tranquil springtime
close to your fine virgin snow!
Close to your most chaste of aspects
let me but that one spring know
with the kisses that a sweetheart
when in private would dare show!"

Dressed in lace-frills by the thousand
she was like a field of flowers.
But within her lovely shell was
winter-frozen, dead and dour.
I have asked impossibility
make a marriage bed this hour.

I have asked impossibility
deck herself as bride so chaste.

I have asked of Death a springtime,
Therefore I must be erased.

(1912)

Skabelse

Jeg er ej født endnu, men fødende forløses jeg.
Af Livet i mit Værk jeg aner Livet i mig selv,
berøvet dette Spejl er jeg, saa godt som, lagt i Jord.

Mit Kald har jeg bragt med, og intet yder jeg af mit.
Men jeg forløses, og forløst ser jeg min Gæld betalt
til Kraften, den, jeg stammer fra, og som har udsendt mig.

Det Rige, som har indkaldt mig, og som jeg stammer fra,
er det en ufødt Magt, der fødende forløser sig?
Er det en Guddomspragt, hvis Væld er idel Herlighed?

Jeg ved det ej, men i mit Blod er alle Længslers Mod.
Jeg hamrer Ild af Mørket, udfrir de afmægtige.

(1925)

Creation

I am unborn as yet, but am delivered giving birth.
From the life in my work I sense the life in myself,
robbed of this mirror, I am as good as laid in earth.

My calling I have brought with me, of my own I perform nothing,
But I am delivered, and delivered see my debt is paid
to the force from which I derive, and which has delegated me.

The kingdom that has summoned me and from which I derive –
is it an unborn power that delivers itself while giving birth?
Is it a divine splendour, whose fount is sheer glory?

I do not know, but in my blood is the courage of all longings.
I hammer fire out of darkness, liberate the helpless.

(1925)

JEPPE AAKJÆR (1866-1930)

Aften

Stille, Hjerte, Sol gaar ned,
Sol gaar ned paa Heden,
Dyr gaar hjem fra Dagens Béd,
Storken staar i Reden.
Stille, Hjerte, Sol gaar ned.

Tavshed over Hedesti
og langs Veje krumme.
En forsinket Humlebi
ene høres brumme.
Stille, Hjerte, Sol gaar ned.

Viben slaar et enligt Slag
over Mosedammen,
før den under Frytlens Tag
folder Vingen sammen.
Stille, Hjerte, Sol gaar ned.

Fjerne Ruder østerpaa
blusser op i Gløden,
Hededamme bittesmaa
spejler Aftenrøden.
Stille, Hjerte, Sol gaar ned!

(1916)

JEPPE AAKJÆR (1866–1930)

Evening

Still, my heart, now sets the sun,
While the moor is resting,
   Herds now homeward are begun,
And the stork is nesting.
   Still, my heart, now sets the sun.

   O'er the moor-path silence falls
As on roads so winding.
   A late bumblebee is all
Keenest ears are finding.
   Still, my heart, now sets the sun.

   Briefly now the lapwing flies
O'er the bog-pond's blushes,
   Ere it folds its wings and lies
'Neath a roof of rushes.
   Still, my heart, now sets the sun.

   Eastern window-panes afar
Flare up in the gloaming,
   Moorland ponds like tiny stars
Catch the sunset's homing.
   Still, my heart, now sets the sun!

(1916)

Majnat

Naar Vildgaasen larmer Valborgnat,
hvem lægger sig da til at sove?
Da vandrer man ensomt med Dug paa Hat
langs Fjord og knoppende Skove.

Derude straaler en Stjærne saa stor,
at helt den fylder mit Øje;
den samme Stjærne forvist jeg tror,
jeg saa over Barndommens Høje.

Og Vibeskriget rækker saa langt;
dog længere Længslerne rækker.
Hvor bliver éns Hjærte bitterlig trangt,
naar Klyden i Majnatten trækker!

Det pipper i Mos, og det pibler i Græs,
det sprætter i hældende Kroner;
der kommer en Duft fra det yderste Næs
af tusinde smaa Anemoner.

Saa ensomt bræger det spæde Lam
paa Bakken langt i det fjærne,
og Frøerne kvækker fra Pyt og Dam,
som sang det fra Stjærne til Stjærne.

(1916)

May Night

When wild geese honk on Walpurgis night
who thinks then of going to rest?
With dew-beaded hat you roam out of sight
through fjordland and woods newly dressed.

Way out there gleams so mighty a star
that all of my eye it now fills;
I'm sure that same star I once saw afar
when I gazed o'er my childhood hills.

And the peewit's cry is borne on the wind,
though longing's borne farther away.
How bitterly close one's heart is confined
when the avocet migrates in May!

There's trickling in grass and cheeping in moss,
the tree-tops twitch out of their slumber;
from the farthermost cape the scent wafts across
of anemones countless in number.

The lonely young lamb on the hill far beyond
can be heard with its plaintive small baa,
and the frogs all croak from puddle and pond,
as if star now were singing to star.

(1916)

HELGE RODE (1870-1937)

Sne

Der er ingenting i Verden saa stille som Sne,
naar den sagte gennem Luften daler,
dæmper Dine Skridt,
tysser, tysser blidt
paa de Stemmer, der for højlydt taler.

Der er ingenting i Verden med en Renhed som Sne,
Svanedun fra Himlens hvide Vinger.
Paa Din Haand et Fnug
er som Taaredug.
Hvide Tanker tyst i Dans sig svinger.

Der er ingenting i Verden, der kan mildne som Sne.
Tys, du lytter, til det Tavse klinger.
Oh, saa fin en Klang,
Sølverklokkesang
inderst inde i Dit Hjerte ringer.

(1896)

HELGE RODE (1870-1937)

Snow

There is nothing in the world that's as silent as snow
when gently through the air it's descending,
muffles each step you take,
hushes, shushes makes
quiet the voices that the air are rending.

There is nothing in the world with the pureness of snow,
Swan-down from the whitest wings of heaven
On your hand a flake
tear-dew seems to make.
White thoughts silently a dance are treading.

There is nothing in the world that can soften like snow.
Hush, you're listening to what's silent singing.
Oh, a sound so fine,
silver bells sublime
in the inmost reaches of your heart are ringing.

(1896)

JOHANNES V. JENSEN (1873-1950)

Paa Memphis Station

Halvt vaagen og halvt blundende,
Slaaet af en klam Virkelighed, men endnu borte
I en indre Gus af danaidiske Drømme
Staar jeg og hakker Tænder
Paa Memphis Station, Tennessee.
Det regner.

Natten er saa øde og udslukt,
Og Regnen hudfletter Jorden
Med en vidløs, dunkel Energi.
Alting er klægt og uigennemtrængeligt.

Hvorfor holder Toget her Time efter Time?
Hvorfor er min Skæbne gaaet i Staa her?
Skal jeg flygte for Regnen og Aandsfortærelsen
I Danmark, Indien og Japan
For at regne inde og raadne i Memphis
Tennessee, U.S.A.?

Og nu dages det. Lyset siver glædeløst
Ind over dette vaade Fængsel.
Dagen blotter ubarmhjærtigt
De kolde Skinner og al den sorte Søle,
Ventesalen med Chokoladeavtomat,
Appelsinskaller, Cigar- og Tændstikstumper,
Dagen griner igennem med spyende Tagrender
Og et evigt Gitter af Regn,
Regn siger jeg fra Himmel og til Jord.

Hvor Verden er døv og uflyttelig,
Hvor Skaberen er talentløs!
Og hvorfor bliver jeg ved at betale mit Kontingent
Til denne plebejiske Kneippkur af en Tilværelse!

JOHANNES V. JENSEN (1873-1950)

On Memphis Station

Half awake and half dozing,
Struck by a drear reality, but still lost
In an inner sea fog of Danaidean dreams
I stand teeth chattering
On Memphis Station, Tennessee.
It is raining.

The night is so desolate and extinguished,
And the rain flays the ground
With a senseless, dark energy.
Everything is clammy and impenetrable.

Why does the train wait here hour after hour?
Why has my lot ground to a halt here?
Am I to flee from rain and mind-numbingness
In Denmark, India and Japan
Only to be rained in and rot in Memphis
Tennessee, U.S.A.?

And now the day is dawning. Light dismally
Seeps in over this wet prison.
The day exposes mercilessly
The cold rails and all the black mud,
The waiting room with the chocolate vending machine,
Orange peel, cigar stubs and burnt-out matches,
The day gapes through with spewing gutters
And an eternal grid of rain,
Rain I say from heaven to earth.

How deaf and irremovable the world is,
How devoid of talent its creator!
And why do I keep on paying my dues
To this plebeian water cure of an existence!

Stille! Se hvor Maskinen,
Den vældige Tingest, staar rolig og syder
Og hyller sig i Røg, den er taalmodig.
Tænd Piben paa fastende Liv,
Forband Gud og svælg din Smærte!

Gaa saa dog hen og bliv i Memphis!
Dit Liv er jo alligevel ikke andet
End et surt Regnvejr, og din Skæbne
Var altid at hænge forsinket
I en eller anden miserabel Ventesal –
Bliv i Memphis, Tennessee!

For inde i et af disse plakathujende Huse
Venter Lykken dig, Lykken,
Hvis blot du kan æde din Utaalmodighed –
Ogsaa her sover en rund ung Jomfru
Med Øret begravet i sit Haar,
Hun vil komme dig i Møde
En fin Dag paa Gaden
Som en Bølge af Vellugt
Med et Blik, som om hun kendte dig.

Er det ikke Foraar?
Falder Regnen ikke frodigt?
Lyder den ikke som en forelsket Mumlen,
En lang dæmpet Kærlighedspassiar
Mund mod Mund
Mellem Regnen og Jorden?
Dagen gryede saa sorgfuldt,
Men se nu lyser Regnfaldet!

Under du ikke Dagen dens Kampret?
Det er dog nu lyst. Og der slaar Muldlugt
Ind mellem Perronens rustne Jærnstivere
Blandet med Regnstøvets ramme Aande –
En Foraarsanelse.
Er det ikke trøstigt?

Quiet! See how the engine,
That enormous contraption, stands calmly seething
Enveloping itself in smoke – it is patient.
Light your pipe on an empty stomach,
Curse God and swallow your pain!

Go on then and stay in Memphis!
After all, your life is nothing else
Than a soggy downpour, and it was always
Your lot to hang around delayed
In some miserable waiting room or other –
Stay in Memphis, Tennessee!

For inside one of these poster-yelling houses
Happiness awaits you, happiness,
If only you can devour your impatience –
Here too a curvaceous young maid sleeps
With her ear buried in her hair,
She will come to meet you
One fine day in the street
Like a wave of perfume
With a look as if she knew you.

Isn't it spring?
Doesn't the rain fall lushly?
Doesn't it sound like an amorous murmuring,
A long muted billing and cooing
Mouth to mouth
Between the rain and the earth?
The day dawned so mournfully,
But look – the rainfall gleams now!

Do you grudge the day its right to fight?
After all, it is light now. And the smell of soil
sets in between the rusty iron struts of the platform
Mixed with the rank breath of the rain-dust –
A hint of spring.
Isn't that consoling?

Og se nu, hvor Mississippi
I sin Seng af oversvømmede Skove
Vaagner mod Dagen!
Se hvor Kæmpefloden nyder sin Bugtning!
Hvor den flommer kongeligt i Bue og svinger Flaader
Af Træer og laset Drivtømmer i sine Hvirvler!
Se hvor den fører en uhyre Hjuldamper
I sin Syndflodsfavn
Som en Danser, der er Herre paa Gulvet!
Se de sunkne Næs – O hvilken urmægtig Ro
Over Landskabet af druknende Skove!
Ser du ikke, hvor Strømmens Morgenvande
Klæder sig milebredt med Dagens tarvelige Lys
Og vandrer sundt under de svangre Skyer!

Fat dig ogsaa du, Uforsonlige!
Vil du aldrig glemme, at man lovede dig Evigheden?
Forholder du Jorden din arme Taknemlighed?
Hvad vil du da med dit Elskerhjærte?

Fat dig og bliv i Memphis,
Meld dig som Borger paa Torvet,
Gaa ind og livsassurer dig imellem de andre,
Betal din Præmie af Lumpenhed,
At de kan vide sig sikre for dig,
Og du ikke skal blive hældt ud af Foreningen.
Gør Kur til hin Jomfru med Roser og Guldring
Og start et Savskæreri som andre Mennesker.
Se dig ud, smøg din vise Pibe
I sphinxforladte Memphis,
Hank rolig op i Gummistøvlerne.

Ah, der kommer det elendige Godstog,
Som vi har ventet paa i seks Timer.
Det kommer langsomt ind — med knuste Sider,
Det pifter svagt, Vognene lammer paa tre Hjul,
Og de sprængte Ruf drypper af Jord og Slam.

And see now how the Mississippi
In its bed of flooded forests
Wakes to the day!
See how the huge river enjoys its winding!
How regally it gushes in curves, swinging flotillas
of trees and tattered driftwood in its eddies!
See how it leads a huge paddle steamer
Into its Deluge-embrace
Like a dancer that masters the dance-floor!
See the sunken headlands – Oh what a vast calm
Over the landscape of drowning forests!
Can't you see how the morning waters of the current
Dress themselves a mile wide in the day's paltry light
And soundly journey under the rain-heavy clouds!

Compose yourself, you too, implacable one!
Will you never forget that eternity was promised you?
Do you withhold from the earth your poor gratitude?
What do you want then with your lover's heart?

Compose yourself and stay in Memphis,
Seek citizenship on the market square,
Go in and take out a life insurance among the others,
Pay your premium of meanness,
So that they can feel secure,
And you won't be thrown out of the association.
Court that maid with roses and a gold ring
And set up a sawmill like everyone else.
Look around, smoke your pipe of wisdom
In sphinx-abandoned Memphis,
Hitch up your rubber boots without a qualm.

Ah, there comes that miserable freight train
That we have waited six hours for.
It comes in slowly – with crushed sides,
It whistles feebly, the cars limping on three wheels,
And the stove roof dripping with earth and mud.

Men paa Tenderen mellem Kullene
Ligger fire stille Skikkelser
Dækket af blodvaade Frakker.

Da pruster vor store Ekspresmaskine,
Gaar lidt frem og standser dybt sukkende
Og staar færdig til Spring. Sporet er frit.

Og vi rejser videre
Gennem de oversvømmede Skove
Under Regnens gabende Sluser.

(1904)

But on the tender among the coals
Lie four motionless figures
Covered with blood-drenched coats.

Then our great express train snorts,
Moves slightly forwards and stops with a deep sigh
Ready to leap forward. The track is clear.

And we journey on
Through the flooded forests
Beneath the gaping floodgates of the rain.

(1904)

Solhvervssang

Vor Sol er bleven kold,
vi er i Vintervold
og dunkle Dage.
    Men nu er Nedgang endt
    og Haabet tændt –
    ja, Haabet tændt,
    for nu er Solen vendt,
nu kommer Lyset og den lange Dag tilbage.

Det grønne, skønne Træ
forjætter Sommerlæ
og søde Skove.
    I Julelysets Skær
    som Stjerners Hær,
    ja, Stjerners Hær,
    er Solens Under nær
og alle gule Blomstersole smaa som sove.

I Granens brændte Duft
faar svundne Somre Luft
og de der kommer.
    Det danske svale Aar
    i Ringgang gaar,
    ja, Ringgang gaar,
    omkring en evig Vaar.
Syng alle Sjæle med om Danmarks fagre Sommer!

(1917)

Solstice Song

Our sun has now grown cold,
we are in winter's hold
the days are waning.
    Now, past the deepest night,
    our hope burns bright –
    yes, hope burns bright,
    for now the sun will right,
now light will soon return, the days again are gaining.

The lovely fir tree green
betokens summer's screen
of woods imposing.
    In Christmas candlelight
    like star-hosts bright,
    yes, star-hosts bright,
    sun's wonder is in sight
and all the yellow flower-suns that now are dozing.

The fir-tree's charry scent
gives air to summers spent
and each newcomer.
    Cool Danish years all swing,
    dance in a ring,
    yes, in a ring
    round an eternal spring.
Let all souls also sing of Denmark's lovely summer!

(1917)

THØGER LARSEN (1875-1928)

Middag

Et heftigt Ildstænk mod det haarde Blaa
staar Middagssolen hed i strittende Straalen.
Den tørre Muldbrink er saa pulvergraa,
Insekter summer over Agerkaalen.

Den stille Dag sig strækker vidt og højt
Omkring mig Myg og Sommerfugle svirrer.
Fra Luft og Løv der pibler klare Fløjt.
I glarfin Dis de fjerne Flader dirrer.

– –

I Søens blanke, afmagtstunge Vand
staar Fisken stiv og dum fra Gab til Hale.
Nu slog den Snuden mod den bratte Strand
og nøs og dasked hen i Dybets Dale.

Der ligger den paa Bund i Søen klar,
og fra dens Snude gaar tilvejrs en Boble:
den stirrer op mod Overfladens Glar,
hvor Solen gynger som en ildgul Gople.

– –

En Bondepige sidder i en Grøft –
med korte Særkeærmer, nøgne Arme.
Man ser det øverste af Barmens Kløft –
der ligger Draaber, Sol og Kødets Varme. – –

Det er saa varmt og godt ved Muld og Strand.
Det er en Sommerdag i Danmarks Land.

(1904)

THØGER LARSEN (1875-1928)

Midday

A violent splash of fire against hard blue,
the midday sun stands hot in bristling rays.
The bank of earth's so powder-grey in hue,
Each insect above navew hums and sways.

The still day stretches out both far and high.
Around me butterflies and midges whirl.
Clear song-notes trickle from the leaves and sky.
In glassy haze the far expanses swirl.

– –

Down in the glassy lake with sluggish maw
the fish stands stiff and dull from mouth to tail.
It snuffed its snout now on the sudden shore
and sneezed and flapped down to the deepest dale.

In clearest water it reposes there,
the bubbles from its snout rise on a wire:
it stares up at the glassy surface where
the sun rocks like a jellyfish on fire.

– –

A peasant girl sits in a ditch and rests –
with short-sleeved shift and with her brown arms bare.
You glimpse the topmost cleavage of her breasts –
with glistening beads and sun and warm flesh there.

It is so fine and warm near soil and sand.
It is a summer's day in Denmark's land.

(1904)

Septembernat

Venlig, men usalig
vandrer langsomt Maanen
en Septembermidnat.
Storm forvirrer Mørket.

I den øde Stue
ligger jeg alene
vaagen paa min Sofa.
Mørket om mig lever.

Over Bord og Vægge
over Gulvets Flade
ligger Maaneruders
matte stille Skærsild.

Maanelyset lever,
er forbrændte Drømme,
stiger lidt og falder,
falder lidt og stiger.

Snart imod mig skinner
Lampens Maanemessing,
snart en Sky for Maanen
slukker Messingskæret.

Udenfor i Hegnet
vaander sig og stønner
Hyldens hæse Grene
som i Hændervriden.

Gennem Himlen iler
Efteraarets Skyer,
ængstet Flugt af Øer
mod en anden Verden.

September Night

Friendly, but unblest
the moon slowly roams
a September midnight.
A gale disturbs the darkness.

In the deserted living room
I lie alone
unsleeping on my sofa.
The darkness round me is alive.

Over table and walls
the surface of the floor
lies the dull still purgatory
of the moonlit panes.

The moonlight is alive,
is charred dreams,
slowly rises and falls,
slowly falls and rises.

Soon the lamp's moon-brass
will shine towards me,
soon a cloud before the moon
will snuff out the brassy gleaming.

Outside in the hedgerow
the elder's hoarse branches
moan and groan
as if wrung by hands.

Across the sky the
autumn clouds chase,
fearful flight of islands
towards another world.

Murens Rosengrene
banker paa min Rude,
Sommernattens Roser
faldt, og Grenen ræddes.

Nattens Angst og skønne
Underverdens-Klage.
Maanens Ild af Ælde
fanger alt mit Væsen.

Stormen fylder Luften,
Nattens Vidder gyser,
mejende gaar Vindens
maaneblanke Leer.

Høst er endt, og Løvfald
kommer, Nat og Løvfald.
Maaneskin og Løvfald,
Suk og Sorg og Løvfald.

Og jeg ligger ensom,
vaagen paa min Sofa,
nylig var det Ungdom,
Leg og lyse Nætter.

Har nu Verden lukket
Livets lyse Sale?
Kom, aa kom tilbage,
Gøge, Nattergale!

(1925)

The wall's rose-branches
knock on my window,
the summer night's roses
fell, and the branch is afraid.

The night's fear and lovely
underworld's complaint.
The moon's ancient fire
captures my whole being.

The gale fills the air,
night's expanses shiver,
the moon-bright scythes of
the wind go reaping.

Harvest is over, and leaf-fall
approaches; night and leaf-fall.
Moonlight and leaf-fall,
sighing and sorrow and leaf-fall.

And I lie alone,
unsleeping on my sofa,
just now there was youth,
playing and bright summer nights.

Has the world now closed
life's bright halls?
Return, oh return,
cuckoos and nightingales!

(1925)

OTTO GELSTED (1888-1968)

September

Traverne staar tunge og lodne
som en Drift vældige Okser.

Køer græsser
ved Bredden af Havet
og ligger langt borte
som et Baand over Bakken.
Luften er lysende klar.

Sorte Brombær langs Vejene!
Og inde i Skovens Dyb
skinner de hvide Blækhatte
som Vokslys i Mørket.

Jord og Hav vælder over af Frugtbarhed.
I Haverne det dumpe
Fald af Gravenstener,
der eksploderer af Saft mod Jorden.
Store Laks, paa Vej efter en Aa,
løber i Fiskerens Garn.

Havren køres ind,
og Dværgmusens Unger,
der ikke er større end en Negl,
røde, haarløse og med blaa Pletter til Øjne,
rives op af deres Rede i Kornet.

Edderkopperne er ude at flyve,
der gaar som en Maanebro over Marken
af Solen, der spejler sig i deres Spind.

OTTO GELSTED (1888-1968)

September

The stooks of corn stand shaggy and heavy
like a drove of mighty oxen.

Cows graze
down by the shore
and lie far away
like a band over the hill.
The air is bright and clear.

Blackberries line the roadside!
And in the depths of the wood
the white ink caps glisten
like wax candles in the dark.

Earth and sea brim with fruitfulness.
In the gardens the dull thud
of falling gravensteins,
exploding with juice against the ground.
Large salmon, seeking up-river
run into the fisherman's net.

The oats are gathered in,
and the harvest mouse young,
no bigger than a fingernail,
red, hairless and with blue spots for eyes,
are raked out of their nest in the corn.

The spiders are in flight,
like a moon-bridge over the fields
there is sun, reflected in their web.

Vældige hvide Skyer
sejler hen over Verden.
Dagen skrider,
og nu staar Møllerne stille.
Jorden drejer ind i Mørket,
og Karlsvognen svinger frem
over sorte og susende Træer.

At gaa Vinteren i Møde
som en Mark fuld af Frø –
at gaa ind i Natten
som en Himmel, hvis blaa Muld
er fuld af tindrende Stjerner –
at dø som en Dag i September
mættet af Liv og Lys!

(1920)

Massive white clouds
sail across the world.
The day slips past,
and the mills are now still.
The earth spins into the dark,
and the Plough swings forward
over black, soughing trees.

To go to meet winter
like a field full of seed –
To enter the night
like a sky whose blue soil
is full of glittering stars –
to die like a day in September
replete with life and light!

(1920)

BODIL BECH (1889-1942)

I Sporvognen

Hvorfor er jeg mon saa sært lykkelig?
Det er, som boede der to Fugle
bag mine spændte Bryster –
gylden Sødme stiger og falder,
naar jeg trækker Vejret –
næsten pinefuld er denne ømme Bæven –
mine Fødder har Lyst at slippe Jorden,
og mine Arme at ro op i Himlene.

Jeg er saaledes
ingen almindelig Dame –

Eller maaske er jeg
yderst almindelig –
for sidder jeg ikke her
i Sporvognen
og betaler Konduktøren
og vender en rolig Profil
mod Vinduet?

Maaske er der mangen en Kvinde,
der ogsaa vender en rolig Profil
mod Vinduet
og er ligesaa dybt lykkelig som jeg.
Sidder vi alle
med Fugle bag Brysterne
og med et Skød, der bæver
som en Ildrose?

(1938)

BODIL BECH (1889-1942)

In the Tram

Why I wonder am I so strangely happy?
It's as if two birds were living
behind my tense breasts –
golden sweetness rises and falls
each time I breathe –
this tender quivering is almost painful –
my feet have an urge to leave the ground,
and my arms to row up into the heavens.

So I am
no ordinary lady –

Or maybe I am
extremely ordinary –
for am I not sitting here
in the tram
paying the conductor
and turning a calm profile
towards the window?

Perhaps there are many such women,
also turning a calm profile
towards the window
who are just as profoundly happy as I am.
Are we all sitting
with birds behind our breasts
and with a lap quivering
like a fiery rose?

(1938)

TOM KRISTENSEN (1893-1974)

Angst

Asiatisk i Vælde er Angsten.
Den er modnet med umodne Aar.
Og jeg føler det dagligt i Hjertet,
som om Fastlande dagligt forgaar.

Men min Angst maa forløses i Længsel
og i Syner af Rædsel og Nød.
Jeg har længtes mod Skibskatastrofer
og mod Hærværk og pludselig Død.

Jeg har længtes mod brændende Byer
og mod Menneskeracer paa Flugt,
mod Opbrud, som ramte Alverden,
og et Jordskælv, som kaldtes Guds Tugt.

(1930)

TOM KRISTENSEN (1893–1974)

Angst

Human angst has dominion that's Asian.
It's matured during immature years.
In my heart it's a daily sensation,
as if mainlands each day disappear.

But my angst must be turned into longing,
into visions of dread and distress.
I have longed for mid-ocean disasters
and for wanton destruction and death.

I have longed for great cities on fire
and for races in flight's headlong surge,
for break-ups the whole world was cursed by
and an earthquake that's known as God's scourge.

(1930)

Det er Knud, som er død

Var jeg en Rype i Dag, løfted jeg Vingen til Slag,
fyldte jeg Lungen med Luft og fløj baade Nat og Dag
over et vinterligt Hav, som sortner bag hvidligt Skum,
gennem den mørke Decembers skyomtumlede Rum.

Kun som en Rype i Storm, Kastebold for al Blæst,
men med et Uvejrs Budskab fløj jeg da mod Nord-Vest.
Hjærtet sprængfærdigt af Smerte, maned jeg saa fra mit Bryst
Sangen, der snart som et Uvejr tuder langs Grønlands Kyst.

Videre skulde den tone over den halve Jord,
følge Kamikkernes Fodtrin og Slædernes lange Spor,
tude i Hudson-Bugten helt ud til King William's Land,
hviske i hver en Boplads langs Jordens yderste Rand.

Alle hans gamle Venner skulde da ruskes af Blund,
Pilekvisten og Klaringen, Auá med den snehvide Hund,
alle de skønne Piger med brede og skinnende Smil
skulde forvirret staa op og glemme det sorgløse Hvil.

Alle skulde de vækkes. Sorgen er knap begyndt.
Snart skal den brede sig ud til Alaskas fjærneste Pynt.
Den store Fortryller er død! Den store Troldmand er død!
Hørte I alle min Sang? Forstod I, hvad den betød?

Øer og Lande og Floder ligger med Islænker lukket.
Glæden, som varmed Jer alle, den brændende Glæde er slukket.
Frys, som vi andre fryser i Dag uden Ild og Glød,
for nu er han død. Det er Knud, som er død.
Forstaar I?

(1936)

It Is Knud Who Is Dead

Were I today a grouse, I'd flex my wings for flight,
I'd fill my lungs with air and fly both day and night
over a winter sea blackening behind whitish foam,
through the cloud-chased December sky I'd roam.

But as a wind-tossed grouse, the sport of every gale,
north-west I'd fly to warn of storms that now hoist sail.
My heart brimful of pain, lured from within my breast
The song that soon will howl the length of Greenland's coast.

On it would echo, covering half the world,
follow sealskin boots and all sledge tracks now unfurled,
howl in Hudson Bay as far as King William's Land,
whisper in settlements and every distant strand.

All his old friends should be roused from a doze so light,
Clearing and Willow Twig, Auá with dog snowy-white,
all the beautiful girls with smiles broad and bright
would rise in confusion, forgetting their carefree respite.

All of them must be awakened. Sorrow's but started,
Soon it will spread to where all Alaska's uncharted.
The great magician is dead! The mighty wizard is dead!
Did you all hear my song? Did you all get the thread?

Islands, lands and rivers are locked with chains of ice.
The joy that warmed you all has paid the final price.
Shiver, as we all do today, our fire is dead,
for he's forever dead, it is Knud who is dead.
Do you all understand?

(1936)

HULDA LÜTKEN (1896-1975)

Hvor har du gjort af dit blaa Blik

Hvor har du gjort af dit blaa Blik?
Engang var dine Øjne som Himlen.
Nu er dine Øjne fulde af graa Ligegyldighed,
naar de ser paa mig.
Og dine Hænder ligger urørlige paa Bordet.
Din Elskov er gammel.
Jeg selv er gammel.
Men mit Hjerte skælver af Ungdom.
Men mit Hjerte – det ser du ikke.
Du kan ikke se mit Hjerte
med dine ligegyldige Øjne.

(1934)

HULDA LÜTKEN (1896–1975)

What Have You Done With Your Blue Look

What have you done with your blue look?
Once your eyes were like the sky.
Now your eyes are full of grey indifference
when they look at me.
And your hands lie motionless on the table.
Your love has grown old.
I myself am old.
But my heart quivers with youth.
But my heart – that you don't see.
You cannot see my heart
with your indifferent eyes.

(1934)

PAUL LA COUR (1902-1956)

Nu gaar jeg

Nu gaar jeg ind i Stenen,
snart er jeg Bjerg og Kulde,
kan jeg ikke aabne mit Dyb,
da maa jeg blive Laas.
Engang skal Bjergene briste,
engang skal Laasene springe,
Stenen løfte sit drømmende Øje
og underligt bryde i Sang.
Kan jeg gaa gennem Klippen,
glemme min Uro i Mørket,
vente mit Stenliv til Ende,
da skal min Laas springe op,
da skal jeg nøgen i Græsset
vende forvandlet tilbage,
da er det navnløs jeg kommer,
da er min Haand blevet Vinge,
da er jeg Ord som er stumme,
svævende Stilhed, Uskyld,
Strømme af Ubevidsthed,
da er mit Flodliv inde.

(1950)

PAUL LA COUR (1902-1956)

Now I Pass

Now I pass into the stone,
soon I am mountain and cold,
if I cannot open my depths,
I must become a lock.
One day the mountains will break,
one day the locks will spring open,
the stone lift its dreaming eye
and strangely burst into song.
If I can pass through the rock,
forget my unrest in the dark,
wait out my stone life until the end,
then my lock will spring open,
then naked in the grass
I will return transmuted,
then I will come nameless,
then my hand will have become a wing,
then I am words that are silent,
floating stillness, innocence,
streams of unconsciousness,
then my spring-tide has come.

(1950)

JENS AUGUST SCHADE (1903-1978)

Paa Café

En god Sang,
et lille skørt Mirakel
udgaar af Grammofonen,
mens jeg tier.
Og til alles Forbavselse
rykker jeg Stolen bort under mig,
og bliver siddende i Luften.

Foran mig sidder en Pige
med grimme Tænder
og flygtige Øjne.
Hun tier.
– Vi to véd,
hvad der foregaar inden i hinanden,
og stærke som Løver kysses vore Sjæle.

Hun stiger op i Luften,
og jeg med,
vi finder hinanden
dér over Bordene.
Og til Drøn og Klapsalver
over Sangens Mirakel
vikler vi os om hinanden
og karrussellerer ud af Caféen.

(1930)

At the Café

A good song,
a crazy small miracle
comes from the gramophone
while I stay silent.
And to everyone's amazement
I push back my chair
and stay sitting in the air.

In front of me sits a girl
with ugly teeth
and flighty eyes.
She stays silent.
– Both of us know
what's going on inside the other,
and strong as lions our souls kiss.

She rises into the air,
and I do too,
we find each other
there above the tables.
And to roars and applause
at the miracle of the song
we intertwine
and roundabout out of the café.

(1930)

Sne

Naa, saa fik vi da Sne,
og jeg, som troede, vi ikke skulde have Sne,
og saa ser det virkelig ud til, at vi skal have en ordentlig Bunke Sne,
og ikke gaa og tænke paa Sne evig og altid, uden at den kommer.

Ogsaa *Luften* har Sne i sig,
den er ligesom *ladet* med Sne,
maaske er der en Snetykning langt borte,
som man saadan kan *mærke* i sig,
uden at man direkte *ved* det,
men som *kommer*, saa at man kan *se* det.

Jeg har hele Tiden haabet paa Sne,
det er dog sjovt, at den kom.
Ja, nu ligger den der –
se, hvor hvid den er,
jeg er saftsusemig glad for den,
jeg har jo hele Tiden nok tænkt, at den vilde komme.

Og saa ligger den der lige med ét –
det er dog sjovt, at den saadan kommer,
uden at man gør noget som helst for det,
jeg har ikke halet den ud af Luften,
det er kommet saadan af sig selv.

(1934)

Snow

So, we got snow after all,
and there I was thinking we wouldn't get any snow,
and it really looks as if we're in for a right load of snow,
and not go on eternally thinking about snow without it coming.

The *air* too has snow in it,
it's almost *laden* with snow,
perhaps there's heavy snowfall far off,
that you can sort of *feel* inside you
without directly *knowing* it,
but that *comes* so that you can *see* it.

I've been hoping for snow all the time,
it's funny even so that it came.
Yes, there it lies now –
look how white it is,
I'm really bloody pleased about it,
I've probably been thinking all the time that it would come.

And then all of a sudden there it is –
it's funny even so that it comes like that
without you doing anything to make it come,
I haven't plucked it out of the air,
it's sort of come by itself.

(1934)

Pædagogisk Gruk
til Mogens Lorentzen

Den, som kun
tar Spøg for Spøg
og Alvor
   kun alvorligt,
han og hun
har faktisk fattet
begge Dele
   daarligt.

(1940)

Pedagogical Grook
for Mogens Lorentzen

Taking fun
as simply fun
and sternly
   taking sternness
such a one
has not discerned
just which is which
   in earnest.

(1940)

GUSTAF MUNCH-PETERSEN (1912-1938)

Marts

Sneen ligger
fast og hvid —
Havet straaler
sommerblaat —
Flammende Sol
og isklar Luft
brænder i trætte Øjne —
Havfugle yngler,
hæse Stære skriger —
Natten kommer
sort og dyb —
Baade følger
stimende Sild —
Over Landet i Vest
gnistrer en Stjærne grønt —

(1937)

March

The snow lies
firm and white –
The sea gleams
summer-blue –
Flaming sun
and ice-clear air
burn in tired eyes –
Sea-birds breed,
hoarse starlings screech –
The night comes
black and deep –
Boats follow
shoals of herring –
Over the land in the west
a star sparkles greenly –

(1937)

en lykkelig dag

i dag er det en lykkelig dag -
jeg har faaet et nyt slips af gud.
det er rødt og jeg binder det i en stor knude,
en fugl har skidt paa min nye frakke,
paa den højre skulder
paa min grønne frakke,
ja, det er en lykkelig dag.
den var sort, før den blev ny og grøn,
det betyder lykke, saadan noget,
som det med fuglen og slipset.–
jeg blir berømt i dag, sikkert;
det regner, men jeg sidder her
med sort og stærk kaffe –
iskoldt vand og pive
foran mig.–
en lykkelig dag,
med fugle, slips og regnvejr
og kaffe, berømmelse og iskoldt vand,
ja, det er underligt.

(1931)

a lucky day

today is a lucky day—
i have got a new tie from god.
it is red and i tie it with a big knot,
a bird has shat on my new coat,
on the right shoulder
of my green coat,
yes, it's a lucky day.
it was black before it became new and green.
that means luck, something like that,
like with the bird and the tie.—
i'll be famous one day, sure to;
it's raining, but i'm sitting here
with strong, black coffee—
ice-cold water and pipe
in front of me.—
a lucky day,
with birds, tie and rainy weather
and coffee, fame and ice-cold water,
yes, it's strange.

(1931)

TOVE MEYER (1913-1972)

Fremmed i storbyens efterår –

Fremmed i storbyens efterår –
Oktober med de døde blomster slængt
over øde altaner.
Vemodig skulle jeg trampe hen over broerne
til de højtidelige toner af Chopins sørgemarch –
Jeg, der hader storbyen! Betragte
– så bistert som en halvgammel pige nu formår –
sommerens affald, træernes forrevne faner
og de hovmodige svaner
der spejlvendt sejler, sejler i de lange tingrå søer.
Og alle disse vordende skulpturer af Robert Jacobsen
der stikker deres skæve sømhoveder
halte trekanter og dæmoniske ellipser op alle vegne –
Bagved dem en stakkels kuldslået sol
nu kun en plade rustent jern, der hastigt opløses,
forstøves i en sky af okker.

Ud fra en af de sidste baggårde runger sommerens
schlager: Du skal lytte til dit unge hjerte!
Jeg lytter
og hører en beskeden banken under venstre ribben
straks overdøvet
af en regn af faldende blade og sporvognens hvinen
gennem Dronningens Tværgade.
Det er mærkeligt med denne stilhed
midt i myldretiden. – Stemmerne stimer
ind gennem gadernes tragte, støder med mørke finner
mod huse – og krænger tilbage med lysende bug
som fisk i en ruse.

TOVE MEYER (1913-1972)

A Stranger in the Big City's Autumn –

A stranger in the big city's autumn –
October with the dead flowers sprawling
over deserted balconies.
Mournfully I was to stomp over the bridges
to the solemn notes of Chopin's funeral march –
I who hate the big city! Consider –
as grimly as an elderly spinster's capable of –
the refuse of summer, the trees' torn pennants
and the haughty swans
sailing as reflections, sailing in the long pewter lakes.
And all of these emergent sculptures by Robert Jacobsen
that stick up their skewed nail-heads
lame triangles and demonic ellipses everywhere –
Behind them a poor sun stricken with cold
now just a sheet of rusty iron that quickly disintegrates,
pulverises in a cloud of ochre.

From one of the last courtyards the summer's song hit
booms out: You must listen to your young heart!
I listen
and hear a modest beating under my left rib
immediately drowned out
by a rain of falling leaves and the screech of the tram
through Dronningens Tværgade.
It is strange with this stillness
in the middle of rush hour. – The voices crowd
in through the streets' funnel, run with black fins
against houses – and careen back with glistening bellies
like fish in a trap.

Ja, jeg ved godt, hører godt
resignationens lavmælte klokker, der kimer, kimer.
De trætte øjne, hænderne, der én gang bar den elskede
på deres stærke vingepar. Stive nu –
Foldet sammen som gamle aviser. – Alt dette
endnu levende bag de ridsede ruder.
Vinden i taget som et kor af forladte børn –
Højt oppe: Fugletrækkets røgsky i drift gennem rummet.
Noget der kalder fjernt skønt forstummet.
Kastanjernes pindsvinehuder –
Også de krampagtigt lukket om denne sommers
udødelige schlager.

Og så denne anden vældige klokkeklang!

(1961)

Yes, I know well, hear well
the subdued bells of resignation that chime, chime.
The tired eyes, the hands that once bore the beloved
on their strong pair of wings. Stiff now –
Folded like old newspapers.– All this
still alive behind the scratched window panes.
The wind in the roof like a choir of abandoned children –
High up: The smoke-cloud of migrating birds swirling through space.
Something that calls distantly though silenced.
The hedgehog skins of the chestnuts –
They too labouredly closed round this summer's
immortal hit.

And then this other tremendous ringing of bells!

(1961)

HALFDAN RASMUSSEN (1915-2002)

Noget om at finde forståelse...

Jeg danser med en pige
gennem salens tomme støj.
Jeg er en ganske lille mand,
men hun er svær og høj.
Hun kløver luft og røg og larm
med ord, som aldrig når mig.
Jeg konverserer hendes barm,
der nikker og forstår mig.

(1952)

HALFDAN RASMUSSEN (1915–2002)

Something about Finding Understanding...

Through empty noise I'm dancing
with a woman round the hall.
I'm not that big a man but she's
voluminous and tall.
She cleaves the air and smoke and din
with words I sense she sends me.
With her great bosom I converse
that nods and comprehends me.

(1952)

TOVE DITLEVSEN (1917-1976)

Blinkende Lygter

I Barndommens lange og dunkle Nat
brænder smaa blinkende Lygter
som Spor, af Erindringen efterladt,
mens Hjertet fryser og flygter.

Her lyser din vildsomme Kærlighed
fortabt gennem taagede Nætter,
og alt hvad du siden elsked og led
har Grænser som Viljen sætter.

Den første Sorg har et spinkelt Skær
som en Taare der skælver i Rummet,
kun den vil være dit Hjerte nær,
naar al anden Sorg er forstummet.

Højt som en Stjerne en vaarlig Nat
brænder din barnlige Lykke,
du søgte den siden, men fik kun fat
dens flakkende Sensommerskygge.

Din Tro tog du med dig saa langt af Led,
for det var det første og sidste,
nu staar den og brænder i Mørket et Sted,
og der er ikke mere at miste.

Og en eller anden kommer dig nær,
men kan aldrig helt forstaa dig,
for dit Liv har du lagt under Lygternes Skær,
og ingen skal siden naa dig.

(1947)

TOVE DITLEVSEN (1917-1976)

Twinkling Lights

In childhood's long night, both dim and dark
there are small twinkling lights that burn bright
like traces memory's left there as sparks
while the heart freezes so and takes flight.

It's here that your pathless love shines clear,
once lost in nights misty and chill,
and all that you've since loved and suffered most dear
has boundaries set by the will.

The first-felt sorrow's a frail, thin light
like a tear that quivers in space;
that sorrow alone your heart will hold tight
when all others time has effaced.

High as a star on a night as in spring
your childhood's first happiness burns,
you sought for it later, only to cling
to late-summer shadow's swift turns.

Your faith you took with you to great extremes,
the first and the last to your cost,
in the dark now somewhere it surely gleams,
and there is no more to be lost.

And someone or other draws near to you but
will never quite manage to know you,
for beneath those small lights your life has been put,
since when everyone must forego you.

(1947)

Ægteskab

I generindret lidenskab,
vakt ved en mindelse om andre favntag,
en fjern berøring med en kølig hud,
en ukendt kvindes drømmende profil
mod byens neonlys —
eller måske:
ved synet af en ung soldat i toget
med klare øjne, i hvis ro han så
et ganske enkelt sind genspejle sit
og slynge det tilbage ufordøjet,
med al dets gådefulde modenhed —
vendes hans sanser søgende imod mig,
sløret af dunkel trang til at bedrage.
Og jeg, der helt befolker dette hus,
befrugter støvet med en spinkel tanke
af eget liv, og dagligt knæler ned,
fortabt i vage bønner, ved en gulvspands
gult emaillerede og tavse troskab —
betragter skjult hans hemmelige ansigt,
pludselig nøgent, næsten forsvarsløst,
som når naturen generobrer forladte haver:
bare et glimt af en vredagtig ømhed,
vantreven, lønligt aftvunget en legal
kærlighedsdød uden påviselig årsag.
Jeg ser det gå bort, og mindes andre kærtegn
af navnløs sødme, muligt hans engang,
men aldrig mere vækkende min lyst
i andet end erindring, aldrig mere.
Ordløst benægter vi, hævngerrigt, ene,
hinandens evne til at vække vellyst.

(1955)

Marriage

In re-remembered passion,
roused by a reminder of other embraces,
a distant contact with a cool skin,
the dreaming profile of an unknown woman
against the city's neon lights —
or perhaps:
at the sight of a young soldier in the train
with bright eyes, in whose calm he saw
a quite simple mind reflect his own
and fling it back undigested,
with all its mysterious maturity —
his senses turn searchingly towards me,
veiled by a dark urge to deceive.
And I, who completely inhabit this house,
fertilise the dust with a frail thought
of own life, and daily kneel,
lost in vague prayers, at the yellow-enamelled
and silent fidelity of a bucket —
covertly consider his secret face,
suddenly naked, almost defenceless
as when nature reconquers deserted gardens:
just a glimpse of an irascible tenderness,
stunted, secretly extorted a legal
death of love for no obvious reason.
I see it go away, and recall other caresses
of nameless sweetness, possibly his once,
but never more arousing my desire
in other than the memory, never more.
Without words we deny, vindictively, alone,
each other's capacity to rouse sensual desire.

(1955)

THORKILD BJØRNVIG (1918-2004)

September

Guldgrund bag Grenene,
Aftenstilhed,
som var jeg alene
med Solsortskriget.
Men alt er til Stede,
Firbenet spejder
vaagent ud
af et Hul i Diget.

Fra Vandet stiger
Goplens rene
Klokkebevægelse
gennem mit Indre.
Nældens Takvinge
lukker sig sort
paa Bjælken, for roligt
at overvintre.

Et nyfaldent Æble
svulmer i Haanden
og glatter Livslinjen
ud en Stund.
Aa, kølige Velsmag,
alt er til Stede,
og strømmer tidløst
gennem min Mund.

Denne sjældne
Ligevægtstime,
som usøgt kommer
er Taalmodsgaven.
Se, Luften er hævet
af Solnedgangen
og svæver gyldent
højt over Haven.

THORKILD BJØRNVIG (1918–2004)

September

Gold ground behind the branches,
Evening stillness,
as if I were alone
with the blackbird's screech.
But everything is present,
The lizard peeks
vigilantly
from a gap in the dike.

From the water
the pure bell-motion
of the jellyfish rises
through my mind.
The small tortoiseshell
shuts itself black
on the rafter, to
quietly winter.

A new-fallen apple
swells in my hand
smoothing out the
lifeline for a while.
Oh, cool savour,
everything is present,
and streams timelessly
through my mouth.

This seldom
hour of composure,
that comes unsought
is the gift of patience.
Look, the air has been lifted
by the sunset
and is hovering high
and golden above the garden.

De fire Vinde
er endelig samlet.
Hvor fjærne Træer
Kronerne breder,
hvor Solen daler,
hviler de ud
som store Fugle
i høje Reder.

(1947)

The four winds
are at last brought together –
where distant trees
spread their crowns,
where the sun sinks,
they find repose
like big birds
in high nests.

(1947)

Lappedykkeren

Med Halsens fuldendte Bøjning,
Næbbets slanke Lanse
sigter den paa mig, svajer
og følger, som vilde den danse,
den mindste af mine Bevægelser,
yndefuld, vagtsom og fin —
men Kroppen blir passivt staaende
lodret, som hos en Pingvin.

Den flyver ikke, som ventet —
en Olieplet paa dens Bryst
er mygt blevet infiltreret,
har lammet dens Evne, Lyst
til at kalde, parres og yngle,
svømme, flyve og dykke,
jage, fange, fortære —
hele dens Legemslykke;
har ramt den som dødelig Sygdom:
en Draabe, en flydende Kim,
og den mineralske Spedalskhed
klistrer dens Fjer som Lim.

Nedskrevet til et Vraggods
blandt Brædder og Dunke paa Sandet,
ubrugelig, kan ikke fiske,
droppet af Luften og Vandet,
paa Vej ned mod Kredsløbets Hades:
de langsomt svindende Ting —
vogter den ufravendt paa mig,
mens jeg gaar om den i Ring.

The Grebe

With the perfect curve of the neck,
the beak's slender lance
it points at me, swaying
and follows, as if it would dance,
the smallest of my movements,
elegant, fine and alert—
but its body is that of a penguin,
held upright, passive, inert.

It does not fly as expected—
on its breast a stain of oil
has gently infiltrated,
has sapped its power and spoilt
its desire to call, to mate and breed,
to swim, to fly and dive,
to hunt, to catch, devour—
its joy at being alive;
has struck like a deadly disease:
a drop, a germ that's afloat,
and the mineral leprosy
glues feathers to sticky coat.

Reduced to just jetsam
midst planks and cans in the sand,
no use at all, unable to fish
dropped by water, air and land,
on its way down to life-cycle's Hades:
each slowly dwindling thing—
it watches my moves intently
as around it I walk in a ring.

Syge lille Guddom,
fortabt paa de ensomme Flader,
endnu har Naturen, den vældige,
aldrig taalt Svækkelsens Grader
fra Fuldkommenhed ned til pur
Udslettelse;– ingen Nød,
som ikke af vilde Dyr fordrer
genvunden Magt eller Død.

Derfor vil jeg ikke prøve
forgæves at rense din Krop,
for du vilde værge din Dødsro
med vild Angst, tog jeg dig op,
som skulde du leve! Nej Maanen
i Nat er dig mere fortrolig
og Skyerne, Luften og dét,
som du afventer rolig, rolig.
Og du vil synke: din sidste
fuldkomne Bevægelse – ned
og ligge uformelig henstrakt
paa dette tilfældige Sted.

(1959)

Sick little deity,
lost on the lonesome expanses,
nature, the mighty, has never as yet
brooked impairment's nuances
from perfection down to pure
obliteration;— no plight
that from wild beasts does not dictate
reasserted power or death outright.

Which is why I will not try in vain
to clean your body of slick,
for you would defend your last rest
with wild fear, were I to pick
you up as if you should live. No,
tonight's moon's a more intimate friend
and the clouds, the sky and what
you so calmly await as your end.
And you will sink down: your last
perfect movement— leaving no trace,
lie outstretched a shapeless form
in this fortuitous place.

(1959)

OLE SARVIG (1921-1981)

Regnmaaleren

Regnmaaleren
med den flade kumme
staar i juninattens bløde regn
paa sin søjle,
fyldes af vand,
mens mørke popler suser
og bevæger deres grene.

Natten kan høres viden om.
Regnen gir genlyd i verden.
Der er tomt. Der er stille.
Alle skabninger sover.

Poplerne suser.

Inat er haven vaagen
og fuld af vellugt.

Ganske stille
som en flad kumme
i juniregnen
vil jeg løbe fuld
af vilje
inat.

(1943)

OLE SARVIG (1921-1981)

The Rain Gauge

The rain gauge
with its shallow basin
stands in the June night's gentle rain
on its column,
is filled with water,
while dark poplars sigh
and move their branches.

The night can be heard far and wide.
The rain finds its echo in the world.
It is empty. It is still.
All of creation is asleep.

The poplars sigh.

Tonight the garden is awake
and full of fragrance.

Quite still
like a shallow basin
in June rain
I shall fill to the brim
with will
tonight.

(1943)

Bjørneklo

Bjørnekloen.
Den staar nede ved havnen,
høj som to mænd,
trives i raadden tang og fisk.

Se dens skærme,
hvor højt den nu er vokset
i denne sommer,
da krigens spil løber over bordet
i de blaa og de graa dage!

Se den,
dens navn er egensind,
og i skærmene har den frygt
og Ahrimans had og fortvivlelse!

En grænseløst elendig,
smudsig og fattig sommer
blomstrer nu med sine kæmpevækster
nede ved havnen.
Og fluerne bestøver dem.

(1943)

Giant Hogweed

The giant hogweed.
It stands down by the harbour,
tall as two men,
thrives in rotten wrack and fish.

Look at its cartwheels,
how tall it now has grown
during the summer,
when the war game sweeps the board
in the blue and grey days!

Look at it,
its name is wilfulness,
and in its cartwheels it has fear
and Ahriman's hatred and despair!

A boundlessly wretched,
dirty and impoverished summer
now flowers with its giant growths
down by the harbour.
And the flies pollinate it.

(1943)

MORTEN NIELSEN (1922-1944)

Døden

Døden, den har jeg truffet da jeg var Dreng.
Men kun som en Stilhed hos nogen som jeg holdt af.
Aldrig som noget omkring mig, en Kulde, en Skygge,
ingen kan nævne ved Navn eller vige fra.

Aldrig som Kulde ved en fremmed Ting.
Som Dyb paa Dyb i stivnede Muskelbaand.
Som om jeg faldt og faldt i en rumløs Kulde
ved at holde en fremmeds kolde Haand i min Haand.

Nu kender jeg den igen, her og allevegne.
Den staar i det tavse Lys over Skovenes Bund.
Den gaar som en svimlende Fjernhed i Sommerhimlen
og ligger som Klager over den sovendes Mund.

Den venter, for altid lidt ved Siden af Tingen,
en Skygge, usynlig, langs Aarer og Sten og Træer.
Den gør det mere rigt med de nye Sekunder
og mere ondt. Og den er mig altid nær.

Men vi fører ingen Samtaler med hinanden,
hverken ved Dagslys eller naar Stjernerne gaar i Flok.
Vi ved det kun begge to, at den anden er der.
Mere er ikke nødvendigt. Vi mødes nok.

(1943)

MORTEN NIELSEN (1922-1944)

Death

Death I encountered when I was a boy.
But only as a stillness in one dear to me.
Never as something around me, a coldness, a shadow
no one can name by name or get to leave.

Never as the coldness of some strange thing
As depth on depth in stiffened muscle band.
As if I fell and fell in a coldness without space
from holding a stranger's cold hand in my hand.

Now I know it once more, here and everywhere.
It stands in the silent light above the forest floors.
It moves like a dizzy distance in the summer sky
above the sleeper's mouth it lies like moans.

It waits, always just to the side of things,
a shadow, invisible, along veins and stones and trees.
It makes it richer with the new seconds
and more evil. And it is always close to me.

But we conduct no conversations with each other,
neither at dawn nor when the stars form fleets.
We just know both of us that the other is there.
No more is necessary. One day we'll surely meet.

(1943)

Øjeblik

Vilde Roser i Dagregn!
    Og Toget er standset,
med Ruder, der løber fulde
    af blændende Regnskær
og Buskenes vilde Lys
    i det vaade og grønne.

Lykkeligt stort og ligetil blir Livet –
Draabe, der rammer Draabe,
    Regn over Regn.
Sekunderne lukker sig op
    for en lang Erindring:
Veje i Hederne, Pigestemmer og Havet.

Jeg smager dem paa min Mund,
    de forsvundne Somre
Kølige, regnfulde Lykke, et Kys af Aar –

Vi rejser i Krigens urolige, fjerde Sommer.
Med eet er der stille
    Vilde Roser i Dagregn,
Ruder, der løber fulde
    blændende Regnskær
og Buskenes vilde Lys
    i det vaade og grønne.

(1943)

Moment

Wild roses in day-long rain!
    And the train has stopped,
with panes streaming
    with dazzling rain-gleam
and the bushes' wild light
    in the wet and green.

Happily great and straightforward life will be –
Drop that strikes drop,
    Rain upon rain.
The seconds open up
    for a long memory:
Paths on the moors, girls' voices and the sea.

I taste them on my tongue
    the vanished summers…
Cool, rainful happiness, a kiss of years –

We travel in the war's restless, fourth summer
Suddenly it is still…
    Wild roses in day-long rain,
Panes streaming
    with dazzling rain-gleam
and the bushes' wild light
    in the wet and green.

(1943)

ERIK KNUDSEN (1922-2007)

Schack Staffeldt

Du tænder lys i alle vinduer
For ikke at se de grinende rovdyr.
Men nattens døtre kalder dig ud, lokker med
            guldæbler og skamløse orkideer.
Din skygge vokser fantastisk, strejfer
Mælkevejen, svinger henover månens torso.
                        Pludselig
Spiller et orgel i susende løvtræer.
Du lytter ind mod dit nøgne hjerte
Og hører ekko fra mindets bjerghuler.

Stjernerne ler med lykkelige øjne.
En af dem er dig. Men hvilken?

Feber i blodet. Hjemve. – Kunne du blot
Slippe din dødvægt! rykke tanken op med rode!

Roligt vugger i det fjerne
Et objektivt fastland. – Turde du blot
Springe ud fra din fordømte vulkanø!

Dit bryst er tungt af lava.

Ingen forløsning, ingen flugt.
Du presses hårdt mellem himmel og jord,
Stønner under vægten af tusind atmosfærer.

Lysene blafrer bag de våde ruder.
Du bar ingen tårer, ingen virkelighed.
Drømmen er dit eneste element.

Men du er vågen og klar.
Uden kikkert
            finder du dig selv:
En slukket planet i et hav af ild.

(1955)

ERIK KNUDSEN (1922–2007)

Schack Staffeldt

You light candles in all the windows
So as not to see the grinning predators.
But the night's daughters call you out, tempt with
                    golden apples and shameless orchids.
Your shadow grows fantastic, grazes
The Milky Way, swings across the moon's torso.
                                        Suddenly
An organ plays in rustling leafy trees.
You listen close to your naked heart
And hear an echo from memory's mountain caves.

The stars smile with happy eyes.
One of them is you. But which?

Fever in the blood. Homesickness.– If only you could
Escape your deadweight! rip thought up by the root!

Calmly in the distance
An objective mainland rocks.– If only you dared
Leap out of your damned volcanic island!

Your chest is heavy with lava.

No deliverance, no flight.
You are hard-pressed between heaven and earth.
Groan under the weight of a thousand atmospheres.

The candles flutter behind the wet window panes.
You have no tears, no reality.
The dream is your sole element.

But you are awake and ready.
Without telescope
            you find yourself:
An extinct planet in a sea of fire.

(1955)

IVAN MALINOWSKI (1926-1989)

Disjecta membra

Blikket søger en klode af fred men ingen
enhed er den sidste ingen grænse urokkelig

selv i evigheden kløves de elskende til roden
kun ilden går aldrig sulten til sengs

frugtens to halvdele udelukker hverandre
og kreperer gladeligt hver for sig

mens solnedgangen pludselig lader masken falde
og du ser ind i en kælder af blod og panik

hvor alting kun består af sine yderpunkter
hvor ingenting følgelig består

hvor en sol af nælder og brændende støv
er prisen for metallers parring og ingenting

står fast end ikke smerten eller længslen
ved vandrende vande under tage af halm

der er ingen løsning eller ligevægt
der er ingen bolig på jorden

men dette splittede blod vil ikke dø
og ukueligt er kødet der klynger sig til sit ben

(1958)

IVAN MALINOWSKI (1926-1989)

Disjecta membra

The gaze seeks a globe of peace but no
unity is the latter no boundary unwavering

even in eternity the lovers are cleft to the root
only fire goes never unsated to bed

the fruit's two halves exclude each other
and happily die on their own

while the sunset suddenly lets slip the mask
and you look into a cellar of blood and panic

where everything only consists of its extremities
and nothing accordingly lasts

where a sun of nettles and burning dust
is the price of the metals' mating and nothing's

for sure not even the pain or the longing
with wandering waters under roofs of straw

there is no solution or balance
there is no dwelling on earth

but this divided blood refuses to die
and the flesh that clings to its bone can't be cowed

(1958)

Myggesang

i juninatten denne drøm

huset båret af kirsebærtræernes skum

til druknende fugles klukkende bølgeslag
under en klokke spinklere end fjordens spejl

min søvn en gærdesmuttes æg: en væg
af kalk og bristefærdigt synsbedrag

dirrende plantet i mørket det hvide en segl
og lydløst hakker et usynligt næb

på spejlets hinde af vind og salt

snart brister alt

(1958)

Mosquito song

in the june night this dream

the house borne on the foam of the cherry trees

to the gurgling wash of the drowning birds
beneath a bell jar frailer than the mirror of the fjord

my sleep the egg of a wren: a wall of
whitewash and optical illusion strained to bursting point

quiveringly planted in the dark the white a sail
and silently there pecks an unseen beak

on the mirror's membrane of wind and salt

the burst is imminent

(1958)

FRANK JÆGER (1926-1977)

Sidenius i Esbjerg

Jeg er her, fordi
jeg skal lære Stormen at kende.

Stormen, som straaler
over de Jyders Land.

Jeg er her, fordi
det i Esbjerg Havn skulle hænde,

at Ord kom strygende
til mig fra oprørt Vand.

Spørgsmaal, som hænger
i Rigning paa skræmte Baade.

Ord, som i Motor stønner,
i Messing ringer:

Hvem kan her skelne
imellem Dom og Naade?

Er Døden tungere Lænker?
Er Døden Vinger?

(1959)

FRANK JÆGER (1926-1977)

Sidenius in Esbjerg

I am here because
the tempest is to be known by me.

The tempest that streams out
over the Jutlanders' land.

I am here because
in Esbjerg harbour it was to be

that words came skimming
from troubled waters to my hand.

Questions that hang
in the rigging of boats scared to start.

Words that moan in engines,
in brass that sing:

Who here judgement
and mercy can tell apart?

Is death yet heavier chains?
Is death wings?

(1959)

Efter Stormen

Mønster i Sandet af Havfruens skællede Hale.
Dérhenne maa saa de første Blodspor være.
De gaar som paa Glasskaar. Kan ikke tale.
Og vores Luft er for dem som Tjære.

Deres Øjne er vandblaa. Ørerne kan de lukke.
Det lange Haar er sort og grønt, det lugter salt.
Deres Bryster er smaa og glatte og meget smukke.
Her ser det ud, som om hun gled og faldt.

Du ser i Sandet, hvor Fingrene er fine,
og Knæene staar støbt som fuldendte Ovaler.
Find hende: Hun tager dine Hænder mellem sine.
Hun rødmer aldrig. Gør stum, hvad du befaler.

Brug hende dristigt. Dejlig fra Haar til Hæl.
Over Jer hviler en smudsig Maage paa Vingen.
Og hvad hun attraar til Gengæld er blot din Sjæl.
Og du har ingen.

(1976)

After the Storm

The sand shows patterns of the mermaid's scaly tail.
There then is where the first blood traces are.
They walk as if on shards of glass. Their voices fail.
And what is air to us to them is tar.

Their eyes are liquid blue. Their ears can tightly fold.
Their waist-long hair is black and green, with salty smell.
Their breasts are small and smooth, most lovely to behold.
It looks as if it was just here she slipped and fell.

The sand reveals her fingers' every bone,
as perfect ovals lie the casts of both her knees.
Find her: She'll take your hands between her own.
She never blushes. Dumbly follows your decrees.

Boldly use her. Delectable from top to toe.
Above you rests in flight a gull that's filthy dun.
And what she craves from you is just your soul.
And you have none.

(1976)

PER HØJHOLT (1928-2004)

Forholdsregler

I

der må begyndes sådan for at sætningen ikke skal løbe (her fra) op i øjnene
eller tilbage hen over sig selv og slette sig ud eller gå igennem (her fx) og
fortsætte på bagsiden eller om 8 år. Der er to sole, en på den anden side
men kun ryggen knæhaserne og huden på overarmene nærer tilliden. Den
som bygger hus mærker det ikke før maden står på bordet. Ørerne? Nej.
Hælene? Til en vis grad. Håret? Nej det vokser ned i æsker. Udsigten ville
kunne nydes hvis her var nogen og det var lidt lysere. Denne sætning den
sidste

II

enhver begyndelse er halvt fuldendt
første råd til fotografen: det er kun på papiret verden ser ud som den gør
blad glider ud af blad: blafrer: en årring
andet råd til fotografen: et stykke papir kan blive meget gammelt
tredje råd til fotografen: længe undervejs er halvt fremme
hvis det ikke var for sent ville jeg begynde på halvvejen eller her

III

du krydsede bækken til hest fortæl mig DET
du købte 20 Snow Flake og en dåse bønner sig DET
du kom forbi et tårn et vandtårn en busk og en dynge våde sten jeg vil høre
   om DET
du sagde ikke noget du sang du var alene hold mund med DET
du gik to skridt frem og 15 skridt frem og stod så her i solen det er DET
   jeg vil vide
du brugte dine sidste kræfter på at nå frem hertil du er meget træt ikke
   min sag DAV

(1966)

PER HØJHOLT (1928-2004)

Precautionary measures

I
it has to start like this so the sentence won't run (from here) up into your eyes
or back over itself and erase itself or go through (here for example) and
continue on the reverse side or in 8 years' time. There are two suns, one on the other side
but only the back, back of the knees and upper arm skin inspire confidence. The person
building a house doesn't notice it before the food's on the table. The ears? No.
The heels? To a certain extent. The hair? No it grows down into boxes. The view could
be enjoyed if there was one here and it was a bit lighter. This sentence the
last one

II
every beginning is half-completed
first piece of advice to the photographer: it's only on paper that the world looks
the way it does leaf glides out of leaf: flutters: a growth ring
second piece of advice to the photographer: a piece of paper can become very old
third piece of advice to the photographer: a long time underway is half-way there
if it wasn't too late i would begin half-way or here

III
you crossed the stream on horseback tell me THAT
you bought 20 Snow Flake and a tin of beans say THAT
you passed by a tower a water tower a shrub and a heap of wet stones and I
    want to hear about THAT
you didn't say anything you sang you were alone keep quiet about THAT
you took two steps forward and 15 steps forward and then stood here in the
    sun it's THAT I want to know
you used the last of your strength to get to here you are very tired nothing
    to do with me HEY

(1966)

Så og så mange lærker

383 lærker er kommet 384

birketræernes kroner syder (385) som balloner faktisk balloner man blæser
   op gasforekomster på stilk nejende som birketræer ja fuldstændig som
   birketræer der syder

388 lærker er kommet og synger over muldvarpeskud 389

vinterens søvnveje blottes vinterens søvnveje ligger blottede og fulde af
   vand solen rammer dem

en morris kører op over bakken og ned og brummer op gennem hulvejen og
   nærmer sig plaskende langs fyrretræer

postens morris kommer til syne under 390 lærker

(1966)

Such-and-such a number of larks

383 larks have arrived 384
the tops of the birch trees are seething (385) like balloons actually balloons
    you inflate gas deposits on stalks curtseying like birch trees yes completely like
    birch trees that are seething
388 larks have arrived and are singing above mole-hills 389
winter's sleep-paths are being uncovered winter's sleep-paths lie uncovered
    and full of water the sun strikes them
a morris drives up over the hill and down again and rumbles up along the sunken road and
    approaches splashingly past the pine trees
the postman's morris comes into sight beneath 390 larks

(1966)

Den tydelige solsort

En solsort kom flyvende
inde fra tågen

den sidder her nu
og synger i en våd bjergfyr

om lidt flyver den tilbage
til naturen

(1977)

The unmistakable blackbird

A blackbird came flying
in from the mist

it's sitting here now
singing in a wet mountain pine

soon it will fly back
into nature

(1977)

BENNY ANDERSEN (1929-)

Svantes lykkelige dag

Se, hvilken morgenstund!
Solen er rød og rund.
Nina er gået i bad.
Jeg spiser ostemad.
Livet er ikke det værste man har
og om lidt er kaffen klar.

Blomsterne blomstrer op.
Dér går en edderkop.
Fuglene flyver i flok
når de er mange nok.
Lykken er ikke det værste man har
og om lidt er kaffen klar.

Græsset er grønt og vådt.
Bierne har det godt.
Lungerne frådser i luft.
Åh, hvilken snerleduft!
Glæden er ikke det værste man har
og om lidt er kaffen klar.

Sang under brusebad.
Hun må vist være glad.
Himlen er temmelig blå.
Det ka jeg godt forstå.
Lykken er ikke det værste man har
og om lidt er kaffen klar.

Nu kommer Nina ud,
nøgen, med fugtig hud,
kysser mig kærligt og går
ind for at re' sit hår.
Livet er ikke det værste man har
og om lidt er kaffen klar.

(1972)

BENNY ANDERSEN (1929–)

Svante's Happy Day

See how the day's begun!
Warm is the round red sun.
Nina is showering at ease.
I'm eating bread and cheese.
Life's not the worst thing around so they say
and the coffee's on its way.

Flowers start to flower once more.
Spiders run down the door.
Birds fly in flocks through the air
when there are birds to spare.
Joy's not the worst thing around so they say
and the coffee's on its way.

Green is the grass and wet.
None of the bees need fret.
Suck in the air till it's spent.
Oh, get that bindweed scent!
Bliss's not the worst thing around so they say
and the coffee's on its way.

In wafts a shower-time song.
She's really going strong.
Outside the sky is quite blue.
I can approve that too –
Joy's not the worst thing around so they say
and the coffee's on its way.

Now Nina comes right in,
naked, with moist warm skin,
kisses me fondly, still bare
goes off to do her hair.
Life's not the worst thing around so they say
and the coffee's on its way.

(1972)

KLAUS RIFBJERG (1931-)

Refshaleøen

Fortiden søger sin overlevelse
bag husrækker, Christianshavn
Amager og en barndom kan ses
algefarvet, hovedpinesprængt mellem bolværk.

Hukommelsen er flyvemaskinebevidst
farvefornemmelsen sort rød
men søsygen af uoplevet tid
kan dårligt elimineres.

Optræk af punkterede skibe
svulstbesatte undervandsbåde
andre overlevede opbrugthedsfænomener
selve passagens absurditet.

Den sædvanlige glappende
intervalstilhed i vandet
en afgjort viden om folk bag hjørnet
skildvagten vender.

Film aldrig oplevet og fremtiden
oplevet som film
i outsider-sektoren følelsen
af tidssvingets stilstand.

Nittelyds ekko er besk om søndagen
pludselig beder man grønhedens
finnebesatte muddereksistenser melde sig
så vi kan få det overstået.

Dok, kran, vagere, råddenskab
selve alderen kvalm
men bevidsthedslykken et turbo-apparat
før tiden, vingeflugt og jubelsmerte.

KLAUS RIFBJERG (1931-)

Refshale Island

The past seeks its survival
behind rows of houses, Christianshavn
Amager and a childhood can be seen
seaweed-coloured, headache-burst between wharfs.

The memory is aware of flying machines
the sense of colour black red
but the sea-sickness of unexperienced time
can hardly be eliminated.

Approach of punctured ships
tumour-possessed submarines
other surviving phenomena of exhaustedness
even the absurdity of the passage.

The usual flapping
interval silence in the water
an incontestable knowledge of people round the corner
the sentry about-turns.

Films never experienced and the future
experienced as a film
in the outside sector the feeling
of the stasis of time's pendulum.

The echo of rivets is harsh on Sundays
suddenly one prays for the fin-possessed
greenness of muddy existences to announce itself
so we can get it all over.

Dock, crane, topmark buoys, putrescence
age itself nauseous
but the happiness of consciousness a turbo machine
before time, wing-flight and rejoicing pain.

Årstallene ét og ligegyldige
men mødet i konstans:
de enorme møllevingers adskillende
understregning af konfrontation.

(1960)

The dates all one and immaterial
but the meeting in constancy:
the enormous windmill sails' separating
underscoring of confrontation.

(1960)

solsort

nu lukkes hospitalets porte op
af rustne hænder det grå
terrassogulv er gummitavst
de levende er endnu mere stille
og ånder gennem sår af sten
mens urets visere af jern
går over deres kinder kullet skrider
mellem husene det regner indadvendt
et sug af præparater stigende og faldende
er spærret inde bag ved gaze står i rør
du sover i de blinde kældre venter bag
en skærm en hånd på lagenet
fingrene blæst hen en grå og fugtig ro
da vokser i dit hjerte spejl som spørgsmål
et skærmet radarminde om en
anden tid da gror i hjerteøret hammerekko
en buet lyd af syn
af dufte farvet moll imellem skyer
da tier ingenlyd du vågner
og har hørt det

(1962)

blackbird

the hospital gates are now being
opened by rusty hands the grey
terrazzo flooring is rubber-silent
the living are even more so
and are breathing through wounds of stone
while the clock's iron hands
pass over their cheeks the coal slips
between the houses it's raining introvertedly
a drag of specimens rising and falling
is confined behind gauze stands in tubes
you sleep in the blind cellars wait behind
a screen a hand on the sheet
fingers blown away a grey and damp calm
then grows in your heart mirror as question
a screened radar memory of an
other time then grows in the heart-ear hammer-echo
an arched sound of sight
of scents coloured minor between clouds
then no-sound falls silent you wake up
and have heard it

(1962)

Remisevej

Visse lokaliteter er svære at placere
i *virkeligheden*, f. eks. Remisevej.

Stedet har intet med sporvogne at gøre.
En remise er en lille skov.

Vejen løber mellem Englandsvej og Røde Mellemvej
på Amager.

Efter denne optakt kommer vers'et:
Remisevej du er krageflagrende
både sommer og vinter.
Du begynder ved Englandsvej
(når man kommer derfra)
du snor dig langs en hæk.
Sundbygaard lå på den ene side,
en gartners jord på den anden.
Remisevej, midt i det hele
er din skov.

Refrain'et gentager bestemte, karakteristiske
træk ved skoven:

Få træer.
Ganske få træer.
Remiseskoven har
ganske få træer.

Flokke af krager,
en stor flok sorte
efterårskrager blæser
mod syd.

Få træer
ganske få.

Remisevej

Certain localities are hard to place
in *reality*. Remisevej, for example.

The place has nothing to do with trams.
A "remise" is a small wood.

The road runs between Englandsvej and Røde Mellemvej
on Amager.

After that prelude comes the main verse:
Remisevej you are crow-flapping
both summer and winter.
You start at Englandsvej
(if you're coming from there)
you wind your way alongside a hedge.
Sundbygaard lay on the one side,
a nurseryman's land on the other.
Remisevej, in the midst of everything
is your wood.

The refrain repeats certain characteristic
features of the wood:

Few trees
Very few trees.
Remise wood has
very few trees.

Flocks of crows,
a large flock of black
autumn crows blows
southwards.

Few trees
very few.

Går man fra Røde Mellemvej
begynder Remisevej ved
Røde Mellemvej.

Det er sent i oktober,
vejen snor sig,
der er pytter uden glas.
Så kommer skoven.
Her holdt de havefest (i kolonien)
for flere år siden
og havde en højttaler i gang
til sent.

Seks træer
måske tyve
lidt græs
en remise.

Det blæser sydfra i dag.
Kasser med glemte tomater.
Kragerne er fløjet
over mod Sundbyøster.

(1965)

If you walk from Røde Mellemvej
Remisevej starts at
Røde Mellemvej.

It is late in October,
the road winds,
there are puddles without glass.
Then comes the wood.
Here they used to hold outdoor parties (in the allotment)
several years ago
and had the loudspeaker in action
until late.

Six trees
twenty perhaps
a little grass
a remise.

It's blowing from the south today.
Boxes with forgotten tomatoes.
The crows have flown
over towards Sundbyøster.

(1965)

Note: The word "remise" means both a small wood and a tram depot

INGER CHRISTENSEN (1935-2009)

juninatten

juninatten findes, juninatten findes,
himlen omsider som løftet til himmelske
højder og samtidig sænket så ømt som når
drømme kan ses før de drømmes; et rum som
besvimet, som mættet med hvidhed, en timeløs

kimen af dug og insekter, og ingen i
denne flyvende sommer, ingen begriber at
efteråret findes, eftersmagen og eftertanken
findes, kun disse rastløse ultralydes
svimlende rækker findes og flagermusens
jadeøre vendt mod den tikkende dis;
aldrig var jordklodens hældning så dejlig,
aldrig de zinkhvide nætter så hvide,

så værgeløst opløste, mildt ioniserede
hvide, og aldrig usynlighedsgrænsen så næsten
berørt; juni, juni, dine jakobsstiger
findes, dine sovende kræ og deres søvndrømme
findes, et svæv af galaktiske kim mellem
jorden så jordisk og himlen så himmelsk,
jammerdalen stille, så stille, og gråden
sunket ned, sunket ned, som grundvand igen

i jorden; Jorden; Jorden i sit omløb
om Solen findes; Jorden på sin rute
gennem Mælkevejen findes; Jorden på vej
med sin last af jasminer, med jaspis og jern,
med jerntæpper, jærtegn og jubel, med Judaskys
kysset i flæng og jomfruelig vrede i
gaderne, Jesus af salt; med jacarandatræets
skygge over flodvandet, med jagtfalke, jagerfly
og januar i hjertet, med Jacopo della Quercias
brønd Fonte Gaia i Siena og med juli

INGER CHRISTENSEN (1935–2009)

June Nights

June nights exist, June nights exist,
the sky at long last as if lifted to heavenly
heights, simultaneously sinking, as tenderly as
when dreams can be seen before they are dreamed; a space
as if dizzied, as if filled with whiteness, an hourless

chiming of insects and dew, and no one in
this gossamer summer, no one comprehends that
early fall exists, aftertaste, afterthought;
just these reeling sets of restless ultrasounds
exist, the bat's ears of jade
turned toward the ticking haze;
never has the tilting of the planet been so pleasant,
never the zinc-white nights so white,

so defencelessly dissolved, gently ionized and
white, never the limit of invisibility so nearly
touched; June, June, your Jacob's ladders,
your sleeping creatures and their dreams exist,
a drift of galactic seed between
earth so earthly and sky so heavenly,
the vale of tears so still, so still, and tears
sinking, sinking like groundwater back

into earth; Earth; Earth in its trajectory
around the sun exists, Earth on its journey
along the Milky Way, Earth on its course with
its cargo of jasmine, jasper, iron,
iron curtains, omens, jubilation, Judas's kiss
kissed right and left, and virgin anger in
the streets, Jesus of salt; with the shadow of the
jacaranda over the river, with gyrfalcons, jet planes,
and January in the heart, with Jacopo della Quercia's
well Fonte Gaia in Siena and with July

så tung som en bombe; med hjemlige hjerner,
med hjertefejl og hjertegræs og jordbær,
med jerntræets rødder i den jordtrætte jord

Jorden Jayadeva besynger i sit mystiske
digt fra det 12. århundrede; Jorden med
bevidsthedens kystlinie blå og med reder hvor
fiskehejren findes, med sin gråblå hvælvede
ryg, eller dværghejren findes, kryptisk
og sky, eller nathejren, silkehejren findes,
og graden af vingeslag hos jernspurve, traner
og duer; Jorden med Jullundur, Jabalpur og
Jungfrau findes, med Jotunheim og Jura
findes, med Jabron og Jambo, Jogjakarta
findes, med jordfygning, jordrøg findes,
med vandmasser, landmasser, jordskælv findes,
med Judenburg, Johannesburg, Jerusalems Jerusalem

(1981)

heavy as a bomb, with domestic brains
heart defects, quaking grass and strawberries
the ironwood's roots in the earthworn earth

Earth sung by Jayadeva in his mystical
poem from the 12th century, Earth with
the coastline of consciousness blue, with nests where
fisherbird herons exist, with their grey-blue arching
backs, or where bitterns exist, cryptic
and shy, or night herons, egrets,
with the wingbeat variations of hedge sparrows, cranes
and doves; Earth exists with Jullundur, Jabalpur and
the Jungfrau, with Jotunheim, the Jura,
with Jabrun, Jambo, Jogjakarta,
with duststorms, Dutchman's breeches
with water and land masses jolted by tremors
with Judenburg, Johannesburg, Jerusalem's Jerusalem

(1981)

Note: Many more words in the original start with or include the letter J

[John Irons has given permission for his own translation to be replaced by that of Susanna Nied, as Inger Christensen's heirs prefer translations of her works by this particular translator to be used in general.]

JØRGEN LETH (1937-)

Kneppe

Det er noget der foregår på øverste etage
hvor fjernsynet står og den store seng.
Det foregår når eftermiddagen er nået til ende
eller efter at fjernsynet har sendt en smadret film
og når det er det der er tilbage at gøre.
Det foregår mellem to kroppe som finder sammen
og har nogle bevægelser at udveksle
og nogle ord at udtale. Kneppe det er et sprog
der bliver brugt og en historie der bliver fortalt
og det er noget der foregår mens havet hvisker
udenfor og himlens stjerner endnu er usynlige
og byens mennesker endnu er i deres huse.
Kneppe det er noget der foregår i den evige eftermiddag
hvor de elektriske pumper og køleskabet er forstummet
og samtaler fra gaden stiger op til den øverste etage
med fjernsynet og sengen. Det er her med det overvældende
lys ind gennem vinduer og døre at det foregår. Det
udstrækker sig i denne time og tager form i dette rum.

(2000)

JØRGEN LETH (1937-)

Fucking

It is something that takes place on the top floor
where the TV is and the big bed,
It takes place when the afternoon is over
or when the TV has shown a beaten-up film
and when that is what's left to be done.
It takes place between two bodies that get together
and have certain motions to exchange
and words to say. Fucking is a language
that is used and a story that is told
and something that takes place while the sea whispers
outside and the stars in the sky are still invisible
and the city dwellers are still in their houses.
Fucking – that's something that takes place in the infinite afternoon
when the electric pumps and the fridge have fallen silent
and conversations from the street rise up to the top floor
with the TV and the bed. It's here with the overwhelming
light in through the windows and doors that it takes place. It
takes up this hour and takes shape in this room.

(2000)

KLAUS HØECK (1938-)

Her er så de ni roser
Til Margit Jean

Her er så de ni roser
som jeg lovede dig
i en natlig seance.
De stammer måske fra, voksede
sig røde i et drivhus eller
et dansk gartneri.
Den første rose er
for forelskelsen, der
sved hjertet med fosfat.

Den anden rose er for
blufærdigheden vi
skjulte os bag gennemsigtig
som krystalvasen, du
anbringer den i nu.
Det er en Crimson Glory,
der vil tabe bladene
eet for eet, som når vi
lagde tøjet stykke for stykke.

Den tredie rose spejler
sin transcendens i
duggdråberne. Den er for
de blide kys, som vi tog
fra hinanden og
den ømhed vi gav
hinanden under
denne vignet, dette
kronblad af scarlagen fløjl.

KLAUS HØECK (1938–)

Here Then Are the Nine Roses
For Margit Jean

Here then are the nine roses
which I promised you
in a nighttime seance.
Perhaps they come from, gained their
redness in a glasshouse or a
Danish nursery.
The first rose is for
the falling in love that
singed the heart with phosphate.

The second rose is for the
chastity behind which
we concealed ourselves transparent
as the crystal vase you
are now placing it in.
It is a Crimson Glory
that will lose its leaves
one by one, as when we
removed our clothes item by item.

The third rose mirrors
its transcendence in
the dew-drops. It is for the
gentle kisses that we took
from each other and the
tenderness we gave
each other under
this vignette, this
petal of scarlet velvet.

Den fjerde rose er for
ilden, er for nattens
ulvehyl, når jeg sprøjtede
sæden ind i din
livmoders våbenhus.
Den er for dine æggestokke,
er for din skedes blod
plettede damask og
klimakteriets rygende hyben.

Den femte rose er for
den store kærlighed,
som kun findes i
digternes fantasi af
frosne smaragder. Dén
kærlighed, der sprænger sin
grænse og sin kerne
og derfor når ind i lidelsens
rene salt, hvorfra den stammer.

Den sjette rose er for
smerten, der brændte
os til den aske,
som nu drysser sagte
ned over vores seng.
Den præger eller
svider sit frygtelige
sigil af calcium
ind i vores huds pergament.

Den syvende rose er for
ensomheden, som gnaver
i alt, der ikke er af jern.
Den beviser, at også
kødet er ubodeligt
ensomt uden sjælens
lyst uden sin
elektriske kortslutning
af gnister og stjerner fra Gud.

The fourth rose is for fire,
is for the wolflike howl
of night when I squirted
my semen up into
the armoury of your womb.
It is for your ovaries,
for your vagina's blood-
flecked damask and for the
smoking rose-hips of the menopause.

The fifth rose is for the
all-consuming love
that only exists in
the poets' fantasy of
frozen emeralds. That
love which bursts its
boundaries and its nucleus
and therefore reaches suffering's
pure salt, from which it is derived.

The sixth rose is for
the pain that burned us
to the ashes
which are now gently sifting down
over our bed.
It is embossing or is
scorching its terrible
seal of calcium
into the parchment of our skin.

The seventh rose is for the
loneliness that gnaws at
everything that is not of iron.
It is proof that the flesh too
is irreversibly
lonely without the soul's
desire without its
electric shortcircuiting
of sparks and of stars from God.

Den ottende rose er for
længslen. Du kan sylte
dens blade i en lerkrukke
eller du kan spise dem.
Det hjælper ikke. Den vil
balsamere dit hjerte med
andre blade så sorte som
den jord, hvorfra de
blomstrede. Denne rose er udødelig.

Den niende rose er for
afskeden, for dette
farvel som ingen ende
vil tage. Den niende
rose er et floragram
af taknemmelighed.
Læg den i pres i Biblen.
Når den visner,
dør også vores kærlighed.

(1985)

The eighth rose is for longing.
You can try preserving its
leaves in a clay pot
or you can eat them.
It will not help.
It will embalm your heart with
other leaves as black as
the earth from which they
once flourished. This rose is immortal.

The ninth rose is for farewell,
for this goodbye
that seems to go on
for ever. The ninth
rose is a floragramme
of gratitude.
Press it in the Bible.
When it withers,
our love will also die.

(1985)

HANS-JØRGEN NIELSEN (1941-1991)

3 stykker om naturen

Af sommerdelen

1

Jord er jord, selvfølgelig, og de bakker dér
ikke andet end de bakker, mægtige lerklumper,
som ikke giver meget efter, men udsigten
ophidser mig; bugtningerne bliver ikke ved med
at være bugtningerne; den hud dér af grønt
korn, grønt græs om kroppen, som ikke er en
krop, men en fjern istids døde sammenskrab,
er spændt af betydning, bølgende og liderlig;
alt er her blødt og elastisk eftergivende,
når øjnene rækker ud, svuuuupp; det er bare
at lade hænderne følge efter mellem baller
og patter, hofter og lårdele, krybende ind til,
forsvindende ned i vældige moar, så enorm
en elskerinde for det vakte lem.

2

Der er en jord at gå på og så ud i, og, senere,
rådne ufølsomt i, renset for enhver betydning,
men her åbner den sit moderskød; den lette fugt
i lavningen hernede, lysets grønnere kvalitet,
klemt inde mellem bakkerne, og jeg opløses blandt
væskepuder i det mørke punkt; kroppen er ikke
andet end én eneste næse for alt, der taler rundt
om, men ikke ud af sig selv, for jorden *er* ingen
mor, selvom hun er talende for manden her, kød
af en mor som afsatte disse kødelige tegn,
tidligt og langt nede.

HANS-JØRGEN NIELSEN (1941-1991)

3 Pieces about Nature

From the summer part

1
Earth is earth, of course, and the hills there
nothing else but hills, colossal lumps of clay,
that do not give way very much, but the view
excites me; the curves do not continue
to be curves; that skin there of green
corn, green grass round the body, which is not a
body but the dead scrapings of a distant ice age,
is taut with meaning, surging and lascivious;
everything here is gently and flexibly yielding,
when the eyes reach out, schwuuup, just let
your hands follow after between buttocks
and breasts, hips and thighs, creeping in to,
disappearing down in mighty ma, so enormous
a lover for the roused limb.

2
There is an earth to walk on and to sow in, and, later,
rot insensibly in, cleansed of every meaning,
but here it opens its maternal lap; the light moisture
in the hollow down here, the greener quality of the light,
squeezed in between the hills, and I am dissolved among
liquid cushions in the dark point; the body is
nothing but one single nose for everything that speaks
around, but not outside itself, for the earth *is* no
mother, even though she speaks for the man here, flesh
of a mother that deposited these carnal signs,
early and deep down.

Af vinterdelen

3
Det kommer væltende gennem timer, bunker sig
på tværs af alt og blinder ruder; en standset
bevidstheds hvidt på hvidt hovedkuls på en stiv
nordvest, så blikket tømmes mellem kroppen og
dens landskab: det er tabet af hukommelse, mens
sneen sletter sneens spor; papiret alt for stort
og kraftfuldt her, hvidt væltende alt der rejser
sig; det sidste lille punkt af mørke, en aldrig
fuldendt sætning, kørt fast og sneet inde gennem
dage i et sammenfoldet ark.

(2000)

From the winter part

3

It comes tumbling through hours, piles up
across everything and blinds window panes; the white
on white of a stopped consciousness head-over-heels on a stiff
northwesterly, so the gaze is emptied between the body and
its landscape: it is the loss of memory, while the snow
erases the snow's traces; the paper far too large
and powerful here, whitely toppling all that rises
up; the last small point of darkness, a never
completed sentence, stuck and snowed in for
days in a folded sheet of paper.

(2000)

PETER LAUGESEN (1942-)

Det jeg vil skrive om

Det jeg vil skrive om
er i den grad småting
at der ikke er ord til det
Ord
er der kun til de ting der er så store
at de ikke betyder noget
Dem er der til gengæld nok af
Men de små ting hvad hedder de
og hvordan kan jeg sige dem
Det er ikke naturen jeg mener
men vores liv
som det er
Naturen er selv skrift den er til at læse
Vejret kan læses
som et digt
Det er ikke prosa det er rytme
almanakken fortæller
Den er poesi
Men det er ikke det jeg vil skrive om
Det er de små ting
der ikke er ord til
eller som alle ord er til for alle ord kommer
af små ting af
at de engang var store og
at alting vender omvendt
at vi vokser os mindre
Planen er for jeg ved ikke hvilken gang
at skrive det hele sammen til EET
LANGT DIGT fordi det er hvad det alligevel
er
og ikke skille det ad
Så længe det foregår er det sådan men indtil nu
er det altid faldet fra hinanden mere og mere
i en anden typografi
og det kan godt være

PETER LAUGESEN (1942–)

What I Want to Write About

What I want to write about
is small things to such an extent
that there aren't any words for it
Words
only exist for things that are so big
that they don't mean anything
Those on the other hand there are plenty of
But the small things what are they called
and how can I express them
It's not nature I'm talking about
but our life
as it is
Nature is itself writing it can be read
The weather can be read
like a poem
It is not prose it is rhythm
the almanack narrates
It is poetry
But it's not that I want to write about
It's the small things
there aren't any words for
or that all words are for since all words come
from small things from
them once having been big and
from everything turning opposite
that we grow smaller
The plan is for the umpteenth time
for me to combine all of it into ONE
LONG POEM for that's what after all it
is
and not to separate it out
As long as it takes place it is like that but until now
it's always fallen apart more and more
into some other typography
and it may well be

det sker igen
Men du skal bare vide at sådan er det ikke
det er EET LANGT DIGT
og det siger alverden
på sin egen måde
som ikke er anderledes
og ikke kan være det
Jeg vil ikke være beruset mere
eller forhindre nogen i noget som helst
bare være den jeg er når jeg ikke er påvirket af andet
end alt det jeg engang som alle andre dengang i den alder
mente var selve døden den triste borgerlige kedsomhed
Nu ved jeg det er løgn og det var osse løgn dengang
Nu ved jeg at der ikke er nogen vej uden om
at leve sit liv
Jeg har lært af de gamle
som de er i mig selv
Jeg har opdaget dem
der hvor de gemmer sig
i tankerne der hvor de sidder
og venter på at nogen skal høre
hvad de hvisker inde under skriget
Jeg har fundet dem og lyttet til dem
både den ene og den anden
og langtfra alle
Der er mange flere i mig
mange jeg endnu ikke har mødt
fordi jeg har set den anden vej
og kaldt den fremad
men de er der
Lige pludselig sidder de i mig og skriver
og jeg ved ikke hvem de er
fordi de er mig og jeg ved ikke hvem jeg selv er
De er en træt og gabende langfredag
og vejret er vildt skiftende her i randen af dalen
Jeg er alle og enhver og ingen af dem
ved hvem jeg er og jeg ved det ikke selv
Det er at komme ud på den anden side med et eller andet i behold
som trods alt ikke er blevet slået i stykker

that'll happen again
But you are to know that that's not how it is
it's ONE LONG POEM
and it says all sorts of things
in its own way
which is not different
and can't be so
I don't want to be intoxicated any more
or prevent anyone from anything
just be the person I am when I'm not influenced by anything else
than all that I once like everyone else then at that age
believed was death itself that sad bourgeois boredom
I now know that's a lie and it was also a lie then
I now know there's no way round
living one's life
I've learnt from the old ones
as they are in my self
I have discovered them
there where they're hiding
in thoughts there where they're sitting
waiting for someone to hear
what they're whispering inside beneath the scream
I have found them and listened to them
both the one and the other
and far from all of them
There are lots more in me
many I haven't met yet
because I've looked the other way
and called it forwards
but they're there
All of a sudden they're sitting inside me writing
and I don't know who they are
because they're me and I don't know who I myself am
They are a tired and yawning Good Friday
and the weather's changing wildly here on the edge of the valley
I am everyone and none of them
know who I am and I don't know myself
It's like coming out on the other side with something intact
that despite everything hasn't been smashed to pieces

Og uden ord
og med alt for mange ord
for ingenting
og alting
Blade aviser tidsskrifter bøger påske igen
Tiden siger bøh og to ukendte forskere har lavet fusion
med et skolekemisæt
i et glas saltvand
Skepsis hos de kloge det vil jo vælte alt for Iran
og Norge
Og naturgassen pump den ind i jorden igen ballonen
er slatten
Solsorte på plænen
Skyerne vandrer og man ser op gennem hullerne mellem dem
Måske
kan man se
de små meteorologiske kameraers øjne i det himmelblå dyb
de små øjne i cellerne de hvide blodlegemers kamp
i sårene
lungernes kraftværk og hjertestationens rørledninger
De små ting
for sproget
Alle de ord der falder ud det er dem nu
der ikke når frem til døren og
dem der får sparket ud med hovedet
i sølvsnoren
Og et helt andet sted samler de sig i et nyt sprog
som er det udstødte selv
som er mytens satan
faldende i rum som Michelangelos skikkelser på loftet
hvor gadelampens lysstråler passerer gennem den åbne dør
om natten
og tankerne hele tiden kredser om det ømme punkt
hvor kroppen lige nu samles
Regnen begynder
Brug kroppens billeder
vinden i vinduet
gardinet og papirerne på væggen
Huden

And without words
and with far too many words
for nothing
and everything
Magazines newspapers periodicals books Easter again
Time says boo! and two unknown researchers have made fusion
with a school chemistry set
in a glass of salt water
Scepticism among the clever that would upset everything for Iran
and Norway
And natural gas pump it back into the earth again the balloon
is limp
Blackbirds on the lawn
The clouds are drifting and you look up through the holes between them
Perhaps
you can see
the eyes of the small meteorological cameras in the sky-blue depths
the small eyes in the cells the fight of the white blood corpuscles
in the wounds
the power plant of the lungs and pipelines of the heart station
The small things
for language
All the words that fall out it's them now
that do not reach the door and
them that are kicked out with their head
in the silver cord
And somewhere else entirely they collect a new language for themselves
that is the expelled thing itself
that is the satan of the myth
falling in space like Michelangelo's figures on the ceiling
where the light-rays of the street lamp pass through the open door
at night
and thoughts constantly circle round the sore point
where the body right now is being assembled
The rain begins
Use the images of the body
the wind at the window
the curtain and the papers on the wall
The skin

Det er ikke et spørgsmål om ondt eller godt
eller smukt og grimt
Skriv igennem
som de små sataner i blodet og lægernes pincetter og vatpinde
Flyv på retorisk vind
Det kommer ikke nærmere
Det gjorte er fortid det ugjorte fremtid
Det er ikke navne men ord
Nøgler
Åbne døre
En rum tid
Et tidsrum
i kroppens billeder når de blir ord og kroppens ord når de blir billeder.

(1990)

It's not a question of evil or good
or beautiful and ugly
Write through
like the small devils in the blood and the doctors' forceps and swab
Fly on rhetorical wind
It won't come any nearer
What's done is past the undone future
It's not names but words
Keys
Open doors
Spacious time
Timely space
in the pictures of the body when they become words and the words of
the body when they become pictures.

(1990)

JOHANNES L. MADSEN (1942-2000)

nedspildt spruttende af syre

nedspildt spruttende af syre
og med alle tanker antændt fægtende
i delte mandariner
skilt og fuldmoden laprende
i grønt lys og flugt
med ligegyldige anslag
suget gennem minuttet
sydende af saft og nedspildt
fra hinkesten og mandariner
hoppende på blomsten
i kejtede kredse over
spejlblanke vandpytter ind
i et ansigt af røg og ingen
ild antændt spruttende
af mandariner men et ansigt
rygende af syre blink
og ætsende i nogens hornhinder

(1969)

JOHANNES L. MADSEN (1942–2000)

spilt out sputtering with acid

spilt out sputtering with acid
and with all thoughts ignited flailing
    in divided mandarins
    separated and fully ripe lapping
in green light and flight
    with indifferent touches
        sucked through the minute
        seething with juice and spilt out
    from hopscotch and mandarins
hopping on the flower
    in clumsy circles above
        mirror-like puddles into
            a face of smoke and no
        fire ignited sputtering
    of mandarins but a face
smoking with acid flash
and corroding in someone's corneas

(1969)

HENRIK NORDBRANDT (1945-)

Kina betragtet gennem græsk regnvejr i café turque

støvregnen
falder i min kaffe
til den bliver kold
og løber over
til den løber over
og bliver klar
så at billedet på bunden
kommer tilsyne.

billedet af en mand
med langt skæg
i Kina, foran en kinesisk pavillon
i regnvejr, styrtregn
der er størknet
i striber
henover den forblæste facade
og over mandens ansigt.

under kaffen, mælken og sukkeret
som er ved at skilles
under den slidte glasur
synes øjnene udslukte
eller indadvendte
mod Kina, i koppens porcelain
koppen som langsomt tømmes for kaffe
og løber fuld af regn
klar regn. forårsregnen

HENRIK NORDBRANDT (1945-)

China observed through Greek rain in café turque

the drizzle
falls into my coffee
until it is cold
and overflows
until it overflows
and becomes clear
so that the picture on the bottom
becomes visible.

the picture of a man
with a long beard
in China, in front of a Chinese pavilion
in the rain, pouring rain
which has stiffened
into streaks
over the windswept facade
and over the man's face.

beneath the coffee, milk and sugar
which are separating
beneath the well-worn glaze
appear eyes, extinguished
or inward-looking
towards China, in the cup's porcelain
the cup slowly being emptied of coffee
and being filled with rain
clear rain. the spring rain

forstøves mod tavernaens halvtag
facaderne på den anden side af gaden
ligner en stor
meget slidt væg af porcelain
hvis skær gennemlyser vinløvet
vinløvet der også er slidt
som indeni en kop. kineseren
ser solen komme tilsyne gennem et grønt blad
der er faldet ned i koppen.

koppen hvis indhold
nu er fuldstændig klart.

(1969)

is atomised against the shed roof of the taverna
the facades on the other side of the street
are like a large
very worn wall of porcelain
whose gleam lights up the vine leaves
the vine leaves that are also worn
like the inside of a cup. the chinaman
sees the sun appear through a green leaf
that has fallen into the cup.

the cup whose contents
are now completely clear.

(1969)

Violinbyggernes by

Hver gang du kommer tilbage
kunne jeg dræbe dig for det
– af misundelse over den udsigt
jeg ikke fik set, floden
der slyngede sig gennem byen og ud
i et blomstrende landskab
med mindre det var en strøm af blå heste
bjergenes sne og de indfødtes
sprog, de indforståede vittigheder
de fortalte om deres konge.
"Violinbyggernes by" har jeg ofte
døbt det sted, hvor jeg leder
efter din sjæls foretrukne tilholdssted
din melankolis skovbund, og den særlige
tone i lyset over din kind
den som gør mig gal sidst på vinteren
eller med andre ord: Om døden ved jeg intet
men en sådan afmagt tillægger jeg de døde
en sådan genstandsløs længsel
at intet billede kan gøres
på trods af rammen, som altid er der:
Hele natten ned ad floden
lå vi ikke desto mindre vågne på dækket
og lyttede til strygermusikken
der blev båret ud mod os fra usynlige bredder.

(1985)

The City of Violin Makers

Every time that you return
I could kill you for it –
out of envy at the view
I never gained a glimpse of, the river
that wound its way through the city and out
into lush countryside
unless it was a stream of blue horses
the snow of the mountains and the local
language, the inside jokes
they made about their kings.
"The city of violin makers" I have often
christened the place where I search
for your soul's preferred haunt
your melancholy's woodland floor, and the special
tint in the light across your cheek
the one that drives me mad in late-winter
or in other words: I know nothing of death
but I ascribe such powerlessness to the dead
such an undirected yearning
that no picture can be made
despite the frame that is always present:
Throughout the night downriver
we nevertheless lay awake on deck
listening to the string music
borne out to us from invisible banks.

(1985)

DAN TURÈLL (1946-1993)

At være beat

"At være beat er at stå på et gadehjørne
og være sindssygt høj"– GREGORY CORSO

At være beat er at stå på et gadehjørne og være sindssygt høj
At være beat er at sidde i et automatvaskeri på Gl. Kongevej og pludselig høre
    Gregory Corsos stemme komme ud af tørretumbleren
At være beat er at løbe hen til en boghandler for at stjæle en blok og en
    speedmarker for at kunne skrive denne tilstand
At være beat er at fyre piben og sætte sig på skraldespandene i baggården mens
    vinden blæser gennem bladene
At være beat er at stå foran automatvaskeriet med psychedeliske øjne og sé
    bilansigter køre forbi
At være beat er at følge med tøjet ind i tørretumblerens og drycleanerens cyklusser
At være beat er at sidde på Spies' kundebænk og recorde og skulle til Algier i
    morgen men uden Spies
At være beat er at acceptere hvad der er at acceptere og opleve hvad der er at opleve
At være beat er at regne med at éns fingre nok er éns eneste fingre
At være beat er at være klar til at springe hélt ud når som helst og aldrig gøre det før
At være beat er hvad som helst og selvfølgelig ingenting
At være beat er uden betydning hvis man enten er det eller ikke er det
At være beat er en af titusind muligheder i sproget
At være beat er at tone ud over gader og hustage via sin egen svimlende hånd
At være beat er en spontan tankerække startet af Gregory Corso en mulig kæde
    som enhver kan tilsætte sit personlige bidrag
At være beat er en tilfældig indkodning som nu sprøjter ud i vilkårlige pletter på
    papiret
At være beat er at være ingenting at være villig til at være hvad som helst selv sig selv
At være beat er at dreje udad uden på forhånd at ha bekymret sig om hvorhen det
    kan gå

29. 4.

(1971)

DAN TURÈLL (1946-1993)

To Be Beat

"To be beat is to stand on a street corner
and be stoned out of your mind" GREGORY CORSO

To be beat is to stand on a street corner and be stoned out of your mind
To be beat is to sit in a launderette on Gl. Kongevej and suddenly hear
　　　　Gregory Corso's voice come out of the spindryer
To be beat is to go over to a bookshop to steal a block and a
　　　　speedmarker to be able to write about this state
To be beat is to make a chillum and sit down on the garbage cans in the backyard while
　　　　the wind blows through the leaves
To be beat is to stand in front of the launderette with psychedelic eyes and watch
　　　　car faces drive past
To be beat is to follow your clothes into the revolutions of the spindryer and the dry-
　　　　cleaner
To be beat is to sit on Spies' customer-bench and record and have to go to Algiers
　　　　the next morning but without Spies
To be beat is to accept what there is to accept and experience what there is to experience
To be beat is to count on one's fingers probably being one's only fingers
To be beat is to be ready to come right out whenever and never do so before
To be beat is anything at all and of course nothing
To be beat is without significance if you either are it or are not it
To be beat is one of ten thousand possibilities in language
To be beat is to fade out over streets and roofs via one's own dizzy hand
To be beat is a spontaneous train of thought started by Gregory Corso a possible chain
　　　　that anyone can add his personal contribution to
To be beat is a chance encoding that now sprays out in random spots on
　　　　the paper
To be beat is to be nothing to be willing to be anything including oneself
To be beat is to turn outwards without having troubled oneself in advance as to where
　　　　one might end up

29. 4.

(1971)

331

MARIANNE LARSEN (1951-)

snehvide

af en eller anden grund kender hun mest til kulde
af grunde hvis naturhistoriske sandhed hun ikke kender
er genstande hun berører kolde
som glas og diverse hårde hvidevarer
på en blæsende strandbred
af en eller anden grund forlader det hende ikke
veje og byer suger sig fast til hende ved hjælp af kulde
og stole senge udflugter penge ansigter binder
uopløseligt
kolde fysiognomier i hendes indre
af en eller anden grund lykke som den må føle
der har fået sin hjerne nedfrosset
for at den ikke for tidligt
skal gå i forrådnelse
af grunde hvis geometri og materiale arbejder
hemmelighedsfuldt
fryser hun ved bevægelser af alting uden for vinduet
som enorme snekrystaller
når hun læser tager sætningerne form
som et frostvejrs dannelse
og frugterne hun spiser følger uoptøede glidebaner
hun mærker næsten ikke den afkølede smag
hendes øjne er stive og glatte
til at berøre direkte af andre
hvis de da også er af is
hun genkendes blandt dukker fremstillet i frysebokse
hendes ur går som siksakdans mellem urolige isflager
hendes hjerte som det underste af et isbjergs synlighed
hun tager ikke egentlige beslutninger

(1974)

332

MARIANNE LARSEN (1951–)

snow white

for some reason or other cold is what she knows best
for reasons whose nature-historical truth she does not know
objects she touches are cold
as glass and various domestic appliances
on a blustery beach
for some reason or other it does not leave her
roads and towns latch onto her with the aid of the cold
and chairs beds excursions money faces bind
indissolubly
cold physiognomies inside her
for some reason or other such as someone must feel
that has had his brain frozen
so that it will not begin
to rot too early
for reasons whose geometry and material work
mysteriously
she freezes by movements of everything outside the window
like enormous snow-crystals
when she reads sentences shape
like the formation of frosty weather
and the fruit she eats follows unthawed slides
she hardly notices the chilled taste
her eyes are stiff and glassy
can be directly touched by others
if they too are of ice
she is recognised among dolls made in freezers
her watch goes like a zigzag dance among restless ice-floes
her heart like the lowest visible part of an iceberg
she does not take real decisions

(1974)

Junidrøm

Den morgen du vil ankomme, rejser jeg mig fra søvnen,
det er juni, og jeg går nøgen,
tungt vuggende hen over gulvet, ikke anderledes
end de køer, der vralter mig i møde,
når jeg på milde aftner dukker op ved hegnet på engen;
jeg er vågen og parat,
de første lysstråler vælter ind
over mavens spidse kuppel, den tronstol
hvorfra du længe har regeret vildt og enerådigt.

Vandet siver varmt ned langs lår og knæ,
ned ad læggene, over fødderne, ud på gulvet,
hører lyden af en bæk langt borte, en klar
og tyst hvisken mellem mosbegroede sten;
kastes dybt ind i mig selv da veerne ruller frem:
Tre sole af sne og en stjerne af frygt,
dykker ned under havet og bæres igen
i en bue op over en gylden bro:
Kun én gang fødes du –

Forundres fra en fjern planet over det vræl
du spænder væggene ud med som hilsen
til den verden, der venter i hvid morgendis,
jeg løfter dig op, ser ind i dine øjne, som jeg kender,
men aldrig har mødt,
forsøger at forstå, hvad de spørger om,
mister blod, men lader din første morgen
være fyldt af lys, af kærtegn og profetiske drømme,
taler til dig og siger:

June Dream

The morning you are to arrive I get up out of my sleep,
it is June, and I go naked
heavily swaying across the floor, no different
from the cows that waddle towards me,
when on mild evenings I appear at the meadow fence;
I am awake and ready,
the first rays of light surge in
over the stomach's pointed dome, the throne
from which you long since have reigned wildly and absolutely.

The water runs warmly down thighs and knees,
down my calves, over my feet, out onto the floor,
I hear the sound of a stream far off, a clear
and silent whispering among moss-covered stones;
am thrown deep into myself when the pains roll in:
three suns of snow and a star of fear,
dive below the sea and am borne up again
in an arch above a golden bridge:
you are only born once –

Am surprised from a distant planet at the roar
you push the walls out with as a greeting
to the world that waits in white morning mist,
I lift you up, look into your eyes, which I know
but have never met,
attempt to understand what they are asking.
lose blood, but let your first morning
be full of light, of caresses and prophetic dreams,
talk to you and say:

En dag skal du gå selv, og livet er dit, min søn,
jorden, der drejer, er til dig, blomsterhaver
med tusinde farver og bare én slange, du skal vogte dig for,
jungler, ørkner og endeløse sletter med brogede dyr,
marker med spirende frø om foråret, om efteråret vildt du
kan jage,
skove med labyrintiske eventyr og høje træer at klatre i,
bjergkæder med slugter og knitrende mineraler,
en flammehimmel med skyer og sværme af fugle,
oceaner med fisk og skatkister fra forliste skibe.

Sne, regn og andre pletfrie spejle,
hvor du år for år kan se dig selv vokse,
byer der vil lokke og lyse dig i møde, og når du bliver større:
Koncertsale der holder angsten borte,
en prinsesse der vil lade sin tunge lege i din mund,
længe før du når at sige noget dumt
– og til det store, tomme rum,
som har overvældet andre før dig,
kan du siden rette dine spørgsmål.

(1998)

One day you will take your own steps, and life is yours, my son,
the earth that spins is for you, flower gardens
with thousands of colours and only one serpent you have to watch out for,
jungles, deserts and endless plains with pied cattle,
fields with germinating seeds in the spring, in autumn game you can hunt,
forests with labyrinthine adventures and tall trees to climb in,
mountain chains with ravines and glittering minerals,
a sky of flame with clouds and swarms of birds,
oceans with fish and treasure-chests from sunken ships.

Snow, rain and other spotless mirrors,
where year for year you can see yourself grow,
cities that will tempt and gleam towards you, and when you are bigger:
concert halls that keep fear at bay,
a princess who will let her tongue play in your mouth,
long before you manage to say something stupid
– and to the huge, empty space
that has overwhelmed others before you
you can then address your questions.

(1998)

F.P. JAC (1955-2008)

jeg har været på spritten

jeg har været på spritten lige siden jeg fandt rede på mig selv,
sen i blomst nægtede jeg krigstruslerne afstod fra for eller imod
kristus og begyndte at tage mine egne billeder rapt ud af huden,
forsvandt i alle afgørende øjeblikke for at finde ro på et ydersted,
finde værd måske ved en pigetinding der tydeligt afspejlede orgasmen,
jeg måtte ud af støjen med en finger i munden og blomster i håret,
finde et hjørne og tømme en balle gin mens bladene sprang fra alle
træerne jeg mener jeg duer bedst på grænsen til whisky og porter,
og intet billede vil kunne overraske i mit vinduetilhold om natten,
nul og nix jeg er dranker men jeg bærer på et af de største og
mest ømme jordiske hjerter det har jeg utallige store sorte katte på,
spørg pigerne på gaden de kender min tilstand de ved hvordan jeg
vil kæles i nakken de ved hvordan tungen skal lægges ud på næsen,
de vil kunne stå inde for mit forfald de vil kunne lyse skønheden,
de vil kunne bekende at jeg er det sidste fra det æstetiske univers,
jeg har været på angsten længere end tulipanen vist står mod til,
jeg har elsket flere glansbilleder end de fleste vil kunne forstå
i sorg og forvirring jeg har set rummene falde ned som krystalis,
jeg har været på spritten længe inden at digtet og kærligheden
blev en mulighed og set en mor der skiftede karakter mens hun græd,
jeg har set dem døende tømme sig mens de kaldte fortvivlet på en
far der ikke fandtes jeg har set pulsen helt åben tidligt en morgen,
og jeg vil ikke ud af det jeg vil ikke dæmpes jeg vil sgu se de
piger når de overlader mig deres kønsåbning og ber mig om at stække,
jeg vil sgu nuancere jeg vil udstråle vrangen jeg vil gøre alle
smukke og alle skal komme til at se at blomsten skyder fra selve
lorteklumpen der er ingen forskel på muld og gødning der er livet,
ingen skal nægte mig min umådelighed jeg hører til i en kulturpause,
jeg hører til i et tomrum inden verden jeg hører til af en verden,

(1980)

338

i've been on the booze

i've been on the booze ever since i could make head or tail of myself,
a late-flowerer i refused war threats abstained from being for or against
christ and began to take my own pictures straight from the skin, dis–
appeared at every crucial moment so as to find peace at some outer place,
find value perhaps next to a girl's temple that clearly reflected orgasm.
i had to get away from noise with a finger in my mouth and flowers in my hair,
find a corner and down a massive finger of gin while the leaves came out on all
the trees i mean i'm best on the whisky and porter boundary,
and no picture will be able to surprise me in my window haunt at night,
nix i'm a drunk but i carry around with me one of the biggest and the
tenderest of earthly hearts i've innumerable black cats on that, just ask the
girls on the street they know what state i'm in they know how i like to have
my neck caressed they know how the tongue's to be laid out along the nose,
they will be able to attest to my decline be able to light up the beauty,
they will be able to admit that i am the last thing from the aesthetic universe,
i've been on fear longer than the tulip would probably put up with,
i have loved more glitter pictures than most people could possibly understand
in sorrow and confusion i have seen the rooms fall down like artificial ice,
i was on the booze long before the poem and love ever became
a possibility and i have seen a mother who changed her nature while she cried,
i have seen them dying emptying themselves while they called out in desperation for a
father who did not exist i have seen the pulse completely open one early morning
and i don't want to get out of it don't want to be subdued i bloody want to see the
girls when they entrust me their genital opening and ask me to clip,
let me be a damned sight more precise i want to radiate the seamy side i want to make
everyone beautiful and they are all to come and see the flower shoot from the very
lump of shit there's no difference between soil and fertiliser there is life,
no one's to deny me my boundlessness i belong to a cultural pause
i belong to an empty space inside the world i belong of a world,

(1980)

BO GREEN JENSEN (1955-)

Svømmeren

Sekunder frosset i skummende ild
Sommerlang svømmerens finner
Skærer hvidguld i det grønne vand.
Han er født i havet. Han
Svømmer med delfinerne mod
Horisontens ring. Deres kroppe
Strejfer hans i et kærtegn
Glat som levende metal. De
Nipper blidt i hans brune arme
Og bærer ham frem under solen.
Han sover i vandet og lever kun
For lysets eksplosion i skum.
Hans fremdrift aflejrer ringe
Og striber, forplanter sig ud
I den finthamrede flade og
Bliver rynker i havets hud,
Signaler som kan ses fra oven,
Men han ved det ikke selv.
Han har skæl nu og svarer
Hverken på fugleskrig
Eller skibssirener. Indkapslet
Er han ene med lyden af
Sine arme i det glatte vand.
Han ænser ikke bølger men
Stryger evigt og uundgåeligt ud
Torpedo mod himmellinien
Hvor dag og nat forbrændes
I et ritual af lys og tid.
Hans rejse er uden stationer,
Der er kun delfinerne og
Solen på det tavse hav.

(1980)

BO GREEN JENSEN (1955-)

The Swimmer

Seconds frozen in foaming fire
Summer-long the swimmer's fins
Slice white-gold in the green water.
He is born in the sea. He
Swims with the dolphins towards
The ring of the horizon. Their bodies
Stroke past his in a caress
Smooth as living metal. They
Gently nibble at his brown arms
And carry him forwards under the sun.
He sleeps in the water and only lives
For the light's explosion into foam.
His forward motion deposits rings
And stripes, spreads out
Over the finely wrought surface, becoming
Wrinkles in the sea's skin.
Signals that can be seen from above.
Though that he does not know himself.
He now has scales and answers
Neither bird cries
Nor ship's sirens. Encapsulated
He is one with the sound of
His arms in the smooth water.
He does not heed the waves but
Sweeps out eternally and inescapably
Torpedo towards the line of the horizon
Where day and night are consumed by fire
In a ritual of light and time.
His journey is without stations,
There are only the dolphins and
The sun on the silent sea.

(1980)

SØREN ULRIK THOMSEN (1956-)

Sol Opgang

Kussens og røvhullets omvendte søer
skyller glinsende over min hud
hårene skilles af springende pis
der tykt og lykkeligt vasker mig varm
              én gang til!
              én gang til!
aldrig før blev jeg slynget så højt
gennem roterende indsøers spejl
slingrende fortsat med hovedet nedad
dybt mod de skrævende skyer.

(1982)

SØREN ULRIK THOMSEN (1956–)

Sun Rise

The upturned lakes of the cunt and the arse
rush gleamingly over my skin
hairs are divided by gushing piss
that thickly and happily washes me warm
       one more time!
       one more time!
never before was I flung so high
via the mirror of rotating inland lakes
reeling still with head pointing down
deep towards straddling clouds.

(1982)

Tandlæge. Gravsted. Vielsesring

– til Michael Strunge

Da jeg kom var det efterår, men da jeg gik fra tandlægen, var det blevet vinter. Jeg standser foran butikkernes ruder og smiler bredt til mit eget spejlbillede, så mine nye guldtænder lyner fra kæbernes lyserøde mørke, og jeg ligner en gammel nazist på film. I nekrologerne skrev de, at sådan måtte det jo gå, men jeg vil ikke være med til at give din død en mening, som alene er livets. Jeg køber en rose og leder efter din grav. "Jeg savner dig," siger jeg og synes, du smiler– men det er jo bare noget, jeg bilder mig ind. Her står jeg med mine første grå hår og mit ønske om en vielsesring. Og der er du, et sted mellem alt for meget jord og alt for meget himmel. I mit urolige hoved.

(1987)

Dentist. Grave. Wedding ring

– for Michael Strunge

When I arrived it was autumn, but when I left the dentist's it had become
winter. I stop in front of the shop windows and smile broadly
at my own reflection, so my new gold teeth flash from
the pink darkness of my jaws, and I look like an old Nazi in
a film. In the obituaries they wrote that that was the way it had to end, but I
refuse to be a party to giving your death a meaning that only belongs to life.
I buy a rose and look for your grave. "I miss you,"
I say and seem to see you smile – but that is just something I imag-
ine. Here I stand with my first grey hairs and my wish
for a wedding ring. And there are you, somewhere between far too much
earth and far too much sky. In my restless head.

(1987)

MICHAEL STRUNGE (1958-1986)

Livets hastighed

Knuser uret
med mine tanker
– jeg lever kun
med livets hastighed

Skifter hurtigt
til ny forklædning
– jeg behøver forandringer
med livets hastighed

Danner kontrast
behøver ingen camouflage
– død og træt af
ikke at være mig selv

Skifter farve
anarkistisk kamæleon
– kaster masken
ændrer leveform

Mit sind
gror ud af mit hoved
– skiftede sind
efter at have været død

Endelig
det lader til at jeg ved nu
– at jeg ikke har
et uforgængeligt selv

Hvem ved
ved hvad ens selv er lig?
– jeg er ligeglad
skaber selv mit selv

MICHAEL STRUNGE (1958-1986)

Speed of Life

Smash the clock
with my thoughts –
I only live
at the speed of life

Swiftly change
to a new disguise –
I need transformations
at the speed of life

Form contrasts
need no camouflage –
sick and tired of
not being myself

Change colour
anarchist chameleon –
throw off my mask
change life-form

My mind
grows out of my head –
changed minds
after having been dead

Finally
it would seem I now know –
that I do not have
an indestructible self

Who knows
knows what one's self is like?
I couldn't care less
myself create myself

Skifter fart
jeg har brug for fartskift
– jeg ændrer mit liv
før det ændrer mig

(1978)

Change speed
I need a change of speed —
I transform my life
before it transforms me

(1978)

Natmaskinen

Langsomt oplades natten af byens lys.
Stjerneknapperne blinker
og på måneskærmen ses de første billeder.
Åh, jeg vugges som på en damper,
et tungt exprestog gennem mørket,
flyver højt i natmaskinen.
Skyerne af drømmedamp
hvisker hvidt til jorden.
Natmaskinen arbejder og absorberer menneskenes sjæle.
Mørket fyldes tæt af en summen af energi ...

Jeg er til koncert i Rockmaskinen.
Ugens overlevende trænges om den lille scene
luften er hed af musik.
Vi er i trance og trang
transcenderende
grænserne mellem køn,
mellem dimensioner af virkelighed,
dansende i tranceformationer
et sted i den sovende by.
Vi er forkomne englebørn
med vinger af fremtidssang,
med barnet i blodet og smøgen i kæften.

Vi har hud af den sarteste drøm
og hjerter der lyser mere end neon.
Vi er kvæstede af dagens skarpe lyde,
blødende lyserød sne,
spiddet af avisoverskrifter.
Vi er en del af Natmaskinen
transformerer angst til venskab.
Vi bærer vore hjerner med stolthed
bytter drømme og cigaretter,
fylder os med rus og musik
bytter køn og masker ...

The Machinery of Night

Slowly the night is charged by the city's lights.
The star buttons blink
and on the moon-screen the first images can be seen.
Oh, I am lulled as on a steamer,
a heavy express train through the dark,
fly high in the Machinery of Night.
The clouds of dream-steam
whisper whitely to the earth.
The Machinery of Night works away, absorbing human souls.
The dark is packed tight with a buzz of energy…

I am at a concert in the Machinery of Rock.
The week's survivors crowd around the small stage
the air is hot with music.
We are in trance and urge
transcending
the boundaries beween the sexes,
between dimensions of reality,
dancing in trance-formations
somewhere in the sleeping city.
We are exhausted little angels
with wings of future-song,
with the child in our blood and a fag in our mug.

Our skin is of the frailest dream
and our hearts gleam brighter than neon.
We've been blighted by the harsh lights of day,
bleeding pink snow,
speared by newspaper headlines.
We are a part of the Machinery of Night
transform fear into friendship.
We wear our brains with pride
exchange dreams and cigarettes,
fill ourselves with ecstasy and music
change sex and masks…

Senere tager vi hjem hver for sig
drager gennem Natmaskinen med nye identiteter
ad offentligt fastlagte ruter.
Der falder sorte klumper af søvn
fra oliehimlen ned i vore øjne.
Vi sover ind som éncellede organismer
fra dengang jorden var hav.

(1981)

Later we go home our separate ways
pass through the Machinery of Night with new identities
along publicly determined routes.
Large black lumps of sleep fall
from the oil-sky into our eyes.
We fall asleep as single-cell organisms
from the time when the earth was sea.

(1981)

19. juni 1983, 25 år. København.

Kupeen stille, alting …

Berlin, mit hoved …
zigzag gennem erindringens by
der står som en stille dam med guldfisk.
Hybrider af ideer skinnende i en billig farve,
på bunden rådner årenes planter.
Mit hoved, Berlin, en planet i sig selv –
der er områder lukket for levende
og steder hvor alting brænder   sammen.
Berlin, mit syn, glimt af gløder i natten,
cigaretternes grå lugt
og pistolernes metalsmæld i begge halvdele.
For fanden, mine knæ, Berlin, det golde guldlys
en kunsteufori, en glæde købt og ædt.
Berlin, mit ansigt, en by uden plan,
linier uden mål,
for hvad skal jeg se hen til
og hvor skal jeg danse
når musikken presses gennem filtre
mens køn passes til form i nylon.
Berlin, mit hjerte, en pumpe for blod, ikke andet!
Og blodets veje kan forudsiges
som turisternes rejser efter souvenirs.

Berlin, måske findes der et aldrig fremkaldt billede
af en pige på Kurfürstendamm
der i et sekund så mig som mennesket i verden, Berlin,
mit hoved er så uklart
hvordan skal jeg finde hendes læber i alt det støv?

(1984)

19 June 1983, 25 Years Old. Copenhagen.

The compartment silent, everything…

Berlin, my head…
zigzag through the city of recollection
that stands like a still pond with goldfish.
Hybrids of ideas gleaming in a cheap colour,
on the bottom the plants of the years rot.
My head, Berlin, a planet in itself—
there are areas off-limits for the living
and places where everything burns   fuses.
Berlin, my vision, glimpses of embers in the night,
the grey smell of cigarettes
and the metallic crack of pistols in both hemispheres.
Dammit, my knee, Berlin, the barren golden light
an art euphoria, a pleasure bought and eaten.
Berlin, my visage, a city without a plan,
lines without aim or measure,
for what am I to look forward to
and where am I to dance
when the music is pressed through filters
while sex is form-fitted to nylon.
Berlin, my heart, a pump for blood, nothing else!
And the ways of blood are predictable
as are the tourists' trips for souvenirs.

Berlin, perhaps a never developed photo exists
of a girl on the Kurfürstendamm
who for a second saw me as man in the world, Berlin,
my head is so unclear
how am I to find her lips in all that dust?

(1984)

SIMON GROTRIAN (1961-)

Ode til et egetræ

Egetræ, jeg hylder dig
og stiller mig ved siden af
du hilser, jeg kan høre suset, lavt som boulevarderne
silende om parkens ro.
Vi læser blad for blad din mening, før du taber sommeren
med dynger til en storm og blir skelet.
Rødderne er skyggegrene, fire dimensioner har du
verdens hjørner mødes i din krone
hvor de strides
jeg kan høre bruset, højt som en tablet.
Og en vidtforgrenet tøjrepæl for kæmper er din smukke stamme
grønne skud kan eksplodere lydløst i dit overstel.
Gamle ven, din stemme lå begravet i en mose
men din fleksibilitet har gjort dig sort som klodens skyggevæsner.
Potentielle kister, borde venter på en motorsav
du store brændte foto af min sorg
der krænger over.
For du lander ved min fod, og jeg blir stående, alene.

(1993)

SIMON GROTRIAN (1961-)

Ode to an Oak Tree

Oak-tree, I pay homage to you
and place myself next to you
you greet me, I can hear the low murmur, like the boulevards
seeping round the peace of the park.
We read your opinion leaf by leaf, before you lose the summer
in folios to a gale and turn into a skeleton.
Your roots are shadow-branches, you have four dimensions
the corners of the earth meet in your crown
where they tussle
I can hear the sizzling, loud like a tablet.
And your trunk is an extensive tethering stake for giants
green shoots can explode inaudibly in your overframe.
Old friend, your voice lay buried in a bog
but your suppleness has made you black as the earth's shadow-beings.
Potential coffins, tables wait for a chain saw
you great burnt photo of my sorrow
that keels over.
For you land at my feet, and I remain standing, alone.

(1993)

PIA JUUL (1962-)

Men jeg ville heller ikke det jeg ville

Men jeg ville heller ikke det jeg ville
Og det jeg ville vidste jeg ikke hvad var
Jeg ville så gerne ha dig
Så fik jeg minsandten det
jeg ville ha, og hvad gør man så
Så råber man *lykken* og
græder sig i søvn ved højlys dag
Man siger man går gennem
engen, og engen er ikke en
eng, men noget helt andet
Kan man måske plukke
blomster hvor ingen gror?
Ja. Og så kaster man sig
derind, bider
den lykke i stykker, smasker, gnaver og
raller, stakåndet, slikker den
af og får kvalme. Snubler
over ordene, sluger maden,
bruger de tre ønsker for
hurtigt og forkert. Dum og bedåret.

(1993)

But I Didn't Want What I Wanted Either

But I didn't want what I wanted either
And I didn't know what it was I wanted
I so much wanted to have you
Then I got what I wanted
well and truly, and what do you do then
Then you shout out *happiness* and
cry yourself to sleep in broad daylight
You say you saunter through
the meadow, and the meadow isn't a
meadow, but something completely different
Can you perhaps pick
flowers where none are to be found?
Yes. And then you throw yourself
into it, bite that happiness
into a thousand pieces, smack your lips, gnaw and
rattle out of breath, tongue it
off and feel sick. Stumble
over the words, swallow the food,
use your three wishes too
quickly and wrongly. Insane and infatuated.

(1993)

NAJA MARIE AIDT (1963-)

Fjerde april

Engang var parken skov engang var byen koloni engang var Wall
Street mur engang var indianerne på den anden side af muren
engang var Brooklyn agerbrug engang var alle sorte slaver engang
var jeg et æg i min mors ovarium engang blev Martin Luther King
skudt på et luset motel netop i dag for enogfyrre år siden dengang var
jeg lige fyldt fire engang blev John Lennon skudt og Kennedy blev
skudt engang kom tyve millioner mennesker i karantæne på Ellis
Island engang byttede Frankrig Frihedsgudinden for Eiffeltårnet
engang var der borgerkrig engang blev en sort mand præsident
dengang sang man i gaderne engang var byen farlig engang var den
bange dengang tårnene faldt var den bange engang satte man alle
sindssyge i fængsel engang mødte min mor min far engang landede
jeg i Newark med et ordentligt bump engang bar jeg kærligheden
som et smykke ved mit bryst engang var min tipoldemor en pige der
skrev et hemmeligt brev i denne stol som jeg nu sidder i og skriver og
udenfor: solen i et barns øjne

(2009)

NAJA MARIE AIDT (1963–)

April 4th

Once the park was woodland once the city a colony once Wall
Street was a wall once the Red Indians were on the other side of the wall
once Brooklyn was farmland once all blacks were slaves once
I was an ovum in my mother's womb once Martin Luther King
was shot at a lousy hotel exactly forty-one years ago today when
I had just turned four once John Lennon was shot and Kennedy was
shot once twenty million people were put in quarantine on Ellis
Island once France exchanged the State of Liberty for the Eiffel Tower
once there was civil war once a black man became president
once people would sing in the streets once the city was dangerous once it was frightened
when the towers fell it was frightened once all
the insane were put in prison once my mother met my father once I landed
in Newark with quite a bump once I wore love
like a jewel at my neck once my great-great-grandmother was a girl who
wrote a secret letter in the chair I am now sitting in and writing and
outside: the sun in a child's eye

(2009)

The Sources of the Texts

Medieval Ballads

The two popular medieval ballads are reproduced from *Danmarks gamle Folkeviser* (1853-), in which the ballads have been numbered and classified (with letters) into various categories of ballad-types. Orthography and punctuation have been standardised according to the principles followed by Erik Dal in *Danske viser*, 1962, and by Jørgen Lorenzen in *Folkeviser*, 1978.

"Ebbe Skammelsøn", *Danmarks gamle Folkeviser* 354 A, Jens Bille's manuscript, c. 1555.

"Jomfruen i fugleham", *Danmarks gamle Folkeviser* 56 C, Svaning's manuscript, c. 1580. Line 2 in stanza 4 inserted from *Danmarks gamle Folkeviser* 56 D – following Lorenzen 1978.

Leonora Christina Ulfeldt (1621-1698)

"Guds goedhed imod mig at ihuekomme", *Jammers Minde*, 1674; diplomatic edition by Poul Lindegård Hjorth and Marita Akhøj Nielsen with the collaboration of Ingelise Nielsen, Det danske Sprog- og Litteraturselskab, C.A. Reitzels Forlag, Copenhagen, 1998, p. 196.

Thomas Kingo (1634-1703)

"Keed af Verden, og kier ad Himmelen", *Aandelige Siunge-Koors Anden Part*, 1681; *Samlede Skrifter* III, ed. Hans Brix, Paul Diderichsen and F.J. Billeskov Jansen, Det danske Sprog- og Litteraturselskab, 2nd edition, 1975, p. 214.

"Hver har sin Skæbne", 1681; *Samlede Skrifter* III, p. 233.

Jens Steen Sehested (c. 1640-c. 1697)

"Sonnet", Gks. 4° 2526, p. 65, c. 1690; checked against *Verdslig barok*, ed. Niels Simonsen, 1982, p. 27. Towards the end of Georg Stiernhielm's Swedish version of this poem, the following note appears: "Min Wän är en Fiol di gamba" (My friend is a viol). Both poems are most likely based on a French original, where the "instrument" is a lute, see Peter Brask, "Danske Studier", 2000.

Hans Adolph Brorson (1694-1764)

"Op! all den ting, som Gud har gjort", *Troens rare Klenodie*, 1739; *Udvalgte salmer og digte*, ed. Steffen Arndal, Det danske Sprog- og Litteraturselskab, 1994, p. 99.

"DEn yndigste Rose er funden", 1732; *Udvalgte salmer og digte*, p. 28.

Ambrosius Stub (1705-1758)

The poems of Stub were published posthumously. They are reproduced from *Ambrosius Stubs Digte* I and II, ed. Erik Kroman, 1972.

"Du deylig Rosen-Knop"; *Digte* I, p. 102.

"Den kiedsom Vinter gik sin Gang"; *Digte* I, p. 122.

Johan Herman Wessel (1742-1785)

"Gravskrift", 1785; *J.H. Wessels samlede Digte*, ed. J. Levin, 2nd revised edition, 1878, p. 270.

"Digterens Gravskrift over sig selv", 1785; *J.H. Wessels samlede Digte*, p. 272.

Johannes Ewald (1743-1781)

"Da jeg var syg", 1771; *Udvalgte digte*, ed. Esther Kielberg, Det danske Sprog- og Litteraturselskab, 1998, p. 37.

"Rungsteds Lyksaligheder. En Ode", 1775; *Udvalgte digte,* p. 54.

"Johannes Ewalds sidste poetiske Følelser nogle Timer før hans Død", 1781; *Udvalgte digte,* p. 106.

Jens Baggesen (1764-1826)

"Da jeg var lille", *Jens Baggesens Samtlige Værker* I, 1801, p. 326.

Schack Staffeldt (1769-1826)

"Indvielsen", *Digte*, 1804; *Samlede digte,* ed. Henrik Blicher, Det danske Sprog- og Litteraturselskab 2001, Vol. 1, p. 238.

"Det Eene", *Nye Digte*, 1808; *Samlede digte* 2, p. 133.

"Aftenrøden", *Nye Digte*, 1808; *Samlede digte* 2, p. 142.

Adam Oehlenschläger (1779-1850)

"Guldhornene", *Digte*, 1803, p. 75.

"Hvor blev I røde Roser dog", *Prometheus*, 1, 1832, p. 31.

Steen Steensen Blicher (1782-1848)

"Præludium", *Trækfuglene. Naturconcert*, 1838, p. 3.

"Stæren", *Trækfuglene*, 1838, p. 15.

N.F.S. Grundtvig (1783-1872)

Grundtvig has had his poems reprinted many times and almost always with variations. For scholarly purposes, the sources below should therefore be supplemented by Grundtvig's bibliography.

"De levendes Land", 1824; *Poetiske Skrifter*V, ed. Svend Grundtvig following "det oprindelige Manuskript" (the original manuscript), 1883, p. 283.

"Den signede Dag med Fryd vi seer", *Danske Høitids-Psalmer til Tusindaars-Festen*, 1826, p. 3.

"Et jævnt og muntert, virksomt Liv paa Jord", 1841; *Udvalgte digte*, Hans Reitzels Forlag, 1963, p. 107.

B.S. Ingemann (1789-1862)

"I Østen stiger Solen op", *Morgensange for Børn*, 1837, p. 8.

"Der staaer et Slot i Vesterled", *Aftensange*, 1839, p. 3.

Carsten Hauch (1790-1872)

"Dødens Genius", *En polsk Familie*, Anden Deel, 1839, p. 77.

Johan Ludvig Heiberg (1791-1860)

"Barcarole", *Prindsesse Isabella eller Tre Aftener ved Hoffet*, 1829, p. 177.

Emil Aarestrup (1800-1856)

"Til en Veninde", *Digte*, 1838; *Samlede Skrifter* III, ed. Hans Brix and Palle Raunkjær, Det danske Sprog- og Litteraturselskab, 1922, p. 75.

"Paamindelse", 1835; *Samlede Skrifter* II, p. 121.

Hans Christian Andersen (1805-1875)

"Det gamle Træ, o lad det staa", *Hyldemoer*, 1851, p. 19.

Holger Drachmann (1846-1908)

"Sakuntala", *Ranker og Roser*, 1879, p. 8.

J.P. Jacobsen (1847-1885)

"Regnvejr i Skoven", c. 1869; *Lyrik og prosa*, ed. Jørn Erslev Andersen, Det danske Sprog- og Litteraturselskab, 1993, p. 82.

Viggo Stuckenberg (1863-1905)

"Ingeborg", *Sne*, Det nordiske Forlags smaa Digtsamlinger, 1901, p. 50.

Ludvig Holstein (1864-1943)

"Det er i Dag et Vejr", *Digte*, 2nd edition, Gyldendal, 1903, 24.

Sophus Claussen (1865-1931)
"Se,jeg mødte paa en Gade", *Danske Vers*, 1912; *Sophus Claussens lyrik* IV, ed. Jørgen Hunosøe, Det danske Sprog- og Litteraturselskab, 1983, p. 60.
"Skabelse", *Heroica* 1925; *Sophus Claussens lyrik* VI, p. 129.

Jeppe Aakjær (1866-1930)
"Aften", *Vejr og Vind og Folkesind,* 1916, p. 28.
"Majnat", *Vejr og Vind og Folkesind,* 1916, p. 31.

Helge Rode (1870-1937)
"Sne", *Digte,* 1896, p. 81.

Johannes V. Jensen (1873-1950)
"Paa Memphis Station", *Tilskueren*, 1904, p. 195.
"Solhvervssang", 1917; *Digte*, Gyldendal, 3rd edition, 1921, p. 85.

Thøger Larsen (1875-1928)
"Middag", *Jord*, 1904; *Fire digtsamlinger 1904-1912*, ed. Lotte Thyrring Andersen, Det danske Sprog- og Litteraturselskab, 1995, p. 36.
"Septembernat", *Limfjords-sange*, 1925, p. 23.

Otto Gelsted (1888-1968)
"September", *De evige Ting*, Nyt Nordisk Forlag, 1920, p. 13.

Bodil Bech (1889-1942)
"I Sporvognen", *Granit og Dugg,* Jespersen og Pio, 1938, p. 18.

Tom Kristensen (1893-1974)
"Angst", *Hærværk*, Gyldendal, 1930, p. 59.
"Det er Knud, som er død", *Mod den yderste Rand*, Gyldendal, 1936, p. 7.

Hulda Lütken (1896-1975)
"Hvor har du gjort af dit blaa Blik", *Elskovs Rose*, Gyldendal, 1934, p. 25.

Paul La Cour (1902-1956)
"Nu gaar jeg", *Mellem Bark og Ved*, Gyldendal, 1950, p. 52.

Jens August Schade (1903-1978)
"Paa Café", *Hjerte-Bogen*, Nyt Nordisk Forlag, 1930, p. 12.
"Sne", *Kællingedigte,* Thaning & Appel, 1944, p. 44.

Piet Hein (1905-1996)
"Pædagogisk Gruk", *Gruk*, 1st collection, Politiken, 1940, p. 79.
Piet Hein © gruk. Reproduced with kind permission from Piet Hein a/s, Middelfart.

Gustaf Munch-Petersen (1912-1938)
"Marts", *Nitten digte*, 1937, p. 25.
"en lykkelig dag", *Vild Hvede*, November 1931; *Samlede skrifter* I, ed. Torben Brostrøm, 1959, p. 34.

Tove Meyer (1913-1972)
"Fremmed i storbyens efterår –", *Havoffer,* Gyldendal, 1961, p. 22.

Halfdan Rasmussen (1915-2002)
"Noget om at finde forståelse …", *Tosserier*, 2nd collection, Hasselbach, 1952, p. 25.

Tove Ditlevsen (1917-1976)
"Blinkende Lygter", *Blinkende Lygter,* Athenæum, 1947, p. 8.
"Ægteskab", *Kvindesind*, Hasselbach, 1955, 2nd impression, 1956, p. 47.
© The heirs of Tove Ditlevsen.

Thorkild Bjørnvig (1918-2004)
"September", *Stjærnen bag Gavlen*, Gyldendal, 1947, p. 75.
"Lappedykkeren", *Figur og ild*, Gyldendal, 1959, p. 67.

Ole Sarvig (1921-1981)
"Regnmaaleren", *Grønne digte*, Branner, 1943; Gyldendal's Spættebøger 1966 edition with a few emendations by the author, p. 15.
"Bjørneklo", *Grønne digte*, Branner, 1943; Gyldendal's Spættebøger 1966 edition with a few emendations by the author, p. 88.

Morten Nielsen (1922-1944)
"Døden", *Krigere uden Vaaben,* Athenæum, 1943; *Digte*, p. 44.
"Øjeblik", *Efterladte Digte,* Athenæum, 1945; *Digte*, p. 92.

Erik Knudsen (1922-2007)
"Schack Staffeldt", *Digte 1945-58*, Nordisk Forlag A/S, 1958, p. 90.
"Schack Staffeldt", *Minotauros*, 1955, p. 9.

Ivan Malinowski (1926-1989)
"Disjecta membra", *Galgenfrist*, Arena, 1958, p. 5.
"Myggesang", *Galgenfrist*, Arena, 1958, p. 25.

Frank Jæger (1926-1977)
"Sidenius i Esbjerg", *Cinna og andre Digte*, Gyldendal, 1959, p. 89.
"Efter Stormen", *Lyrik 76*, ed. Anne Marie Bjerg and Erik C. Lindgren, 1976, p. 76.

Per Højholt (1928-2004)
"Forholdsregler", *Min hånd 66*, Schønberg, 1966, p. 15.
"Så og så mange lærker", *Min hånd 66*, Schønberg, 1966, p. 36.
"Den tydelige solsort", *PRAKSIS, 1: Revolver*, Schønberg, 1977, p. 65.

Benny Andersen (1929-)
"Svantes lykkelige dag", *Svantes viser*, Borgen, 1972, p. 58.

Klaus Rifbjerg (1931-)
"Refshaleøen", *Konfrontation*, Schønberg, 1960, p. 43.
"solsort", *Voliére – Et fuglekor på femogtyve stemmer*, Gyldendal, 1962, p. 28.
"Remisevej", *Amagerdigte*, Gyldendal, 1965, p. 17.

Inger Christensen (1935-2009)
"juninatten", *alfabet*, Gyldendal, 1981, p. 19.

Jørgen Leth (1937-)
"Kneppe", *Billedet forestiller*, Gyldendal, 2000, p. 32.

Klaus Høeck (1938-)
"Her er så de ni roser", *Hjem*, Gyldendal, 1985, p. 280.

Hans-Jørgen Nielsen (1941-1991)
"3 stykker om naturen", *Nielsen sort på hvidt*, Tiderne Skifter, 2000, p. 291.

Peter Laugesen (1942-)
"Det jeg vil skrive om", *Kulttur*, Borgen, 1990, p. 57.

Johannes L. Madsen (1942-2000)
"nedspildt spruttende af syre", *nedspildt spruttende af syre*, privately printed, 1969, unpaginated. Reissued by Arena, 2003.

Henrik Nordbrandt (1945-)
"Kina betragtet gennem græsk regnvejr i café turque", *Syvsoverne*, Gyldendal, 1969, p. 11.
"Violinbyggernes by", *Violinbyggernes by*, Gyldendal, 1985, p. 17.

Dan Turèll (1946-1993)
"At være beat", *Manuskrifter om hvad som helst*, Arena, 1971, p. 227.

Marianne Larsen (1951-)
"snehvide", *Cinderella*, Swing, 1974, p. 18.

Pia Tafdrup (1952-)
"Junidrøm", *Dronningeporten*, Gyldendal, 1998, p. 121.

F.P. Jac (1955-2008)
"jeg har været på spritten", *Misfat*, Borgen, 1980, p. 104.

Bo Green Jensen (1955-)
"Svømmeren", *Requiem & messe*, Borgen, 1981, p. 87.

Søren Ulrik Thomsen (1956-)
"Sol Opgang", *Ukendt under den samme måne*, Vindrose, 1982, p. 47.
"Tandlæge. Gravsted. Vielsesring", *Nye digte*, Vindrose, 1987, p. 24.

Michael Strunge (1958-1986)
"Livets hastighed", *Livets hastighed*, Borgen, 1978, p. 9.
"Natmaskinen", *Vi folder drømmens faner ud*, Borgen, 1981, p. 26.
"19. juni 1983, 25 år. København.", *Væbnet med vinger*, Borgen, 1984, p. 105.

Simon Grotrian (1961-)
"Ode til et egetræ", *Livsfælder*, Borgen, 1993, p. 31.

Pia Juul (1962-)
"Men jeg ville heller ikke det jeg ville", *En død mands nys*, Tiderne Skifter, 1993, p. 23.

Naja Marie Aidt (1963-)
"Fjerde april", *Alting blinker*, Gyldendal, 2009, p. 7.